Second Edition

Developmental and Adapted Physical Activity Assessment

Michael Horvat, EdD
University of Georgia

Luke E. Kelly, PhD
University of Virginia

Martin E. Block, PhD
University of Virginia

Ron Croce, PhD
University of New Hampshire

SHAPE America SOCIETY OF HEALTH AND PHYSICAL EDUCATORS®

health. moves. minds.

HUMAN KINETICS

Library of Congress Cataloging-in-Publication Data

Names: Horvat, Michael A., 1947- author.
Title: Developmental and adapted physical activity assessment / Michael
 Horvat, Luke E. Kelly, Martin E. Block, Ron Croce.
Description: Second Edition. | Champaign, Illinois : Human Kinetics, [2019] |
 Includes bibliographical references and index.
Identifiers: LCCN 2017041138 (print) | LCCN 2017038344 (ebook) | ISBN
 9781492543923 (e-book) | ISBN 9781492543800 (print)
Subjects: LCSH: Physical education for children with disabilities. |
 Ability--Testing.
Classification: LCC GV445 (print) | LCC GV445 .H665 2018 (ebook) | DDC
 371.9/04486--dc23
LC record available at https://lccn.loc.gov/2017041138

ISBN: 978-1-4925-4380-0

The web addresses cited in this text were current as of October 2017, unless otherwise noted.

Acquisitions Editor: Ray Vallese; **SHAPE America Editor:** Joe McGavin; **Senior Developmental Editor:** Melissa Feld; **Senior Managing Editor:** Amy Stahl; **Copyeditor:** Patricia L. MacDonald; **Indexer:** Nancy Kopper; **Permissions Manager:** Dalene Reeder; **Graphic Designer:** Whitney Milburn; **Cover Designer:** Keri Evans; **Cover Design Associate:** Susan Rothermel Allen; **Photograph (cover):** Getty Images/iStock/FatCamera; **Photographs (interior):** © Human Kinetics, unless otherwise noted; p. 9 © SolStock/Getty Images; **Photo Asset Manager:** Laura Fitch; **Photo Production Manager:** Jason Allen; **Senior Art Manager:** Kelly Hendren; **Illustrations:** © Human Kinetics, unless otherwise noted; **Printer:** Edwards Brothers Malloy

SHAPE America – Society of Health and Physical Educators
1900 Association Drive
Reston, VA 20191
800-213-7193
www.shapeamerica.org

Printed in the United States of America   10 9 8 7 6 5 4 3 2 1

Human Kinetics
P.O. Box 5076
Champaign, IL 61825-5076
Website: www.HumanKinetics.com

In the United States, email info@hkusa.com or call 800-747-4457.
In Canada, email info@hkcanada.com.
In the United Kingdom/Europe, email hk@hkeurope.com.

For information about Human Kinetics' coverage in other areas of the world,
please visit our website: **www.HumanKinetics.com**

E6938

I would like to dedicate this book to the memory of my mother and father, who taught me the value of hard work and doing the right thing. It is also dedicated to my wife, Glada, and children, Ian, Kala, and Michael, who make life worth living.

M.H.

I would like to dedicate my sections of this book to my wife, Beth, and to my children, Luke Andrew, Zachary, and Melissa, for being the source of my inspiration and for their ongoing support.

L.K.

This book is dedicated to my father, Dr. Herbert Block, who recently passed away at the age of 100. His guidance and support throughout my life have truly shaped me into the man I have become.

M.B.

To those who have instilled in me a dedication to academic excellence: my parents, Josephine and Frank; my brother, Michael; my mentor, Dr. Frank Papcsy; and my dear colleague and friend, Michael Horvat.

R.C.

Contents

Chapter 1   Who You Are Assessing   1

Chapter 2   Why You Are Assessing   9

Chapter 3   Getting to Know the Student   31

Chapter 4 — Selecting an Appropriate Assessment Instrument — 47

Chapter 5 — Selecting and Administering Tests — 63

Chapter 6 — Assessing Motor Development and Motor Skill Performance — 89

Chapter 10 Assessing Behavior
and Social Competence   **197**

Preface

Meeting the needs of individuals with disabilities requires the contribution of physical education teachers, coaches, special education teachers, athletic trainers, physical therapists, and occupational therapists. We refer to this group as the motor performance team (MPT) and recognize that a variety of information is needed to serve individuals with disabilities. Although the text targets practicing adapted physical educators, the information is useful for general physical educators, physical and occupational therapists, adapted physical education and activity researchers, special education administrators, and parents. Teachers and researchers in adapted physical education regularly select, administer, and interpret assessments for numerous purposes. Characterized by enormous variability in purpose, content, difficulty, and format, assessment instruments (including their selection, administration, and interpretation) generate a vast array of questions that require answers. Often, simply knowing the questions is the beginning of wisdom. Unfortunately, few resources that clarify assessment-related issues are available to teachers of adapted physical education in professional preparation programs. In fact, this textbook is the only book currently on the market that focuses solely on assessment, details the assessment process and how to use assessment data when making programming decisions, and reviews specific assessment tools for adapted physical educators and physical therapists. We regard assessment as the cornerstone of individual instruction. Assessment is like a puzzle that requires us to fit the pieces together to present a true picture of overall functioning and capabilities. The purpose of this text is to present assessment information as a systematic, multifaceted process of gathering and interpreting information about a student. Concepts and procedures are explained, and assessment problems are presented via case studies that emphasize critical thinking and present real-life situations that teachers encounter on a daily basis. Specific assessment tools are presented and reviewed in detail so that members of the MPT have a better understanding of available tools and have a better understanding of how assessment works.

In each chapter, students are required to discuss case studies as well as learn specific assessment instruments. Assessment information will help the MPT develop a written recommendation regarding placement and instructional programming. Key terms, key concepts, and review questions are included at the end of each chapter. From our perspective, assessment in physical activity—while always challenging—need never be confusing when sound principles are applied and understood. All the chapters have been updated to emphasize the decisions needed in the assessment process and articulate the rationale about educational and physical decisions.

Chapters reviewing specific assessment tools have also been updated. For example, chapter 6 (Assessing Motor Development and Motor Skill Performance) has been upgraded to emphasize motor function. In this context, newer versions of instruments such as TGMD-3 and Bruininks-Oseretsky have been included. Other tests such as the Gross Motor Function Measure (GMFM) and Hawaii Early Learning Profile (HELP) are used by physical therapists but relate to motor functioning. Chapter 7 (Assessing Physical Function) includes updated versions of FitnessGram and the Brockport Physical Fitness Test. In addition, the Functional Movement Screen (FMS) and Special Olympics Alaska Functional Performance Test have been added to address physical functioning. Chapter 8 includes updates on posture assessment, the Berg Balance Scale, Performance Oriented Mobility Assessment (POMA), and the STAR Excursion Balance Test as well as the Balance Error Scoring System (BESS), which is used for balance and concussion symptoms. Also, more specific tests used in sports for disabilities and Special Olympics have been included, emphasizing other disciplines that work with physical education personnel. Perceptual motor tests have been moved to a new chapter titled Assessing Perception and Cognition (chapter 9). We are especially excited about cognition assessment, not only for assessing head injuries and concussions but also for planning and initiating movement. All teachers, coaches, and therapists need to understand how these concepts can be integrated into their teaching or rehabilitation programs.

Teachers, coaches, and therapists who use the concepts presented in this book will gain credibility as diagnosticians who are able to provide thoughtful tests and results that can be used in planning their intervention programs. Readers will understand what to do when tests are not available or are inappropriate for the environment or population and will be able to apply assessment solutions to their problems. Our continuing goal is to meet a need for clarifying assessment-related issues surrounding physical and motor assessments of persons with disabilities. Specifically, we realize that assessment is the cornerstone of the instructional process and seek to provide an updated version for professionals in adapted physical education and other professionals who make up the MPT. The development of this text represents a continuing effort to provide an authoritative treatise on assessment in adapted physical education. This allows us to understand the needs and level of functioning of students in order to address their concerns in processing information and planning a movement. The text is intended for undergraduate and graduate programs in adapted physical education as well as all individuals who are interested in assessment of physical activity.

eBook available at HumanKinetics.com

Accessing the Web Resource

The web resource includes digital versions of forms in the book and links to other assessment tools. You can download and print the forms or use them as models for creating your own forms. This online content is available to you for free upon purchase of a new print book or an ebook. All you need to do is register with the Human Kinetics website to access the online content. The following steps explain how to register.

Follow these steps to access the web resource:

1. Visit www.HumanKinetics.com/DevelopmentalAndAdaptedPhysical ActivityAssessment
2. Click the second edition link next to the corresponding second edition book cover.
3. Click the Sign In link on the left or top of the page. If you do not have an account with Human Kinetics, you will be prompted to create one.
4. After you register, if the online product does not appear in the Ancillary Items box on the left of the page, click the Enter Pass Code option in that box. Enter the following pass code exactly as it is printed here, including capitalization and all hyphens: **HORVAT-BR2S-WR**
5. Click the Submit button to unlock your online product.
6. After you have entered your pass code the first time, you will never have to enter it again to access this online product. Once unlocked, a link to your product will permanently appear in the menu on the left. All you need to do to access your online content on subsequent visits is sign in to www.HumanKinetics.com/DevelopmentalAndAdaptedPhysical ActivityAssessment and follow the link!

Click the Need Help? button on the book's website if you need assistance along the way.

Acknowledgments

We are excited to share this version of our textbook with our colleagues in adapted physical education and other professionals who work with individuals with disabilities. We especially thank those who have continued to use this textbook in their classes. We would be remiss not to acknowledge Dr. Judy Werder and Dr. Len Kalakian. They began the process with the first treatise on physical and motor assessment of persons with disabilities more than 30 years ago, and their pioneering efforts appeared in an earlier edition with another publisher. I was fortunate enough to work on a subsequent text revision with Dr. Kalakian and enjoyed the experience immensely. Dr. Luke Kelly, Dr. Martin Block, and Dr. Ron Croce have provided their expertise to develop an outstanding product and resource in our field. I would like to recognize and thank them for all their work as we develop our current edition.

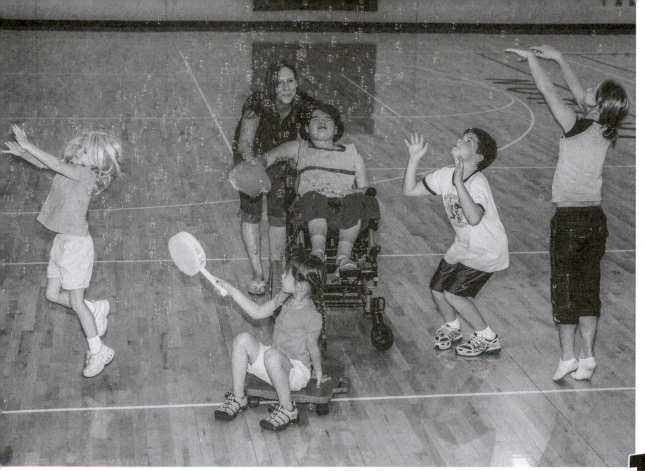

Chapter 1

Who You Are Assessing

Assessment is a multifaceted process that is critical in determining whether a student qualifies for special education services under federal law and, more important, whether the student's disability significantly affects educational performance. The evaluation process sets boundaries to determine the eligibility of a student and what types of special education services should be provided. These services include teachers, coaches, therapists and other relevant personnel. We refer to this group as the **motor performance team (MPT)** and recognize that a variety of information is needed to serve individuals with disabilities.

Assessment in adapted physical education (APE) is similarly a complex process that focuses on identifying whether a student qualifies for services, developing appropriate goals for those students who do qualify, implementing appropriate instructional activities and supports to achieve goals of the individualized education plan (IEP), and determining the most appropriate placement for students in physical education. As is the case with special education assessments, before you can begin to assess the development of goals, instructional activities, and appropriate placement, the question of who qualifies for services must be answered. However, students with disabilities must not only be addressed for participation in regular or adapted physical

Case Study 1
Reevaluation of Services

Josiah, a nine-year-old fourth grader at Atlantic Beach Elementary School, was diagnosed with Duchenne muscular dystrophy while in kindergarten. He was able to walk independently until the end of third grade but is currently using a manual wheelchair. Although Josiah has adapted fairly well to his wheelchair, he has trouble in physical education, especially in tagging and fleeing games. He also has difficulty with throwing and striking patterns because he can no longer stand when doing these skills. Originally Josiah did not qualify as disabled within the parameters of IDEA. However, he did have a disability as defined by Section 504 of the Rehabilitation Act (he has a 504 plan rather than an individualized education plan, or IEP). Under this act he receives special transportation and physical therapy services. Although he has never received adapted physical education services, his parents and teachers have determined that APE services combined with regular physical education will help facilitate activities of daily living and independence.

education but also provided services for long-term functioning in the transition process, participation in adapted sports, and rehabilitation from injuries or illness and overall health.

The purpose of this chapter is to review the basic information regarding who qualifies for adapted physical education as well as other factors and services related to the student that may affect assessment. It also looks at the needs of individuals with disabilities who are receiving early intervention services that are developmentally appropriate, participating in disability sports, or recovering from an injury or illness during the formative school years, especially as students transition from a school to community setting. Decisions regarding qualification, curriculum, placement, and instruction are discussed in chapter 2.

QUALIFYING FOR APE SERVICES

Most educators think of the **Individuals with Disabilities Education Act (IDEA)** and the **Americans with Disabilities Act (ADA)** as vehicles that determine whether an individual qualifies for special education services. To qualify for adapted physical education services under IDEA, a student must have a condition that meets the criteria for one of the eligible disabilities. However, simply having one of these disabilities does not automatically qualify a student for special education services. To be eligible for special education services, the disability must significantly affect the individual's educational performance, even with accommodations. In other words, a label of "hearing impairment" or "other health impairment" may be a real diagnosis given by a doctor, but if students perform sufficiently, they may

Case Study 2
Recovery From Injury

Kala is a high school student who recently tore her ACL while playing soccer. After surgery, she received physical therapy to rehabilitate her knee. At this point, she is ready to join her team and participate in physical education. The physical education teacher or coach can work closely with her medical personnel to aid in her recovery and training. Although she does not qualify for special education services, her treatment plan is based on restoring her function and allowing her to return to her level of participation. Likewise, Michael, 16, who suffered a concussion during football, will go through the same process by following concussion protocols implemented by teachers and coaches who work with the medical community to ensure he can safely return to participation.

not qualify for special education services. Students can in many cases adjust to their disability and thus perform at expected levels. In addition, some students may incur injuries from accidents or sports participation. These are viewed as temporary disabilities that don't qualify for special education services but require services from the physical education teacher or coach. Therefore, the decision of whether or not a student qualifies as having a disability under IDEA is based solely on educational needs as determined through assessment, as opposed to a label (Horvat, Kalakian, Croce, and Dahlstrom, 2011).

ATTRIBUTES AND DIMENSIONS THAT AFFECT THE STUDENTS YOU ASSESS

Many factors influence how a particular student will react to the assessment process. Students may have limited endurance and cannot physically complete the entire test battery in one testing period. Another student may not cognitively understand what to do, and still another student may be frightened of all the new sensory experiences in the testing environment. Anyone attempting to test students must fully understand that students react differently and need to focus successfully to complete the various test items in order to get a true representation of their abilities. For example, a student may demonstrate a lack of physical fitness, be overweight, or, as in case study 1, be generally inefficient in movement. In addition, a lack of vision results in restrained gait and balance difficulties in unknown situations (Horvat, Ray, Ramsey, Miszko, Keeney, and Blasch, 2003). Likewise, cognitive or behavioral difficulties may cause students to elicit poor responses or exert minimal effort. Each dimension may affect testing in physical education and how an examiner might accommodate students at many levels of functioning. The examiner should find out as much as possible about each student from teachers, parents, and

Case Study 3
Head Injury From Auto Accident

Jillian is 12 years old and in seventh grade at Highland Springs Middle School. She is recovering from an automobile accident and has residual effects from a head injury. She now qualifies as a student with a disability under IDEA, and the motor performance team (MPT) has asked several specialists to assess Jillian's physical and cognitive function. Areas that have been targeted for assessment include physical therapy, speech therapy, occupational therapy, and adapted physical education, all of which aid in the rehabilitation process.

other relevant persons to ensure the environment is appropriate for valid testing. Students should be aware of the test items and given opportunity to practice them. This helps students understand what is expected of them. The tester should always praise students for their effort and ensure they feel comfortable during the procedure.

In case study 3, the diagnosis of traumatic brain injury qualifies Jillian as a student with a disability under IDEA, a decision that enhances Jillian's chances for rehabilitation. Her condition must have been such that it significantly affected her educational performance. The question now is whether her condition significantly affects her ability to be successful in physical education. To make this determination, the physical educator or movement performance team needs to assess Jillian's physical and motor functioning. Testing might include motor abilities, physical fitness, sports skills, and behavior and social skills as they relate to her success in physical education. If it can be determined that Jillian has significant deficits, then she would qualify for APE services. She may perform well enough to participate in regular class activities and may not require a special class placement.

ZERO EXCLUSION AND ZERO FAILURE

Two important concepts of IDEA are zero exclusion and zero failure. Virtually every student with a disability who qualifies for special education under IDEA also qualifies for physical education services. These physical education services may need to be specially designed to meet the student's unique motor and health needs, and the services may need to be provided in restrictive settings such as at home or in a hospital. In addition, these physical education services must be provided to everyone with disabilities regardless of the severity of the disability. This concept is known as **zero exclusion**.

Once a student with disabilities has qualified to receive physical education services, the program should be created and implemented in such a way as to ensure the student's success. Each student's unique abilities and needs should be addressed, and a carefully constructed, individually determined program should then be implemented. This is the concept of **zero failure**. Assessment is critical to ensure the success of each student with a disability in physical education. For example, a student with autism may need picture schedules and picture prompts as well as a quiet small-group setting to be successful. Another student with a physical disability may need several different types of adapted equipment plus rule modifications for various sports and games played in physical education to ensure success. The key is to determine through assessment each student's unique abilities and strengths as well as unique concerns and needs in order to create a program or situation that provides the best chance for the student to be successful. For example, students may participate in clinical (rehabilitation) or sport-specific (recreational or elite) programs that are based on individual needs, interests, or skills.

SPORT PARTICIPATION

Disabled Sports USA, Paralympics, Special Olympics, and BlazeSports America are organizations at local, regional, national, and international levels that provide instruction and training in disabled sport activities. Assessment in this case is not for meeting needs or qualifying for services but for determining athletes' level of functioning and specific sports or events in which they can participate. Chapter 7 discusses the Special Olympics Alaska Functional Performance Test which tracks performance training and documents the overall health of participants. The following groups provide training and organization in disabled sport activities.

- *Paralympics.* The International Paralympic Committee serves as the global governing body of the Paralympic Movement. The **Paralympics** include elite-level sport opportunities for individuals with physical disabilities, intellectual disabilities, and visual impairments. The Paralympic Games are held directly after every Olympic Games, bringing together athletes from around the globe to represent their countries.

- *Disabled Sports USA.* **Disabled Sports USA** provides opportunities for individuals with disabilities to participate in community sports, recreation, and education programs. The main goal of the programs is to improve the lives of soldiers, youth, and adults with disabilities. The program is community based so it provides opportunities for students to engage in their community both during and after school.

- *BlazeSports America.* The mission of BlazeSports is to use adaptive sports and recreation to change the lives of individuals with physical disabilities. BlazeSports offers recreational sports programming for children and serves as an introductory organization for Paralympic sports. It allows children with physical disabilities to sample sport opportunities as well as participate in recreational and competitive disability sports programming that aligns with the programming of the Paralympics.

- *Northeast Passage.* Northeast Passage is a state program in New Hampshire that allows individuals with disabilities to participate in recreational opportunities alongside their nondisabled peers. The program provides barrier-free recreation and health programs such as recreational sports, disability

Case Study 4
Assessment After Amputation

Matthew is a high-school-age long distance runner who recently lost his leg below the knee in an accident. After watching the Paralympics, he became interested in opportunities in his community that would let him continue to participate in the sport. With help from his school's physical education teacher and physical therapist, Matthew was able to regain his function and movement patterns used in running. With hard work and the support of his teacher and therapist, he is now competing in Paralympic events with the dream of participating in future Paralympic Games. In this context his assessment would be based on determining his level of functioning and what he would need to do to reach his goals and dreams.

sports, programs for military and veterans, and recreational therapy in both school and home-based settings.

- *Special Olympics.* The **Special Olympics** offer movement training and sports programs for individuals with intellectual disabilities on regional, state, national, and international scales. The Special Olympics provide multiple levels of sport participation from Level A programming, which provides training in basic sports skills for those individuals with moderate to severe disabilities, to traditional sport opportunities for both individual and team sports. Programming is centered around community, including programs such as Unified Partners, which pairs able-bodied peers with athletes to compete in traditional sports. Coaching manuals allow coaches to plan sport programming for a wide range of abilities as well as provide individual sport-specific assessments for the athletes. These assessments can be useful in determining gaps in activities of daily living as well as to track progress of athletes throughout the program.

CONCLUSION

Federal legislation determines whether individuals qualify for special education services. The chapter first identifies who qualifies for specific services via the Individuals with Disabilities Education Act (IDEA) and Americans with Disabilities Act (ADA) and its predecessor the Rehabilitation Act of 1973 (Section 504).

The legislation provides rationale for receiving services and qualifying for adapted physical education. However, many students do not qualify under these guidelines but require attention because of specific health disorders (asthma, diabetes) or injuries due to accidents or sport participation that compromise their functional ability. Therefore the question of who you are assessing not only includes those who qualify under federal legislation but also considers other conditions that teachers encounter in the classroom. Teachers or the MPT must evaluate the needs of these individuals and their level of functioning.

What You Need to Know

Key Terms

Americans with Disabilities Act (ADA)

Disabled Sports USA

Individuals with Disabilities Education Act (IDEA)

motor performance team (MPT)

Paralympics

Special Olympics

zero exclusion

zero failure

Key Concepts

1. You should understand how a student qualifies for special education services under the Individuals with Disabilities Education Act. You should also understand the process for determining whether a student with a disability qualifies for adapted physical education services.
2. You should be able to discuss the concepts of zero exclusion and zero failure as they relate to physical education for students with disabilities.
3. You should be able to describe the key attributes and dimensions related to whom you assess in adapted physical education. You should understand how the following dimensions can influence assessment and subsequently program planning: physical and motor, perceptual, learning and cognitive, behavioral, and social.
4. You should be able to provide examples of disability sports and recreational programs available to students on a local, regional, state, and national level.

Review Questions

1. How would you assess Josiah, the fourth grader with Duchenne muscular dystrophy?
2. Which professionals would you contact for assistance in developing a plan for students with short-term disabilities that are not covered by special education legislation?
3. Jillian, the seventh grader who was in an automobile accident and who qualifies as a student with a disability under IDEA, needs to be evaluated to determine whether she qualifies for adapted physical education services. What dimensions and attributes might you consider for inclusion in your assessment plan?
4. Recall that Matthew is a high school student who recently lost his leg below the knee. How would you determine whether Matthew's goals are still appropriate for high school and whether these goals can be implemented in general physical education programs?

Why You Are Assessing

A friend comes up to you and asks if you would like to go downtown and have lunch. How do you make this decision? Do you just jump in your friend's car and go? Maybe, but more likely you ask yourself some questions first. Do you have any other obligations for lunch? Do you have time? Do you have enough money to buy lunch? Are you actually interested in having lunch with this friend? You probably then analyze this information to make an informed decision. Finally, you use this information to shape your response. You might respond that you would love to have lunch, but you will need to be quick because you have to be back at a certain time for your next class.

You may be saying to yourself, "What does making a decision about lunch with a friend have to do with assessment in physical education for individuals with disabilities?" It illustrates how assessment is an integral part of the decision-making process. To make an informed decision about lunch, you had to assess a number of factors, analyze the data you assessed, and then use the assessment data to make an appropriate decision. This simple example also illustrates what can happen when you make decisions without assessing. You could have immediately said, "Sure," jumped in your friend's car, and gone downtown and had lunch. Of course it was embarrassing when you found you did not have enough to pay for your meal and had to borrow money from your friend. Then halfway through lunch you suddenly realized your next class started in 10 minutes, so lunch had to be cut short so your friend could drive you back to school. Finally, when you got to class late, another friend asked why you stood him up for the lunch you had planned the week before. The point here is that when you make decisions without assessing, the odds are that there will be unanticipated negative consequences. For example, you now have two friends upset with you. One is upset because you stood him up for lunch, and the other is upset because you stuck her with the bill and then cut lunch short because you had another obligation.

TERMINOLOGY

The focus of this chapter is to introduce assessment as an integral part of the decision-making process that underlies all teaching behavior. **Assessment** as addressed in this book is an umbrella term to describe the process used by teachers to make informed decisions. There are frequent misconceptions regarding assessment because the term is used in different ways and may be used interchangeably with other terms such as *testing*, *measurement*, and *evaluation*. To avoid any confusion, the following definitions will be used for this book. *Assessing* and *testing* refer to the process of administering an instrument for the purpose of collecting performance data. Although these terms can be used interchangeably, the preferred term is *assessing*. *Testing* frequently has a negative connotation because it is commonly associated with summative forms of evaluation where students are graded.

Instruments, *tests*, *assessments*, *items*, and *tools* all describe the procedures or subsets of the procedures used to collect information on the behavior being assessed. These procedures typically define what will be assessed, the conditions under which the assessment should be performed, the equipment required, the administration instructions, and the scoring. Instruments can range in complexity from simple (e.g., one item to assess one motor skill such as catching) to complex (e.g., several items to assess each of the major components of physical fitness).

Assessment instruments are commonly categorized as either norm referenced or criterion referenced. **Norm-referenced instruments** (NRIs) are generally standardized tests designed to collect performance data that are then compared with reference standards based on normative data provided with the instrument. An example of a norm-referenced assessment is a softball throw for distance, where the distance thrown under standardized conditions is recorded. This score is then looked up in a normative chart to obtain a percentile score that indicates the percentage of students in the normative sample that could throw as far as this individual. **Criterion-referenced instruments** (CRIs) are generally less standardized and involve evaluating performance against an established set of criteria. An example of a simple

CRI for skipping involves observing students and recording whether they correctly do the following:

- Move forward by stepping and then hopping
- Maintain an upright body posture
- Alternate the step–hop pattern between feet
- Move arms in opposition to the legs
- Hold arms around waist level and slightly flexed

Standardized, when used in conjunction with assessment instruments, means that procedures must be followed when administering the instrument. Most NRIs tend to be highly standardized, which means explicit procedures must be adhered to. These procedures usually include how to set up the testing environment, what equipment to use, the administration instructions, how to record the data, and how to score and interpret the results. The reason NRIs need to be so highly standardized is to ensure that any differences found in performances can be attributed to ability and not to differences in how the test was administered and scored. Figure 2.1 shows the administration instructions for the jumping sideways item from the Peabody Developmental Motor Scales 2 (Folio & Fewell, 2000). Note that the tester must demonstrate the item exactly as described and give instructions verbatim to each student when administering this item. CRIs also have standardized procedures for administration and scoring but frequently provide the administrator a little

---

PEABODY DEVELOPMENTAL MOTOR SCALES 2

Jumping Sideways

Position: Standing

Stimulus: Tape starting line (2 in. by 2 ft)

Procedure: Stand with your left side next to the line. With your hands on your hips and keeping your feet together, jump back and forth (sideways) over the line for three cycles without pausing between jumps (left and right equal one cycle).

Say "Jump across the line like I did."

Scoring criteria:

2 = Child jumps back and forth for three cycles with hands on hips, with feet together, and without touching line or pausing between jumps.

1 = Child jumps back and forth one or two cycles with hands on hips, with feet together, and without touching line or pausing between jumps.

0 = Child lands on line or pauses between jumps.

Figure 2.1   Sample standardized instructions for an NRI item.

From Horvat, M., Kelly, L.E., Block, M.E., and Croce, R., *Developmental and adapted physical activity assessment*, 2nd ed. (Champaign, IL: Human Kinetics, 2019). Adapted from M.R. Folio and R.R. Fewell, 2000, *Peabody developmental motor scales*, 2nd ed. (PRO-ED, Inc.), 27. Used with permission.

more flexibility. For example, the administrator may be permitted to model the task or allow more trials. Since the goal of most CRIs is to get an accurate indication of the student's performance in relation to the comparison criteria, the emphasis during administration is on eliciting the best performance.

Reference standards refer to how the data collected during the assessment are interpreted. As implied in the name, NRIs allow scores to be compared with normative data collected under the same conditions on other students with similar characteristics such as age and gender. Table 2.1 shows a simple normative chart for interpreting performance on an agility test by age and

Table 2.1   Shuttle Run for Boys

Percentile	Age							
	9-10	11	12	13	14	15	16	17+
100th	9.2	8.7	6.8	7.0	7.0	7.0	7.3	7.0
95th	10.0	9.7	9.6	9.3	8.9	8.9	8.6	8.6
90th	10.2	9.9	9.8	9.5	9.2	9.1	8.9	8.9
85th	10.4	10.1	10.0	9.7	9.3	9.2	9.1	9.0
80th	10.5	10.2	10.0	9.8	9.5	9.3	9.2	9.1
75th	10.6	10.4	10.2	10.0	9.6	9.4	9.3	9.2
70th	10.7	10.5	10.3	10.0	9.8	9.5	9.4	9.3
65th	10.8	10.5	10.4	10.1	9.8	9.6	9.5	9.4
60th	11.0	10.6	10.5	10.2	10.0	9.7	9.6	9.5
55th	11.0	10.8	10.6	10.3	10.0	9.8	9.7	9.6
50th	11.2	10.9	10.7	10.4	10.1	9.9	9.9	9.8
45th	11.5	11.0	10.8	10.5	10.1	10.0	10.0	9.9
40th	11.5	11.1	11.0	10.6	10.2	10.0	10.0	10.0
35th	11.7	11.2	11.1	10.8	10.4	10.1	10.1	10.1
30th	11.9	11.4	11.3	11.0	10.6	10.2	10.3	10.2
25th	12.0	11.5	11.4	11.0	10.7	10.4	10.5	10.4
20th	12.2	11.8	11.6	11.3	10.9	10.5	10.6	10.5
15th	12.5	12.0	11.8	11.5	11.0	10.8	10.9	10.7
10th	13.0	12.2	12.0	11.8	11.3	11.1	11.1	11.0
5th	13.1	12.9	12.4	12.4	11.9	11.7	11.9	11.7
0	17.0	20.0	22.0	16.0	18.6	14.7	15.0	15.7

Note: Percentile scores based on age. Test scores in seconds and tenths.

SHAPE America - Society of Health and Physical Educators, 1976, *AAHPERD youth fitness test manual* (Reston, VA: Author), 35.

gender. A 12-year-old male who ran the course in 10.3 seconds would be in the 70th percentile, meaning he ran as well as 70 percent of the students in the normative sample that took the test. CRIs, on the other hand, compare the students' performance against established criteria. Figure 2.2 shows a CRI for assessing the catch. In this CRI, the criteria are the five components, henceforth referred to as **focal points** that define the mature catching pattern. The teacher would observe the student's catching behavior and record which of the focal points the students could and could not perform. It should be noted that it is possible for a CRI to have norms. The Test of Gross Motor Development 3 (Ulrich, 2018) is an example of a CRI that also provides age and gender reference standards.

The **measurement** is the data collected by the assessment instrument. Assessment of a motor skill such as throwing could involve several measures. For example, the physical educator could measure the student's knowledge of the key focal points of the overhand throw, how far she throws, how accurately she throws, and if she can perform the key focal points correctly. Each type of measurement produces a different type of data. Knowledge might be measured by a paper and pencil test composed of 10 multiple choice items. The score collected could be a percentage reflecting the number of items out of 10 the student answered correctly. Throwing distance could be measured in meters thrown, and throwing accuracy could be measured in terms of the number of times out of 10 trials the student hit a target. Finally, throwing form could be measured by a checklist that indicates which of the focal points of the throw were performed correctly.

What is measured by an assessment instrument has implications for both psychometrics (e.g., validity, reliability) and how the information can be used to make different types of decisions. Measurement in physical education tends to focus on either the process involved in the performance or the products produced by the performance. **Process measures** are typically related to CRIs, measuring motor skill performance and judging how the skill was performed. For example, when the student threw, did he start with side orientation, did he transfer his weight, and did he follow through after the ball was released? **Product measures**, on the other hand, focus on the outcomes or products of the performance, such as the number of repetitions, distance covered, time needed to complete a task, or number of times a target was hit out of a number of trials. As a general rule, process measures tend to be more subjective and subsequently require more skill to assess than do product measures, which tend to be more objective. Measurement issues are addressed in more detail in chapters 4 and 5.

Evaluation refers to the comparison and interpretation of multiple assessments to explain the changes observed. A common application of evaluation is to compare a student's entry assessment and exit assessment on an objective that was taught, with the intent of determining how much progress was made. Evaluation can be described as either formative or summative. **Formative evaluation** is ongoing and focuses on shaping the performance over time to reach a desired goal. **Summative evaluation** is performed at established intervals, with the purpose of interpreting the performance against established standards. Reassessing a student throughout an instructional unit and giving her feedback on how to improve her performance is an example of formative evaluation.

Equipment and Space Requirements:

- Use an inflatable playground ball that is 6 inches in diameter.
- Catch in an outdoor field or large gymnasium at least 30 feet in length (10-foot staging area plus 20-foot catching distance).

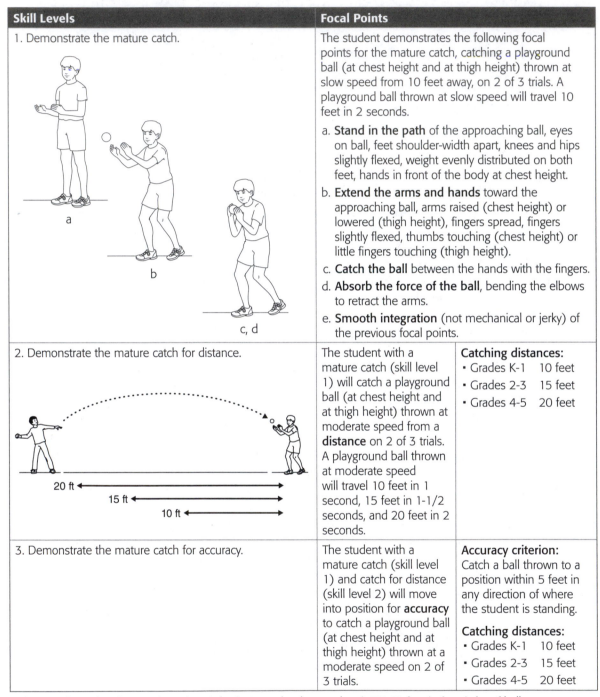

Skill Levels	Focal Points	
1. Demonstrate the mature catch.	The student demonstrates the following focal points for the mature catch, catching a playground ball (at chest height and at thigh height) thrown at slow speed from 10 feet away, on 2 of 3 trials. A playground ball thrown at slow speed will travel 10 feet in 2 seconds. a. **Stand in the path** of the approaching ball, eyes on ball, feet shoulder-width apart, knees and hips slightly flexed, weight evenly distributed on both feet, hands in front of the body at chest height. b. **Extend the arms and hands** toward the approaching ball, arms raised (chest height) or lowered (thigh height), fingers spread, fingers slightly flexed, thumbs touching (chest height) or little fingers touching (thigh height). c. **Catch the ball** between the hands with the fingers. d. **Absorb the force of the ball**, bending the elbows to retract the arms. e. **Smooth integration** (not mechanical or jerky) of the previous focal points.	
2. Demonstrate the mature catch for distance.	The student with a mature catch (skill level 1) will catch a playground ball (at chest height and at thigh height) thrown at moderate speed from a **distance** on 2 of 3 trials. A playground ball thrown at moderate speed will travel 10 feet in 1 second, 15 feet in 1-1/2 seconds, and 20 feet in 2 seconds.	**Catching distances:** • Grades K-1 10 feet • Grades 2-3 15 feet • Grades 4-5 20 feet
3. Demonstrate the mature catch for accuracy.	The student with a mature catch (skill level 1) and catch for distance (skill level 2) will move into position for **accuracy** to catch a playground ball (at chest height and at thigh height) thrown at a moderate speed on 2 of 3 trials.	**Accuracy criterion:** Catch a ball thrown to a position within 5 feet in any direction of where the student is standing. **Catching distances:** • Grades K-1 10 feet • Grades 2-3 15 feet • Grades 4-5 20 feet

Reference data: The distance from the pitcher's mound to home plate is 35-40 feet in fastpitch softball.

Figure 2.2   Sample Everyone Can! CRI for catching.

From Horvat, M., Kelly, L.E., Block, M.E., and Croce, R., *Developmental and adapted physical activity assessment*, 2nd ed. (Champaign, IL: Human Kinetics, 2019). Reprinted, by permission, from L.E. Kelly, J. Wessel, G. Dummer, and T. Sampson, 2010, *Everyone can online resource* (Champaign, IL: Human Kinetics), 7. Illustrations reprinted from J. Wessel, 1976, *I CAN: Object control* (North Brook, IL: Hubbard Scientific Company), 89. By permission of J. Wessel.

Computing average percent mastery on the objectives taught during a unit or reporting a student's progress on a report card in the form of a letter grade for physical education are examples of summative evaluation.

ASSESSMENT DECISIONS

In this book, assessment is a dynamic process that precedes and informs all teaching behavior. This approach to assessment may be in marked contrast to the stereotypical view held by many teachers that assessment is a static process performed periodically to fulfill certain requirements but is not directly related to their teaching. This belief is commonly adopted when teachers do not understand the importance of collecting assessment information that matches the decision to be made.

Case Study 1
Using the Right Tool for the Job!

Before starting a soccer unit, Mr. Davis wants to assess kicking performance. He selects a kicking test he found in one of his college textbooks that is relatively easy to set up, administer, and score and has age and gender norms. He spends one class period administering this test and collecting his data. That night he converts the raw scores into percentiles using the age and gender norms and learns that the students' abilities range from the 10th to the 95th percentile, with most of the class performing around the 50th percentile. Based on this information, what aspect of kicking do you think he should address next class?

What is the problem with Mr. Davis' assessment? The problem is that the assessment test he selected does not match the decision he needs to make. He might be able to infer from his data that the students need work on this objective since the majority of the class performed around the 50th percentile, but he does not know what part of the skill the students specifically need to work on. For example, a student who is five inches (12.5 cm) taller and 20 pounds (9 kg) heavier than the other students in the class could score in the 95th percentile but have an immature kicking pattern that could benefit from instruction, regardless of his size. What Mr. Davis should use is a criterion-referenced instrument that allows him to judge which focal points of a mature kicking pattern his students are able to perform. This assessment data would provide him with the focal points of the kick that students are underachieving, giving him the necessary information to develop appropriate learning activities. Since the assessment he used did not provide any useful information, he erroneously concludes that testing is a waste of time and that in the future he will just start teaching kicking without a prior assessment. Of course this incorrect conclusion is based on using the wrong type of assessment for the decision to be made.

Although it may appear obvious in this example that Mr. Davis did not select the appropriate assessment, it is difficult to match assessments with a wide range of abilities. For students with disabilities, teachers must make numerous decisions based on a host of factors. For example, Mary is eight years old and is recovering from a traumatic brain injury (TBI) that occurred when she was four. To teach her to catch, several decisions need to be made, including the following:

- Is Mary developmentally ready to learn this skill?
- Does Mary possess the prerequisite skills needed to learn catching (e.g., can she visually track a moving object)?
- Does Mary have any neuromuscular limitations imposed by her TBI that are interfering with her ability to perform the catch?
- What are the key focal points of catching that Mary must be able to perform in order to successfully catch?
- Which, if any, of the key focal points of the catch can Mary already perform?
- What is Mary's best learning modality?
- Does Mary have any unique communication needs that must be accommodated during assessment and instruction?
- Does Mary have any behavior issues that may interfere with assessment and instruction?
- What type of ball (e.g., size, weight, texture, color) should be used when assessing and for instruction?
- What are Mary's experience with and attitude toward physical education in general and toward catching specifically?
- Will Mary be able to work on this skill in the general physical education setting?
- What alternative approaches can be used if Mary refuses to work on catching?

The previous example highlights the wide range of instructional decisions a teacher will likely need to make when working with just one student on one motor skill. How these decisions are made and operationalized is the focus of this book. The first step in the assessment process is defining what decision needs to be made. Physical educators working with students with disabilities can be called on to make decisions in four areas: qualification, curriculum, placement, and instruction.

Qualification Decisions

Qualification decisions, which may also be referred to as eligibility or classification decisions, involve determining whether a student's level of performance warrants special attention. This could involve deciding whether a student's physical fitness performance is good enough to qualify for a national physical fitness award, determining what sport classification is needed for participation in a disabled sports event, or determining whether the deficits in a student's physical and motor abilities are significant enough to qualify him to receive special education services. In each case, there are established rules that govern how performance must be assessed as well as qualifying standards that must be met. For example, included in figure 2.3 are the federal regulations stipulating the procedures that must be followed when evaluating students to determine whether they qualify for special education services.

Adapted physical educators should be part of the school's multidisciplinary assessment team that evaluates students referred for special education (SE), especially when the nature of the disability (e.g., autism spectrum disorder, intellectual disorder, visual impairment) is known to be associated with significant motor delays. This team assesses students to determine their present level of performance (PLOP) and then interprets the results to determine whether the delays are significant enough to qualify for one of the 13 special education categories in IDEA (see IDEA Sec 300.306 and Sec 300.308).

When physical educators are called on to participate in qualification decisions, they must be able to both select and administer appropriate assessments that meet these requirements. NRIs are typically used when making qualification decisions because they provide normative interpretive data that can show the magnitude of the differences found in a student's performance compared with standards. A school could require, for example, that a student's performance be greater than two standard deviations below the mean on a standardized test to qualify for adapted physical education services. Most schools have well-defined procedures for making qualification decisions. Physical educators should familiarize themselves with these procedures so they understand their specific responsibilities as well as their roles as part of the overall assessment team.

It should be noted that in many school districts, APE specialists collaborate with other professionals who evaluate students in the motor domain such as physical and occupational therapists. This group, commonly referred to as the **motor performance team**, will frequently assess a student as a team to maximize efficiency and reduce the time and stress on the student being evaluated. Although the specialists evaluate their own domains, working as a team facilitates the sharing of information and frequently provides additional valuable insights that provide a more comprehensive picture of the students' attributes and needs. This group also frequently confers when creating their IEP goals and coordinating the provision of their services so that they maximize the benefits for the students they all serve.

Curriculum Decisions

When students qualify for SE, **curriculum decisions** are then required to determine what modifications will address the students' unique needs in the various curricula areas. Some students qualify for SE because the nature of their disability affects their development in some curricular areas but not in others. For example, Zachary, a student born Deaf, may be behind enough in language development to require SE, but physically and motorically he can perform in the normal developmental range. In this situation it is probably feasible for Zachary to follow the general physical education (GPE) curriculum, but he will likely need support services to compensate for his communication

SEC. 300.304 EVALUATION PROCEDURES

(a) Notice. The public agency must provide notice to the parents of a child with a disability, in accordance with Sec. 300.503, that describes any evaluation procedures the agency proposes to conduct.

(b) Conduct of evaluation. In conducting the evaluation, the public agency must:

(1) Use a variety of assessment tools and strategies to gather relevant functional, developmental, and academic information about the child, including information provided by the parent, that may assist in determining:

(i) Whether the child is a child with a disability under Sec. 300.8; and

(ii) The content of the child's IEP, including information related to enabling the child to be involved in and progress in the general education curriculum (or for a preschool child, to participate in appropriate activities);

(2) Not use any single measure or assessment as the sole criterion for determining whether a child is a child with a disability and for determining an appropriate educational program for the child; and

(3) Use technically sound instruments that may assess the relative contribution of cognitive and behavioral factors, in addition to physical or developmental factors.

(c) Other evaluation procedures. Each public agency must ensure that:

(1) Assessments and other evaluation materials used to assess a child under this part:

(i) Are selected and administered so as not to be discriminatory on a racial or cultural basis;

(ii) Are provided and administered in the child's native language or other mode of communication and in the form most likely to yield accurate information on what the child knows and can do academically, developmentally, and functionally, unless it is clearly not feasible to so provide or administer;

(iii) Are used for the purposes for which the assessments or measures are valid and reliable;

(iv) Are administered by trained and knowledgeable personnel; and

(v) Are administered in accordance with any instructions provided by the producer of the assessments.

(2) Assessments and other evaluation materials include those tailored to assess specific areas of educational need and not merely those that are designed to provide a single general intelligence quotient.

(3) Assessments are selected and administered so as best to ensure that if an assessment is administered to a child with impaired sensory, manual, or speaking skills, the assessment results accurately reflect the child's aptitude or achievement level or whatever other factors the test purports to measure, rather than reflecting the child's impaired sensory, manual, or speaking skills (unless those skills are the factors that the test purports to measure).

(4) The child is assessed in all areas related to the suspected disability, including, if appropriate, health, vision, hearing, social and emotional status, general intelligence, academic performance, communicative status, and motor abilities;

(5) Assessments of students with disabilities who transfer from one public agency to another public agency in the same school year are coordinated with those children's prior and subsequent schools, as necessary and as expeditiously as possible, consistent with Sec. 300.301(d)(2) and (e), to ensure prompt completion of full evaluations.

(6) In evaluating each child with a disability under Sec. Sec. 300.304 through 300.306, the evaluation is sufficiently comprehensive to identify all of the child's special education and related services needs, whether or not commonly linked to the disability category in which the child has been classified.

(7) Assessment tools and strategies that provide relevant information that directly assists persons in determining the educational needs of the child are provided.

(Authority: 20 U.S.C. 1414(b)(1)-(3), 1412(a)(6)(B))

Figure 2.3 IDEA evaluation procedures.

deficits, until these deficits are addressed in SE. The nature of the needs of other students who qualify for SE may mean that the GPE curriculum is not appropriate for them. In these instances, a specially designed curriculum will address their needs.

For example, Jennifer qualified for SE because she has a severe intellectual disability (ID) and is functioning physically and motorically four years behind her chronological age of seven. In Jennifer's case, it is highly unlikely that the GPE curriculum will be appropriate—she is developmentally already four years behind and will learn at a significantly slower rate because of her ID. This should not be misinterpreted to mean she cannot learn many of the motor skills taught in GPE; it means that given her delay and learning rate, there will not be enough time for her to learn enough of the content in the GPE curriculum to develop the functional fitness and lifetime sport and recreational skills she will need to lead a physically active life after her school years. This means a specially designed curriculum needs to be developed for Jennifer that delimits the number of PE curriculum goals and objectives to compensate for her current PLOP and learning rate.

Figure 2.4 illustrates the relationship between the GPE curriculum and different levels of specially designed APE curricula. GPE curricula typically include around 150 objectives leading to the achievement of 10 to 12 goals by the end of the program, such as demonstrated ability to develop and carry out a fitness program or play a functional game of tennis, volleyball, basketball, or golf (Kelly & Melograno, 2004). For most students with mild and moderate disabilities, there is significant overlap between their APE curricula and the GPE curriculum. This is illustrated by the smaller pyramid within the larger GPE pyramid. The APE pyramids would contain proportionally few objectives and goals. Although the APE pyramids have a smaller base, they still share the same apex with the GPE curriculum, indicating the students in the smaller pyramid will still leave the program with functional competency, just on fewer goals. However, as the severity of the disability increases, the degree of overlap with the GPE decreases and more unique content is included in the APE curricula. The apex of these pyramids may also be

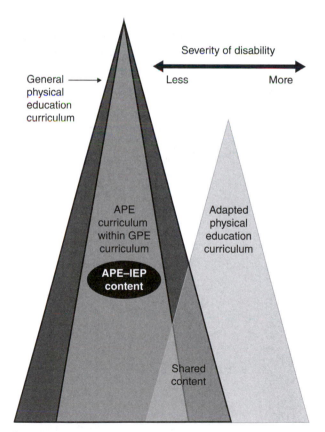

Figure 2.4 Relationship between the GPE and APE curricula.

lower, indicating the functional competency of these students will be lower or modified. For example, their functional level for bowling may be independently pushing a bowling ball down a bowling ramp instead of using a traditional three-step approach and an underhand roll.

The most efficient method for making curriculum decisions is to conduct a curriculum needs assessment (CNA). A CNA is created from the content in the GPE curriculum (for more information on step-by-step procedures for creating and conducting a CNA, see Kelly, 2011). Figure 2.5 shows the summary report from a CNA. The CNA can be designed to include any number of grades but in most cases is delimited to the first three or four years, when most students are identified and evaluated for SE. This report covers the first three years (K-2) of the GPE curriculum and evaluates whether this student is ready to be placed in the third grade GPE curriculum. The first wide column under each grade indicates the objectives that students are expected to master in the GPE curriculum that year. Next to each objective are five narrow columns labeled #, M, A, C, and E. The # column indicates the student's score on that objective. Since all the items in this CNA are CRIs, # represents the number of focal points the student successfully demonstrated when assessed. The number of focal points required for mastery is shown in parentheses after each objective [e.g., Run (5)]. The column labeled *M* indicates with a "Y" for yes or an "N" for no whether mastery was achieved.

The last three columns contain ratings of the student's attention, comprehension, and effort during the assessment. At the bottom of each grade column are calculations of the student's mastery level for that grade and cumulative mastery across the grades. These values are used to interpret whether the GPE curriculum will be appropriate for the student being evaluated. The value in the bottom right of the report, 51.5%, indicates that this student has currently mastered only approximately half the objectives the majority of students entering third grade will have already mastered. Looking across the bottom line of the report, it is clear that this student still needs to master two kindergarten objectives and has been falling further behind each year.

Given this performance profile, what is the likelihood this student will be able to remediate the 16 objectives that have not previously been learned while working on the next 11 objectives targeted for achievement in third grade? It should be abundantly clear that this student will never catch up in the GPE curriculum and that this student will need a specially designed APE curriculum. The million-dollar question is what is the critical cutoff score that determines when the GPE curriculum is appropriate? This is a complicated question that is influenced by many factors such PE class sizes, teacher competency, instructional time for PE, and available support services. As a result, this value must be set by each school district. A common cutoff score for the CNA method is 70 percent. The logic here is if students at the lower elementary grades are already 30 percent or more behind on mastering the basic physical and motor skills, which are the building blocks for more advanced skills, they are going to require both a modified curriculum and specialized instruction.

The take-home point here is that failure to assess and address the PE curriculum needs of students with disabilities will doom them to failure if the

NEEDS ASSESSMENT SUMMARY

Student's name _____ Date: _____ Assessor: _____

Goal/grade	K					1						2						Goal %
Body awareness	#	M	A	C	E		#	M	A	C	E		#	M	A	C	E	Mastery
Parts (5)	5	Y	A	A	A	Planes (5)	5	Y	A	A	A	Personal space (6)	6	Y	A	A	A	100%
Actions (6)	6	Y	A	A	A	Directions in space (6)	6	Y	A	A	A							
General space (6)	6	Y	A	A	A													
Locomotor																		00.0%
Run (5)	3	N	A	B	B	Hop (6)	2	N	B	B	C	Skip (6)	2	N	B	B	C	
Gallop (6)	3	N	A	B	C	Slide (6)	2	N	B	B	C							
Object control																		60.0%
Underhand roll (5)	5	Y	A	A	A	Kick stationary (6)	6	Y	A	A	A	Kick moving (5)	3	N	B	B	B	
Underhand throw (5)	5	Y	A	A	A							Catch (5)	2	N	B	B	C	
Body control																		16.7%
Log roll (4)	4	Y	A	A	A	Shoulder roll (5)	0	N	B	B	C	Backward roll (5)	0	N	B	B	C	
						Forward roll (5)	0	N	B	B	C	Two-point balances (4)	1	N	B	B	C	
						Balance beam walk (5)	1	N	B	B	C							
Rhythm dance																		80.0%
Even beat (4)	4	Y	A	A	A	Accent beat (4)	4	Y	B	B	B	Polka (6)	2	N	B	C	C	
Uneven beat (4)	4	Y	A	A	A	Communication through movement (5)	5	Y	B	B	B							
Social																		100%
Follow instruction (5)	5	Y	A	A	A	Work habits (6)	6	Y	A	A	A							
Fitness																		25.0%
												Partial curl-ups (4)	2	N	B	B	C	
												Stretching (5)	5	Y	A	A	A	
												Warm-up (6)	3	N	B	B	A	
												Cardiorespiratory exertion (6)	3	N	B	B	C	
Grade % mastery	9/11 = 81.8%					6/11 = 54.5%						2/11 = 18.2%						
Overall % mastery	9/11 = 81.8%					15/22 = 68.2%						17/33 = 51.5%						51.5%

Key for column headings: Goal = the name of the objective with the total number of focal points in (); # = the number of focal points the student successfully demonstrated two out of three times; M = an indication of mastery of all the focal points, demonstrated by Y or N; A = a rating of the student's level of attention during the assessment; C = a rating of the student's apparent comprehension of what skill should be performed; E = a rating of the effort the student exhibited performing this item; ratings: A = above average, B = average, C = below average.

Figure 2.5 Sample curriculum needs assessment summary report.

From Horvat, M., Kelly, L.E., Block, M.E., and Croce, R., *Developmental and adapted physical activity assessment*, 2nd ed. (Champaign, IL: Human Kinetics, 2019). Reprinted, by permission, from L.E. Kelly, 2011, *Designing and implementing effective adapted physical education programs* (Urbana, IL: Sagamore), 60.

GPE curriculum is used as the default basis for their instruction. If Jennifer, discussed earlier, was taught the GPE content, even with an APE teacher to assist her, she would continue to fall further behind each year because the GPE curriculum requires her to learn too much content in too little time. After 12 years of physical education in the GPE curriculum, she would still be at the base of the pyramid—trying to master the fundamental motor skills—and would finish her K-12 schooling without achieving any of the GPE goals needed to maintain her health and fitness. On the other hand, if an MPT assesses her needs at the start of her program, develops an appropriate APE curriculum, and implements it with ongoing assessment to ensure she learns the target content, Jennifer will leave the program having achieved her goals and with the functional physical and motor skills to maintain her fitness and participate in physical and recreational activities.

Placement Decisions

The previous curriculum decisions focused on determining the students' PLOP in physical education, in relation to the GPE curriculum content, and then how the curriculum would need to be modified to meet their unique needs. Once the curriculum is defined, **placement decisions** determine the best instructional setting for students who have qualified for SE. For students with disabilities, this means determining the most appropriate and least restrictive environment (LRE) where the physical education goals and objectives in their specially designed PE curricula and IEPs can be addressed and achieved. Figure 2.6 shows the federal regulations that pertain to LREs. The goal of the LRE mandate is to educate students with disabilities to the maximum extent possible in the general education environment, with the use of support services.

The placement decision process starts with reviewing the objectives targeted for instruction in the students' APE curricula for the coming year. These objectives become the basis for their annual goals and short-term objectives in their IEPs. Once the content to be taught for the year has been identified from the students' APE curricula, the next step is determining the LRE for the students to learn this content. The goal is to teach the APE curriculum content in GPE to the maximum extent possible. With this in mind, the students' target APE objectives for the year are compared with the GPE content. For most students with mild disabilities and many students with moderately severe disabilities, there will be a lot of overlap in the objectives between the APE and GPE curricula. The major difference will be that the APE students will have fewer objectives because their curricula have been adjusted to accommodate for their developmental delay and learning rates.

Note that there does not always need to be an exact one-to-one match when making a placement decision. For example, Luwanda has one locomotor skill, the gallop, targeted to be mastered this year in her APE program. Her target GPE class is working on galloping and sliding. Luwanda could be easily included in GPE to work on her galloping by making one simple modification. When everyone else is practicing galloping and sliding or using those skills in any game or activity, Luwanda always gets to gallop. By making just this simple adjustment, Luwanda will receive twice as much practice on the objective she needs to work on, and she will be able to practice with her classmates during physical education.

The more overlap there is between APE students' objectives and the target GPE placement, the greater the likelihood of GPE being an appropriate placement, with minor modifications as needed to address the APE students' needs. As the severity of the disability of the students increases, the likelihood of curriculum objectives overlapping decreases. However, even in these cases, every opportunity should be explored to find situations where the students can be included in GPE and still work on their APE curriculum objectives. For example, a student confined to a wheelchair could work on wheelchair skills in GPE while the GPE students work on their locomotor skills, or a student with cerebral palsy could work on a personal fitness routine while the GPE class practice their fitness skills.

LEAST RESTRICTIVE ENVIRONMENT: SEC. 300.114 LRE REQUIREMENTS

(a) General

(1) Except as provided in Sec. 300.324(d)(2) (regarding children with disabilities in adult prisons), the State must have in effect policies and procedures to ensure that public agencies in the State meet the LRE requirements of this section and Sec. Sec. 300.115 through 300.120.

(2) Each public agency must ensure that:

(i) To the maximum extent appropriate, children with disabilities, including children in public or private institutions or other care facilities, are educated with children who are nondisabled; and

(ii) Special classes, separate schooling, or other removal of children with disabilities from the regular educational environment occurs only if the nature or severity of the disability is such that education in regular classes with the use of supplementary aids and services cannot be achieved satisfactorily.

(b) Additional Requirement—State Funding Mechanism

(1) General

(i) A State funding mechanism must not result in placements that violate the requirements of paragraph (a) of this section; and

(ii) A State must not use a funding mechanism by which the State distributes funds on the basis of the type of setting in which a child is served that will result in the failure to provide a child with a disability FAPE according to the unique needs of the child, as described in the child's IEP.

(2) Assurance. If the State does not have policies and procedures to ensure compliance with paragraph (b)(1) of this section, the State must provide the Secretary an assurance that the State will revise the funding mechanism as soon as feasible to ensure that the mechanism does not result in placements that violate that paragraph.

(Authority: 20 U.S.C. 1412(a)(5))

Figure 2.6 IDEA (2004) least restrictive environment regulations.

From Horvat, M., Kelly, L.E., Block, M.E., and Croce, R., *Developmental and adapted physical activity assessment*, 2nd ed. (Champaign, IL: Human Kinetics, 2019). Information from *Federal Register,* August 23, 1977, PL 94-142, The Education for All Handicapped Children Act.

Relationship Between the APE Curriculum, IEP, and Placement

An IEP is a one-year snapshot of a student's comprehensive APE curriculum designed to meet his or her unique physical education needs. In theory, if you were to take the 12 years of a student's IEP objectives and lay them out in sequence, you should see the developmental sequences defined in the APE curriculum progress and build on each other until they culminate in the achievement of the student's physical education goals. For this to occur, the physical educator must follow the curriculum and placement decisions just described.

The culmination of making assessment-based curriculum and placement decisions produces an annual series of functional IEPs. The APE curriculum defines the students' scope and sequences and the objectives to be mastered each year during the program that will lead to the acquisition of the lifetime sport, recreation, health, and wellness goals they will need to live and maintain a healthy life. The content targeted for mastery in each year of the APE curriculum becomes the basis for the IEP instructional goals and the objectives for the coming year. The subsequent placement decisions then determine the LRE where these students can best achieve their IEP goals while being included to the maximum degree appropriate with students without disabilities.

Unfortunately, when appropriate assessment procedures are not followed, a meaningful IEP cannot be created. All too often, physical educators fail to assess the curriculum implications of the students' PLOP, developmental delays, and learning deficits and jump directly into making a placement decision. Now instead of making their placement decisions based on the students' physical and motor needs, the decision is made on which GPE class they think the students will fit into the easiest. In this case, the placement has nothing to do with addressing their physical and motor needs but is based solely on finding a placement where hopefully the students can at least be safe and will have an opportunity to participate with their peers without disabilities. Since the IEP requires some content-specific goals and objectives for physical education, a common practice is to just copy some generic objectives from other sources such as IEP databases of PE objectives, picking a few of the GPE objectives in the target placement, or from other published sources such as the SHAPE national PE standards. Of course the problem with this approach is little progress is made on learning these objectives, so the next year another random set of objectives is selected and included in the IEP.

The bottom line is that SE students receiving APE need to work on the objectives in their APE curricula so they can achieve their PE goals by the end of their programs. To ensure this happens, APE teachers must make sure

- each APE student has an appropriate APE curriculum,
- APE students are provided the requisite time and instruction to acquire the target skills,

- APE students are placed in the least restrictive PE environment possible, and
- the APE curriculum content is the basis of the IEP content.

The key to making appropriate placement decisions is ongoing assessment of the APE students' progress on the objectives targeted to be mastered each year in their curricula. If the APE students are making satisfactory progress on their target objectives in GPE, then the GPE placement should be continued. If they are not making satisfactory progress, other alternative placement options should be considered.

Instructional Decisions

Instructional decisions are the most common type of decision teachers must make. As indicated in the example of Mary, the eight-year-old recovering from traumatic brain injury, almost every action a teacher performs when teaching requires an instructional decision. These decisions can involve a wide range of assessment tools, from standardized instruments to teacher-developed checklists. The common element is that they all involve collecting data that is used to make an informed instructional decision. An important distinction is that most assessments for instructional decisions can be built into the ongoing instruction. That is, assessment is part of the instructional process and not a separate stand-alone activity.

A stereotypical view of physical education assessment is that the teacher introduces a skill to be learned, such as the underhand serve in volleyball. The teacher typically demonstrates the underhand serve and explains how the skill is used in various games and sports. She then involves the class in select drills and activities designed to provide students an opportunity to practice and learn the underhand volleyball serve. Finally, at the end of the unit, the teacher tests the students on their underhand serving ability. There are a number of problems with this approach. First, collecting assessment data at the end of the unit is of little value because without preassessment data from the beginning of the unit, there is no way to know if the students' performance on the underhand serve improved or got worse. This method of assessment also puts too much responsibility on the learner. It communicates to the students that the sole purpose of assessment is to test them. For students to learn under the demonstration method, they must be able to watch the teacher's demonstration and then determine the following:

- What are the key focal points of the underhand volleyball serve?
- Which of these focal points can they already perform correctly, and which ones do they need to work on?
- Which component should they try to correct first?
- Of the focal points they need to work on, what specifically are they doing wrong, and what specifically should they do differently to correct their performance?
- Finally, when given a chance to work on this skill, what should they do?

For many students who cannot automatically replicate what they see the teacher demonstrate, all these decisions are beyond their ability. Clearly, it should be the teacher's responsibility to do these tasks. The teacher should explain that in order to learn any motor skill, the students must first know the key components, or focal points, of the skill. The teacher should demonstrate each focal point and explain how the students can self-assess themselves to determine whether they are performing each one correctly. When the students identify that they have a problem with a focal point, they should be encouraged to ask for assistance both from the teacher and from their peers. During all instruction, the teacher should systematically observe and assess all the students and validate or correct their self-assessments. The teacher should also group individuals for instruction and design appropriate learning activities that focus on the specific focal points of the skill being taught. At the end of the unit, the teacher should systemically observe performance during game activities and record these values as the final assessment. When done correctly, students should not perceive that they are being tested but instead should view assessment as a natural part of the learning process. The take-home point is that it is the teachers' responsibility to make assessment-based instructional decisions to facilitate and guide the learning of their students so they achieve the curriculum objectives.

IS ASSESSMENT REALLY NECESSARY?

Are you convinced now that in order to teach you must assess, or are you thinking, *I can see how assessment could be used in conjunction with teaching, but I think I can still teach without assessing*? Let's examine case study 2.

So what can you learn about assessment from Mr. Brady's lesson? First, before instruction, determine what the students need to learn and the content you plan to teach (e.g., how to kick a soccer ball), and choose an assessment instrument to measure how to perform that behavior. Second, use this initial assessment data to identify the students' learning needs, and then design appropriate learning activities and instructional groups to address these needs. Finally, continually assess during instruction to provide students with relevant feedback, to evaluate the effectiveness of your learning activities, and to ensure that students are on task and working on the appropriate focal points of the skill based on their assessed needs.

ASSESSMENT IS ESSENTIAL

Clearly, assessment is important when teaching all students, but it is critical when working with students with disabilities. Although some students with disabilities have excellent physical and motor skills and require no modifications in physical education, many others have multiple factors that interfere with their ability to efficiently learn in physical education. For these students, learning motor skills can be very time consuming as well as physically and emotionally draining. These students frequently start with marked developmental delays and learn at much slower rates than typical of their peers.

Case Study 2
What Is the Key to Effective Teaching?

Mr. Brady elects not to assess his class before a soccer unit because he believes he has a pretty good idea of their soccer skills. For the first lesson, he focuses on the instep kick. He demonstrates the correct kicking pattern several times and calls particular attention to where his laces make contact with the ball. Once during his demonstration, he has to stop and prompt a student to pay attention. This student has a severe learning disability and frequently acts out in class. After Mr. Brady completes his instruction and demonstrations, he divides the class into small work groups and assigns each an activity that involves kicking. During the practice session, Mr. Brady moves around the gym, observing the class. Soon after the session begins, there is a problem with one student who has been picking up the ball and throwing it at others. Mr. Brady has to intervene, remind the student of the class rules, and warn him that not following directions will result in time-out. Mr. Brady continues to observe the class; he notices that another student is performing the skill well, so he stops the class so the other students can observe her kick. Near the end of the class, Mr. Brady runs a group activity that involves kicking. At the end of the activity, he congratulates the class for their good work on kicking and tells them to practice on their own between now and the next class. Realizing he did not have any additional behavior problems, he also mentions he is pleased that the class followed the class rules. How do you think Mr. Brady's lesson went?

If you examine Mr. Brady's class from the perspective of two students, you see a variation in the success of the lesson. Tracy had a great time, loves physical education, and plays on a local youth soccer team. She is one of the better kickers in the class and likes to show off her abilities. During the practice session, she made sure she was the one kicking when Mr. Brady came near their group. She was thrilled when Mr. Brady singled her out to demonstrate her kick. She cannot wait until the next physical education class. The other student, Ben, did not have such a great time. He does not like physical education because he cannot perform as well as other students. The other students also make fun of him. During the practice session, the kids in his group started making fun of his kicking, so he picked up the ball and threw it at them and received Mr. Brady's warning. For the rest of the class, Ben decided to just watch the other kids; he positioned himself so he could keep an eye on Mr. Brady, and whenever the teacher came near, Ben acted as if he were working with the group. At the end of class he was disappointed to hear that they would be working on kicking again next class, but he was glad Mr. Brady didn't yell at him again. He concluded he is better off just staying out of Mr. Brady's sight during physical education rather than trying to do the skills and being laughed at by the other students.

Further, it is impossible for Mr. Brady to know what the students learned during class because he did not collect any pre- or postassessment data. If he had, he would have found that neither student showed any improvement in their kicking. Tracy already had a mature kicking pattern before his instruction and just practiced the skill she already had during class, while Ben had mastered none of the focal points of the kick at the start or end of the class. What Ben learned was a new coping and avoidance behavior. He practiced this new coping and avoiding skill for 20 minutes during the practice session and group activity, and Mr. Brady reinforced Ben's efforts at the end of class.

As a result, many of these students become easily frustrated when learning motor skills and may eventually refuse to even try or will give up after only one attempt if they are not successful. In other words, these students have a low tolerance for failure. If the teacher cannot match the learning activities to their unique needs to ensure success, they will fail and most likely give up.

Once students give up, the teacher must spend a considerable amount of time and energy redirecting and motivating them to try again. When the students do eventually agree to try again, it is imperative that they succeed. Success develops confidence both in their ability to learn and in the teacher's ability to teach them. Failure reinforces their perception that they cannot learn motor skills and also that the teacher cannot help. The key to ensuring success and preventing this failure cycle is assessment. For these students to learn, thrive, and enjoy physical education, the skills they are taught must be task analyzed into small, teachable focal points that are accurately assessed and used to design appropriate learning activities.

What You Need to Know

Key Terms

assessment

criterion-referenced
  instruments

curriculum decisions

evaluation

focal points

formative evaluation

instructional decisions

measurement

motor performance team

norm-referenced instruments

placement decisions

process measures

product measures

qualification decisions

reference standards

summative evaluation

Key Concepts

1. You should be able to explain the differences between norm-referenced instruments and criterion-referenced instruments.
2. You should be able to compare and contrast the four major types of assessment-based decisions teachers need to make in physical education when working with students with disabilities.
3. You should know the role and function of continuous assessment during instruction in physical education.
4. You should understand how student success and failure are controlled through assessment in physical education.
5. You should be able to explain the differences between formative and summative evaluation and when each is used in physical education.

Review Questions

1. Define the purpose of qualification decisions in physical education. When are these decisions made? What type of assessment tools should be used when making this type of decision?
2. Define the purpose of curriculum decisions in physical education. When are these decisions made? What type of assessment tools should be used when making this type of decision?
3. Define the purpose of placement decisions in physical education. When are these decisions made? What type of assessment tools should be used when making this type of decision?
4. Define the purpose of instructional decisions in physical education. When are these decisions made? What type of assessment tools should be used when making this type of decision?
5. Outline the step-by-step procedures a teacher should follow to determine where a new student, who has qualified for special education, should be placed for physical education and what content should be taught to this student this year.

Chapter **3**

Getting to Know the Student

Any proficiency demonstrated by a student today has been shaped by events that make up his or her growth and development history. When assessing performance in any domain, determining performance levels within that domain marks but one phase of the assessment process. As you develop any comprehensive assessment, you must also understand factors that may affect current performance. For example, enrichment activities, deprivation, and traumatic events as well as physical and sensory impairments are several factors that contribute to a person's present level of function. As you extend your decision-making process, you become a detective, gathering relevant background and current information from a variety of sources that can affect decision making and serve as the foundation for selecting instruction strategies. With this information, you will be better positioned to understand and plan for an individual's physical activity future.

Knowing where a student has come from almost always provides insights into present-day performance. These insights, in turn, help lay the foundation for selecting teaching strategies that will enhance the student's potential. Getting to know an individual student is a process that begins not with selecting and administering tests but with a thorough knowledge of the student's background. Background information can be obtained from health and medical records, psychological workups, school files, case studies, and anecdotal reports. The purpose of this chapter is to examine the types of background information gathered before the assessment process. Key topics include the information available in the files of a school district.

CENTRAL AND SCHOOL FILES

Depending on the school district, information about a student's performance may be available to the teacher from the **central file**. Central files are electronic in many school districts and are the primary source of available information and the driving force behind the treatment plan. The central file is kept by the director of special education and may include such items as the following:

- Parent questionnaire and developmental history
- Results of vision and hearing screening
- Referral of concern from school support team
- IEP
- Protocol file (test protocol or history)
- Consent for evaluation
- Doctor form
- ADHD form (available in some school districts)

It also contains the most up-to-date information concerning the student's progress and overall functioning. For the adapted physical education teacher, the director of special education is the link to information that may be required for physical education.

A student's cumulative or special education file may also provide valuable information for assessment and program development. Initial files established for each student follow the student through the school years. Although the precise content of cumulative records may vary among school districts, recent test history and evaluations are available for comparisons. Updated records or assessments can provide information on recent changes in the student's condition or functional ability. Cumulative **school files** may be available electronically and typically include the following:

- Name, address, family status
- IEP
- Consent for placement
- Current psychological assessment
- Copies of classroom modifications
- Release of neuropsychological assessments
- Due process forms

By directing the teacher to problems that may occur in physical education, school files can be extremely valuable in planning an adapted physical education action plan. If a student's file reveals a history of distractibility, for example, such information can help the tester decide on the types of tests to administer and conditions for testing. A student who is distractible may be tested when there are a minimum of distractions in the testing environment. If a student with diabetes is to be assessed on a physical fitness test, the adapted physical education teacher should schedule the test after lunch to avoid problems with blood sugar.

In several states, a web-based program called Easy IEP can be accessed from any location. In addition, confidential hard copies, both current and past, stay in the file at the school.

HEALTH-RELATED RECORDS

To plan an appropriate physical education program, teachers must scrutinize available **health-related records** for relevant information that will aid the assessment process and subsequent program planning. Teachers must clearly understand that such records are confidential and must always be treated in an appropriate manner. In both school and agency settings, the nurse or other health personnel can assist in reviewing available records for a particular student, while parents can also be asked to share health-related material. Health and medical files should be examined for essential information:

- Chronic illnesses (e.g., diabetes, chronic heart condition, chronic asthma)
- Acute illnesses (e.g., appendicitis, chicken pox)
- Record of mild illnesses (e.g., frequency of colds, headaches, earaches) and records of absenteeism due to illness
- Sensory impairments (e.g., vision or hearing loss, speech or language difficulties)
- Physical impairments (e.g., cerebral palsy, muscular dystrophy, amputation)
- Persistence of reflexes or contraindicators to activity
- Written permission from parent or guardian to contact medical personnel in case of emergency
- Phone numbers of parents or guardians in case of emergency
- Medications, including dosages and their purposes

A quick perusal of the health file can be valuable because it often reveals vital information about the student's health history. This preliminary assessment may pinpoint areas in need of further assessment. For example, a health file may indicate that Amy receives physical therapy once per week (see case study 1). It is crucial that the teacher determine reasons for and the nature of the therapy. Such information enables the teacher to work in conjunction with the therapist to provide Amy with experiences that facilitate her physical activity goals.

Case Study 1
Difficulty Rising, Tendency to Fall

Amy is a preschool student of four years of age. She has a tendency to fall while playing and has difficulty rising from a prone position. She also tilts her head to one side while reaching or stepping and has difficulty with object control skills.

A consultation with Amy's doctor revealed that Amy has a mild form of muscular dystrophy. The teacher should assess muscular strength (handheld dynamometer), range of motion (goniometer), and gait (gait analysis) and concurrently develop an intervention for Amy. He can also develop an observational analysis to prompt Amy for correctly throwing, reaching, and stepping as well as rising from a chair. His intervention can then focus on specific exercises such as hand weights or surgical tubing to improve overall strength and movement.

Before obtaining health-related information from the MPT, doctor, or other allied health professional, it is essential to follow due process procedures and secure parental permission for the records to be released. In some school districts, this information may be part of the confidential file available to all school personnel. At this juncture, it may be appropriate for the teacher to contact the parent or guardian, doctor, school or agency nurse, and other therapists and allied health personnel whose names appear in the file. The file should provide an important information base and reveal the student's history, current status, and future needs. It is equally important that the teacher provide (as well as receive) relevant information (e.g., Amy has a low level of muscular strength and fatigues easily). This information will be beneficial in the instructional process to the extent that teachers understand what is required to increase or maintain physical functioning.

Teachers, along with allied professionals on the MPT, the parent or guardian, and the student, must work cooperatively to plan an appropriate program based on assessment information from many sources. Because each person offers a unique perspective of the student's functioning, individual viewpoints are essential in assessing and planning an intervention. Sometimes there is the tendency for one specialist, if acting in relative isolation, to see the student only through the eyes of his or her specialty. For example, the physical therapist may think that a student with cerebral palsy should use an electric-powered wheelchair, while the classroom teacher and parent believe it is essential to promote functional strength and not rely on electronic devices. Generally, the more perspectives available, the greater the likelihood the student will be perceived and subsequently served as a whole person. This whole-person approach reveals a wide spectrum of abilities that are often interrelated and interdependent. Finally, the more individual needs identified, the greater the likelihood that needs can be met and program objectives achieved. Included in figure 3.1 is a sample medical authorization form that can be used to gather

Developmental Adapted Physical Education
Long-Term Disability

Date sent: _____

Students should participate in physical education on a regular basis. If a permanent or long-term disability interferes with participation in the regular physical education program, an individualized physical education curriculum will be planned around the student's motor strengths and abilities. The student shall be enrolled in the *adapted program* based on completion of this form.

Student's name: _____ DOB: _____ School: _____

Grade: _____

Parent/Guardian: _____ Phone: _____

Disability: _____

Characteristics of disability: _____

_____

Expected duration of disability: _____

Medication type (implication for physical activity): _____ Dosage: _____

Concerns: _____

_____

The following activities will be adapted to the student's individual capabilities. Please mark any activity you would **NOT** recommend for the above student.

I. Physical fitness activities
- ☐ arm–shoulder strength
- ☐ abdominal strength
- ☐ flexibility (range of motion)
- ☐ cardiorespiratory endurance
- ☐ leg strength
- ☐ catching

II. Locomotor activities
- ☐ creeping
- ☐ crawling
- ☐ walking
- ☐ running
- ☐ sliding
- ☐ hopping
- ☐ jumping
- ☐ skipping
- ☐ galloping

III. Nonlocomotor activities
- ☐ bending
- ☐ twisting
- ☐ pushing
- ☐ pulling
- ☐ lifting
- ☐ hanging
- ☐ balancing
- ☐ swinging

IV. Aquatics
- ☐ swimming skills
- ☐ water play
- ☐ diving

V. Object control skills
- ☐ kicking
- ☐ striking
- ☐ overhead throwing
- ☐ underhand throwing
- ☐ ball bouncing

Figure 3.1   Sample medical authorization form.

(continued)

MEDICAL AUTHORIZATION FORM *(CONTINUED)*

VI. Other activities not recommended

_____

_____

_____

_____

_____

_____

_____

_____

Comments:_____

Specific activities or motor and fitness goals: _____

_____

Your input will assist us in determining an appropriate instructional program.

Date: _____   Signed: _____, MD

Phone number: _____

Figure 3.1   *(continued)*

From Horvat, M., Kelly, L.E., Block, M.E., and Croce, R., *Developmental and adapted physical activity assessment*, 2nd ed. (Champaign, IL: Human Kinetics, 2019).

activity-related information. When seeking background information about a student, particular attention should be paid to the following:

- Medical diagnosis
- Condition's severity
- Prognosis
- Psychological evaluations
- Medication
- Symptoms or characteristics with potential for impact in adapted physical education settings
- Past and current courses of treatment
- Recommended and restricted activities (source, rationale)

Teachers and members of the MPT who attempt to secure medical information need to be aware that, for a variety of reasons, such information may not always be immediately forthcoming. Although difficulties may be encountered when communicating with doctors, a teacher has the responsibility to secure the information if possible.

The doctor may respond slowly and often cautiously for a variety of reasons. How soon or thoroughly a doctor responds may depend, in part, on how highly he prioritizes the teacher's need for information. Some doctors, concerned about medical malpractice in a society that has become excessively litigious, are hesitant to provide information that could become the basis for future litigation. For the same reason that a doctor may be hesitant to provide information, it may be equally important for the teacher to have information. Finally, a doctor is bound by confidentiality, and her willingness to respond will be better ensured when she has written permission from a parent or guardian to share patient history with the teacher. In case study 1, this is particularly important for the adapted physical education teacher because the doctor can provide valuable information concerning Amy's functional status and any contraindications for exercise.

PSYCHOLOGICAL WORKUPS

In most school settings, it is likely that the student has been referred previously for assessment by a school or agency psychologist. Records of **psychological workups**, both formal and informal, can provide insights that help determine how the student's psychological characteristics might be responsible for his or her performance status. These considerations might also affect decisions regarding types of tests that need to be administered and what environmental conditions might yield reliable and valid information. For example, if cognition is impaired, the student might not understand some of the instructions on a test or the abstract notion of exerting a maximal effort. In addition, memory functions or behavior may interfere with the test setting and with getting adequate responses that can be used to develop instructional strategies. For the MPT, this information may be valuable in understanding the student's psychological frame of reference or the environment in which instruction should occur. It also influences the selection of interventions and the potential to ensure learning.

AGENCY FILES

Whenever a student is served by a particular agency, that agency typically maintains records of that client's participation. Agencies can include hospitals, sports organizations, and social services. Often the kinds of information found in health-related records and school and special education files will be reflected in **agency files**. Depending on the nature of the service provided, information specific to that agency's program emphasis will appear in the file. If the student has completed participation in a given agency's program, the teacher can review pretest results, progress reports, and posttest results recorded during the client's participation. Of particular value are insights from summary reports and anecdotal reports. Summary reports or interviews often afford information that is not apparent when reviewing quantitative assessments. For example, an assessor may place a student in a work-related setting and interview the job supervisor about the employee's work habits, ability to relate, and personality in that environment. The report may also contain information from the individual or parent concerning job satisfaction or problems encountered in that setting. Obviously, these reports may be biased by the person responding or a new person who has little knowledge of the client's background and experience.

INSIGHTS FROM PARENTS AND GUARDIANS

Parents and guardians have the right to be involved in the assessment process and should be encouraged to provide information aside from what is legally mandated. Parents can report information, typically from a naturalistic setting, about their child's history or out-of-school environment. This information may include the student's developmental history, including interviews, complete case histories, and experiences in transition situations or work environments. School personnel may have little or no knowledge of the student's past, and they typically observe behavior only within the context of the educational program. **Parental insights** may include the following:

- *Family history:* name and birth date as well as other siblings (including age and gender)
- *Birth history:* pregnancy history, birth weight, complications during or immediately after birth
- *Physical and health history:* overall health history, including present health status and physical functioning, and developmental history, including milestones (e.g., sitting, walking, toilet training, talking) or lags in development
- *Social interaction and play development:* relationships with friends and siblings; play development and interests; interaction with family, other students, teachers
- *School history:* current performance levels and progress in school; test evaluations and recommendations of teachers, therapists, doctors; current program or transition plan

Interviews should be conducted with sensitivity and their purpose made clear to the parent. The interviewer must encourage the parent or guardian to talk freely while minimizing, to the extent feasible, his or her own participation. This will facilitate the parent's or guardian's ability to reveal essential, focused insights. Interview questions should be objective and reflect the interview's focus. For example, "At what age did Amy walk?" is more appropriate than a subjective question such as "Amy walked by age one, didn't she?" Figure 3.2 provides a useful format for interviewing parents about their child's motor development history.

INSIGHTS FROM OTHER SCHOOL OR AGENCY PERSONNEL

Sources other than those previously cited can provide additional valuable information about a student, particularly if the student was previously in a general (i.e., unmodified) program and has only recently been referred for adapted physical education. Coworkers and others on the MPT will be able to offer insights that shed light on how the current referral for assessment came to be deemed necessary. Classroom teachers, speech therapists, and physical educators may be able to share their observations about a student's motor development, fitness, behavioral and play history, or most efficient modality for learning. Such information can be most helpful if it is systematically recorded.

Adapted Physical Education
Gross Motor Development

Student's name: _____   Interview date: _____

Date of birth: _____   Grade/teacher: _____

Interviewer: _____

Name of parent/guardian: _____

Address: _____   Phone: _____

	A. Motor development	Yes	No	Unsure
1.	First walked without crawling beforehand (creeping on hands and knees)	☐	☐	☐
2.	First walked before 12 months	☐	☐	☐
3.	First walked between 12 and 18 months	☐	☐	☐
4.	First walked between 18 and 24 months	☐	☐	☐
5.	First walked after 24 months	☐	☐	☐
6.	Seemed to sit, stand, and walk late	☐	☐	☐
7.	Walks on toes	☐	☐	☐
8.	Walks flat-footed	☐	☐	☐
	B. Coordination			
9.	Falls frequently	☐	☐	☐
10.	Bumps into things, people frequently	☐	☐	☐
11.	Loses balance easily	☐	☐	☐
12.	Seems to show shaky, jerky movements	☐	☐	☐
	C. Body awareness			
13.	Feels uncomfortable about his or her body	☐	☐	☐
14.	Confused easily about direction (e.g., right, left, forward, sideways)	☐	☐	☐
15.	Understands basic body parts and their relationships (e.g., front, back, arm, foot)	☐	☐	☐
	D. Physical fitness			
16.	Tires easily	☐	☐	☐
17.	Overweight	☐	☐	☐
18.	Seems to lack strength	☐	☐	☐
19.	Lacks vitality (energy, enthusiasm)	☐	☐	☐

Figure 3.2   Suggested format for interviewing parents or guardians about a student's motor development history.

(continued)

PARENT INTERVIEW (CONTINUED)

	E. Social and emotional development			
20.	Enjoys balls, bats, and other movement toys (jump ropes, rebounder)	☐	☐	☐
21.	Plays outdoors often	☐	☐	☐
22.	Plays vigorously with other students	☐	☐	☐
23.	Enjoys gym class	☐	☐	☐
24.	Participates in extracurricular physical activities	☐	☐	☐
25.	Enjoys playing physical games and sports	☐	☐	☐

Figure 3.2   *(continued)*

From Horvat, M., Kelly, L.E., Block, M.E., and Croce, R., *Developmental and adapted physical activity assessment*, 2nd ed. (Champaign, IL: Human Kinetics, 2019).

Case Study 2
Attention Disorder

Ian is a 12-year-old seventh grader who has difficulty remembering the instructions for game activities. He commonly blurts out answers before the teacher is finished but has difficulty completing sequences in the proper order. By consulting with Ian's teacher, the physical educator discovers that Ian's homework is not turned in on time and is often incomplete. His desk is unorganized, and his academic performance is low. Ian has been given a prescription for Adderall but does not take the medication on a regular basis.

   Several red flags suggest a learning or attention disorder. The prescription of Adderall necessitates more information from the doctor or psychologist concerning Ian's difficulties. If Ian takes the medication according to the doctor's recommendation, his problem may be remediated. If not, an alternative medication may be prescribed or more extensive neurological screenings should be utilized. In addition, the teacher should structure the environment and employ behavior management strategies to remediate Ian's performance.

Once the information has been recorded, patterns of behavior, growth, and development become more apparent and will aid in the decision-making process. For example, if Ian has a problem with attention, then this problem should be recorded and used to determine the proper assessment (see case study 2). Likewise, Mickey (case study 3) may need specific medication for his condition. Historical information from school or agency personnel may be gathered through interviews or by use of other informal measures, including rating scales or checklists (e.g., for observing a student's motor skills or social interactions during recess).

Case Study 3
Preexercise Medication

Mickey is a very active nine-year-old fourth grader who is also very athletic. However, during physical activity he sometimes has to stop and cough. After a brief rest, he usually rejoins the activity. During physical fitness testing, he complained of being tired and could not complete a walk/run.

In this context, the teacher should be aware of any medical conditions that affect physical performance as well as any medications Mickey may need. By consulting with the school nurse, the teacher finds that Mickey has asthma and needs to take medication before exercise.

Other school personnel who may provide valuable preassessment information to the adapted physical education specialist include nurses, administrators, teacher aides, and occupational therapists. The school nurse, in particular, might share information not always found in a student's school file. Often, the school nurse will have had meetings or conversations with the student's parents, doctor, or other therapists. In this context, the nurse may provide information on the use of specific medication (e.g., for a student with asthma) or on medications that could affect the student's performance or safety in physical education. Although essential information is usually documented in the health file, the insights of other school personnel should be considered along with other informal assessment information.

Nonschool personnel may also provide valuable information. If the student lives in a group home, the group home supervisor may shed some light on the student's needs, such as behavior prompts or reinforcement strategies. Likewise, an employment supervisor may provide important insights from the workplace perspective on the student's training needs, such as the amount of strength and endurance needed to lift and stack objects in the workplace.

INSIGHTS FROM THE STUDENT

Too often, students are overlooked or underutilized as a source of information, but **student insights** can be invaluable. Students can provide information about their specific needs or self-satisfaction with their situation. Sometimes, however, a person with a disability is not perceived (by those without disabilities) as being capable of determining and articulating his own unique interests and needs (Horvat & Kalakian, 1996). Teachers need to recognize this and go directly to the student for information that typically is reported by others. Any question asked of someone else should also be addressed directly to the student, when appropriate.

It is important to establish a rapport with the student and to show genuine interest in the answers. Rapport helps alleviate anxiety and provides important information on the student's viewpoint. For example, the interviewer might say, "I've asked you to meet with me this morning to share with you what our program has to offer. Just as important, our staff is genuinely interested in what you would like to learn and do as you participate in our program." When interviewing students or persons whose social or mental ages do not roughly equate with their chronological ages, communication should match the individual's developmental status.

ROLES IN THE ASSESSMENT PROCESS

Interpretation of test data provides a major means of getting to know the student. Yet there has not always been clear determination or agreement among allied professionals on the MPT regarding who assesses what. Physical education assessments of persons with disabilities have not historically been undertaken by adapted physical education personnel. It is not particularly uncommon for persons with disabilities to have been assessed for physical education by general physical education teachers, occupational therapists, physical therapists, mainstream classroom teachers, special education teachers, and sometimes psychologists. The person responsible for adapted physical education *must* be thoroughly familiar with the test, test content, and test administration procedures. The person conducting adapted physical education assessments should also be firmly grounded in adapted physical education and its relationship to special education and related services in the school setting.

At times, there will be honest differences of opinion among allied professionals regarding who makes up the MPT. For example, flexibility is one component of physical fitness, and as such, it is typically addressed in a physical education curriculum. Flexibility is also addressed in physical therapy. The occupational therapist may assess throwing because he perceives throwing as a manipulative skill. Yet the same skill might be assessed by an adapted physical education specialist, who sees throwing skill development as being within the purview of her own profession.

Often, there are no clear-cut boundaries for determining if a given activity belongs to a specific profession. This perhaps is how it should be, since professionals who worry more about territorial imperatives than about students may be putting their professions ahead of the very persons whom the professions are trying to serve. Individuals who serve the same students must strive to create a working environment characterized by communication, mutual respect, and, foremost, the development of specific goals in the best interests of the person being served.

Assessment by the Physical Educator

Physical education teachers are involved in assessment at a variety of levels. The elementary physical educator may be responsible for conducting initial posture or scoliosis screening at the preschool or kindergarten levels. Screening is a type of general assessment administered to all students in a class. At early age levels, motor screening becomes part of a larger, more comprehensive screening of general cognitive, affective, psychological, and social development. Individuals diagnosed as having disabilities at early age levels are usually referred for more in-depth diagnostic assessment.

The physical educator and other members of the MPT may also conduct screening tests at the primary and upper elementary grades. General fitness tests, such as FitnessGram, are often administered by the elementary physical education teacher. FitnessGram has health-related items that reflect healthy zones and areas to be improved. Its use as a placement tool among persons who have disabilities may be of somewhat limited value in relation to norm-referenced tests that specifically address individual needs and level of functioning. Teachers make decisions and plan instruction around areas of strength and need. Results of such assessments can help determine whether an individual with a disability meets entry or exit criteria for placement in adapted physical education.

At middle and high school levels, physical educators may administer tests corresponding to certain curricular units of instruction. For example, the teacher may select a soccer skills test for use at the end of a soccer unit. In a skills test, individuals are asked to demonstrate proficiencies in specific skills presented during the physical education class. Secondary-level physical educators may also administer group fitness tests and sometimes may administer written tests to assess knowledge of physical education concepts.

Today, most physical education curricula are objective based, with clearly defined achievement criteria for each grade level (Horvat, Kalakian, Croce, and Dahlstrom, 2011). Objective-based curricula readily lend themselves to ongoing criterion-referenced assessment. In some schools, physical education teachers must report their classes' percentage of mastery on curricular objectives taught during the school year. Objective-based programs with curriculum-embedded assessment provide a clearly defined system for evaluating programs, individualizing instruction, and monitoring pupil progress toward objectives. Objective-based instruction has had tremendous impact on physical education. Curriculum planning, accountability, and curriculum-embedded assessment are now integral parts of a field in which, for some, individualization had seemed next to impossible.

Members of the MPT are faced with the challenge of conducting diagnostic tests. Assessment for diagnostic purposes requires that the teacher gather data that help determine the specific nature of individual motor difficulties or why individuals are having problems in physical education. For example, diagnostic motor testing is utilized to pinpoint particular motor development problem areas such as agility or eye–hand coordination. In-depth diagnostic assessment of motor functioning is usually administered individually. Diagnostic instruments may be formal (e.g., norm referenced) or informal (e.g., criterion referenced). Formal diagnostic tests tend to be more time consuming and may require a separate session for each objective area.

Because diagnostic tests are usually administered to students individually, it is difficult for the general physical educator to find time to test each student. In some school districts, adapted physical educators or other MPT members assume responsibility for all movement-related individual assessments.

The content of skills tests administered by physical educators can vary and may include tests of sports skills, fundamental motor skills, or perceptual-motor abilities. The content of these tests should directly reflect skills taught in the physical education curriculum, and skills in the curriculum should directly reflect skills needed in community- and home-based settings.

Assessments by Specialists Representing Other Therapies

In recent years, schools have become more interdisciplinary in providing opportunities for individuals who have disabilities. An important manifestation of this trend is that occupational therapists (OTs), physical therapists (PTs), and vocational trainers have undertaken contributing roles in public schools. Pursuant to federal mandates, these therapies are provided as related services when determined necessary to facilitate a student's special education program. When therapists are members of the MPT, portions of motor assessment can be conducted by the OT or PT. Traditionally, OTs and PTs have functioned within a medical model, while physical educators have functioned within an educational model. Physical education teachers primarily assess observable, measurable motor skills, while OTs and PTs tend to assess processes underlying movement. For example, the physical educator might assess throwing skill, while the physical therapist might assess range of motion, which to some extent underlies the ability to throw skillfully. The OT might also assess manipulative abilities that facilitate ball handling, which in turn affects throwing proficiency.

These individuals must work together to facilitate appropriate assessments that identify a student's functional performance levels in the following areas:

- Gross and fine motor skills
- Reflex and reaction development
- Developmental landmarks
- Sensorimotor functioning
- Self-help skills
- Prevocational skills
- Social interaction skills
- Ambulatory devices

Several assessment areas overlap between adapted physical education and special education. This sort of overlap of professional responsibilities has been the subject of some controversy. The MPTs, however, can work cooperatively to avoid gaps in both assessment and service. Upon receiving and reviewing the referral of a student for assessment, it is vital that physical educators and therapists cooperatively plan and decide who will administer each type of assessment. Each professional brings unique, relevant information to the team meeting. The MPT approach to assessment emphasizes sharing, respecting, and learning from each team member's contribution. For example, the OT, adapted physical education teacher, and vocational trainer can work together to develop the specific intervention strategies needed for the individualized transition plan (ITP) by assessing components of the tasks required in the workplace and the physical skills needed to accomplish these tasks.

In some schools, physical therapists are available to assist in motor assessment, providing valuable insights for planning appropriate physical activities. For students who have physical disabilities (e.g., cerebral palsy, muscular dystrophy), motor assessment may be based primarily on a medical model. Physical therapists can evaluate tonus and persistence of reflexes that interfere with range of motion, posture, and movement patterns. The results of a clinical evaluation by a physical therapist can then be combined with information gathered by a physical educator to develop the program plan. In cases involving physically disabling conditions when only early diagnostic information is available, an evaluation by a physical therapist may shed light on present functional capacity and subsequent implications for physical education programming (e.g., by determining head movements that may induce a reflex). In addition to identifying physiological (motor), topographical (affected parts of body), and etiological (causative) factors used in classifying physical disabilities, physical therapists can also conduct supplemental evaluations, including the following:

- Posture evaluation
- Eye–hand behavior patterns (eye dominance, eye movements, fixation, convergence, grasp)
- Visual status (sensory defects, motor defects)
- Early reflexes
- Joint range of motion and strength
- Stability skills (locomotor, head control, trunk control)
- Motor symptoms (spasticity, athetosis, ataxia, rigidity, tremors)

All the members of the MPT can provide information vital to the intervention process. Since the therapist's intervention is minimal, the adapted physical education teacher needs to translate relevant evaluative information into appropriate educational goals for each student. Within this context, the objectives defined from the evaluation of MPTs must be observable and measurable, and they must be used to develop an appropriate intervention plan based on individual needs.

CONCLUSION

Determining levels of performance is just one phase in getting to know a student's needs. You must understand the factors that affect performance and the student's level of function. In order to make proper decisions, it is essential to access all the current, background, and relevant information from various sources. In case study 3, Mickey has difficulty breathing and requires preexercise medication that helps him participate in physical activity.

What You Need to Know

Key Terms

agency files

central file

health-related records

parental insights

psychological workups

school files

student insights

Key Concepts

1. You should understand the general role of assessment in developing the intervention program.
2. You should understand medical and psychological parameters that affect the student's functioning.
3. You should be familiar with the medical concerns of students with disabilities.

Review Questions

1. What type of information is available in your local school district? Who has access to this information?
2. What information should the physical education teacher provide at the program intervention meeting?
3. What essential information does the adapted physical education teacher get from other teachers or school personnel?
4. What additional resources are available to physical education teachers and adapted physical education teachers in understanding the needs of their students?

Chapter 4

Selecting an Appropriate Assessment Instrument

The purpose of this chapter is to provide a basic understanding of the essential criteria all assessment instruments must possess: validity, reliability, objectivity, and norms. Once you understand these factors, you can use them to evaluate assessment instruments to determine which are most appropriate for the decisions you need to make. You will also need to use these criteria when creating your own assessment instruments, which is common when working with students with disabilities.

Selecting an appropriate means of assessment is a complex process that starts with understanding the psychometric qualities of the instruments. Once you know what to look for in a sound assessment instrument, you can start the process of matching the instrument to the decision to be made and ensuring that you can competently administer the test. When evaluating the appropriateness of any measurement tool, you must consider validity, reliability, and objectivity. This chapter defines these terms, discusses their role in determining an instrument's trustworthiness, and discusses how these factors interact with each other.

47

The purpose of conducting any assessment is to collect accurate data so that an informed decision can be made. You learned in chapter 2 that teachers need to make four types of decisions (i.e., qualification, curriculum, placement, and instructional) and that each of these decisions determines the type of assessment instrument that should be used. In physical education, particularly when working with students with disabilities, collecting accurate assessment data is not as simple as matching a commercially and readily available test with the type of decision that needs to be made. Consider case study 1.

VALIDITY

Validity is a function of what is measured by the test and how the test results are used. An assessment instrument is considered valid if the scores obtained measure what the instrument was designed to measure, and there is evidence to support this judgment. In physical education, instruments are used to

Case Study 1
Selecting the Right Tool for the Job

A neighbor of Ms. Johanson, knowing she is a physical educator, asks her to evaluate his son Peter's running pattern to see if it is okay. He is concerned that Peter is not as fast as other boys and wants to know what he should be doing to help him.

This sounds like a simple request, but what decisions need to be made in this situation?

- Is Peter's running pattern appropriate for his age?
- If not appropriate, what needs to be worked on?
- Is his running speed appropriate for his age and gender? If not, what are the possible contributing factors, and how can they be addressed?
- Does he lack strength?
- Does he lack balance?
- Does he lack coordination?
- Is he afraid to run for some reason?

Given these basic questions, Ms. Johanson needs to determine what assessment instruments she should use to address them. Task-specific instruments often meet the demands of the task; at other times, the perfect tool cannot be found, and the physical educator must develop an instrument. On the surface, assessment appears very straightforward. If you want to evaluate students' running performance, assess how they run. The complications begin when it comes to selecting the appropriate instrument to do the assessment. Hundreds of assessment tools are available that measure some aspect of physical education. The challenge is knowing how to evaluate these tools to select one that meets the specific demands of the assessment decision.

measure a wide range of attributes—such as beliefs, knowledge, behavior, performance, and ability—across the spectrum of physical education content, which includes physical fitness, body awareness, body management, locomotor skills, object control skills, team sports, and lifetime sports. Given this wide range of attributes and content, no one assessment instrument is universally valid. Several types of evidence can support the validity of a given instrument. Depending on the purpose of the assessment instrument and what is measured, one or more of these sources may be appropriate. Five sources of validity evidence are briefly reviewed here.

Face Validity

Face (logical) validity is the simplest and most subjective source of validity evidence to support an assessment instrument. For face validity, there needs to be a direct connection between what is measured by the instrument and what is being assessed. For example, let's say Mr. Rodriguez is teaching a striking unit to students in third grade and wants to know if they can hit a ball off a batting tee a distance of at least 20 feet (6 m), in fair territory, at least 8 out of 10 times. He could design an assessment instrument that provides 10 striking trials off a batting tee and record the number of times the ball lands in bounds and goes the required distance. Since there is a direct connection between what is measured by this instrument and the objective it is designed to measure, this would be considered strong face validity evidence.

Face validity is easy to judge when the instrument is limited to a few behaviors and the scoring is highly objective. In the striking example, only one behavior, striking, is measured, and the observations involve judging whether the ball is hit, whether it stays in bounds, and whether it goes at least 20 feet. Let's look at the same skill but from a different perspective. What if the objective for conducting the assessment is to determine whether the students are performing the two-hand sidearm strike correctly? The physical educator needs to create an assessment instrument like the example in figure 4.1. This instrument also appears to have face validity in that the components being observed appear to be directly connected to the objective of striking. However, there might be some issues regarding how the components have been defined and whether the number of components is appropriate. The judgments the teacher has to make are also more subjective and competency based. Instead of just judging whether the ball is hit or how far it goes, the teacher must know the seven components and judge, in the less than a second it takes for this skill to be performed, whether the student performs each correctly. For this assessment instrument, additional validity evidence is warranted to address these issues.

Content Validity

Content validity concerns collecting evidence to support that what is measured by the instrument reflects what the instrument is designed to measure. For the batting assessment in figure 4.1, what evidence shows that the seven focal points, or components, of a mature two-hand sidearm strike represent

Equipment and Space Requirements:

- Use a softball (12-inch circumference, official weight) with a no-sting surface and a regulation-size metal or wooden bat that is 26 to 28 inches in length.

- Bat in an outdoor field or large gymnasium at least 70 feet in length (10-foot staging area plus 60-foot throwing distance).

Skill Levels	Focal Points	
1. Demonstrate the mature two-hand sidearm strike. a, b, c c, d, e f	The student demonstrates the following focal points for the mature two-hand sidearm strike while batting (right- or left-handed) a softball that is thrown underhand to the student at slow speed from 20 feet, on 2 of 3 trials. A softball thrown at slow speed will travel 20 feet in 2 seconds. a. **Grip bat** with hands together, nondominant hand palm down near the base of the bat, dominant hand palm up above nondominant hand. b. **Stand sideways**, with nondominant shoulder toward pitcher, feet shoulder-width apart, weight evenly distributed on both feet, eyes on ball, bat behind dominant shoulder, hands at shoulder height. c. **Swing bat forward** in horizontal plane at waist level, with trunk rotation forward. d. **Shift weight** onto batting-side foot, and step forward with opposite foot during bat swing forward. e. **Contact center of ball** with top third of the bat. f. **Follow through** well beyond ball contact. g. **Smooth integration** (not mechanical or jerky) of the previous focal points.	
2. Demonstrate the mature two-hand sidearm strike for distance. 40 – 60 ft 90°	The student with a mature two-hand sidearm strike (skill level 1) will bat a softball thrown at moderate speed from a **distance** on 2 of 3 trials. A softball thrown at moderate speed will travel 40 feet in 2 seconds, 50 feet in 2-1/2 seconds, and 60 feet in 3 seconds.	**Striking (batting) distances:** • Grades K-1 40 feet • Grades 2-3 50 feet • Grades 4-5 60 feet
3. Demonstrate the mature two-hand sidearm strike for accuracy.	The student with a mature two-hand sidearm strike (skill level 1) and sidearm strike for distance (skill level 2) will bat a softball, thrown at moderate speed from a distance, for **accuracy**, on 2 of 3 trials.	**Accuracy criterion:** Within a 90° arc, 45° to the right or left of the student, centered on the person who threw the ball. **Striking (batting) distances:** • Grades K-1 40 feet • Grades 2-3 50 feet • Grades 4-5 60 feet

Reference data: A baseline distance of 60 feet and a distance from the pitcher's mound to home plate of 35 to 40 feet is used in fastpitch softball.

Figure 4.1 Everyone Can! two-hand sidearm strike batting assessment.

From Horvat, M., Kelly, L.E., Block, M.E., and Croce, R., Developmental and adapted physical activity assessment, 2nd ed. (Champaign, IL: Human Kinetics, 2019). Reprinted, by permission, from L.E. Kelly, J.A. Wessel, G.M. Dummer, and T. Sampson, 2010, *Everyone can* (Champaign, IL: Human Kinetics). Illustrations reprinted from J. Wessel, 1976, *I CAN: Object control* (North Brook, IL: Hubbard Scientific Company), 89. By permission of J. Wessel.

the essential parts of this skill and that these components can be assessed by teachers? These issues could be addressed in a number of ways. First, the person developing the assessment instrument could review the literature and cite research to support the stated components and document that these components can in fact be observed by trained teachers. A second option would be to convene a panel of experts and have them review the proposed components to judge their appropriateness. Of course, what constitutes an expert would need to be clearly defined. If the experts' ratings or the documentation from the professional literature supports the proposed components, then this would be considered evidence of content validity.

Although stronger than face validity, content validity is still subjective (i.e., it is based on subjective judgments of whether something is or is not valid). Content validity involves several independent judgments, providing more evidence than the single judgment made in the case of face validity. The concept of content validity can be applied to the assessment of many different aspects of physical education. For example, a paper and pencil test may be used to evaluate whether the students have acquired the necessary knowledge about physical fitness. When creating an assessment instrument to measure physical fitness knowledge, the challenge is to evaluate this knowledge with a reasonable number of questions that accurately represent the content that was taught. Evidence of content validity could be determined in this case by delineating the content taught and the emphasis given to each topic and then keying the test items to this matrix. A panel of experts could then review these materials and judge whether the items on the test accurately reflect the course content.

Concurrent Validity

Concurrent validity statistically measures the relationship between an existing instrument with established validity and a new instrument that assesses the same attribute. Your initial reaction might be why create a new instrument if there is already one that is known to be valid? The answer is usually related to time and cost. For example, Ms. Morris wants to determine the body fat of the students in her school to learn whether obesity is a problem that needs to be addressed. To answer this question, she requires a valid way to assess body fat. She could use a clinical measure that has already been validated, but it may be expensive and require travel to a lab or hospital. A simpler approach is to use a skinfold caliper to measure select skinfolds and then use a regression equation to predict the students' body fat. How does Ms. Morris know the skinfold method is valid? Validity was determined by the people who created the regression equation. They measured the skinfolds of a group of people and compared their results using a clinical measure that serves as a gold standard. By statistically comparing the results, the skinfold assessment correlates highly with the established standard and is considered strong evidence of concurrent validity.

Construct Validity

Construct validity is concerned with demonstrating that what an assessment item measures is representative of a construct. Constructs are traits such as sportsmanship, anxiety, general motor ability, and coordination. There is usually a theoretical basis for the construct and many possible potential measures. The goal is to find a series of measures that are easy and cost effective and that represent the construct. Evidence of construct validity is established by techniques such as factor analysis and tests of group differences. For example, consider an assessment instrument designed to measure coordination. One way to test its construct validity is to assess two groups of people who clearly differ (i.e., high and low) in their coordination and then see if the assessment instrument distinguishes between these two groups. If it does, this would be considered evidence of construct validity.

Criterion Validity

Criterion (predictive) validity examines the degree to which one or more test scores can be used to predict performance on a future related event. For example, can SAT scores predict the success of college students in the United States? Can a soccer volleying test predict who makes the varsity soccer team? To calculate predictive validity, the score on the predictor assessment (e.g., SAT) must be correlated with a score for the criterion factor (e.g., college grade point average). For example, let's say an adapted physical education tool has been created for screening all preschool and elementary students to determine whether they would benefit from adapted physical education services. Depending on their scores, students are referred for additional evaluation and then ultimately placed in various settings such as general physical education (GPE), physical education with support services (e.g., aid provided), GPE with APE support, GPE with APE pullout, or separate APE. To calculate the predictive validity of our APE screening tool, the teacher correlates the students' screening scores with their performance in their ultimate placements. If the correlation is high (e.g., greater than 80%), this would be considered strong evidence of predictive validity for this instrument. The obvious advantage of having an APE screening tool with high predictive validity is that it can assist teachers and parents when making difficult physical education placement decisions, which can frequently be very subjective and prone to bias.

RELIABILITY

Reliability of an assessment instrument refers to the consistency of the result obtained over multiple administrations. On the surface the concept of reliability is very simple. If you give the same assessment twice to the same group of students, a reliable assessment will produce the same results. For example, a physical educator could assess a student's running speed by timing how long she takes to run 50 yards (50 m) today and then administering the same assessment again tomorrow. If the student runs approximately the same time both days, this test would be considered a reliable measure of her running speed. Although the concept of reliability is simple, its application to the measurement of physical education content can be complicated because it can be affected by administration procedures, scoring precision, and student performance variability. Each of these factors is discussed in this section.

Administration procedures define how an assessment should be administered and scored. Ideally, all the conditions should be kept the same during repeated assessments so that any change detected between assessments is the result of changes in student performance. One way to reduce errors related to variability in administrative procedures is to provide explicit instructions on how each item should be set up, demonstrated, explained, and scored. While this process increases administrative consistency between assessments, it also adds to the time and effort required of the teacher to learn and apply these procedures. In addition, it makes the administration of the test more formal, which sometimes adversely affects student performance. This method is most commonly used in the administration of norm-referenced instruments. Another method is to simplify the procedures for each item so that they are easier for the teacher to remember. The teacher can then administer the items in a more relaxed and potentially authentic setting. This second method is most commonly used with criterion-referenced instruments. The shortcoming of this method is that there will be minor differences between how the teacher administers the assessments on separate occasions, which may affect student performance. The bottom line is teachers should strive to standardize the procedures they use when they formally assess and reassess students so that measures obtained can confidently be attributed to changes in performance and not to changes due to other factors. Consider case study 2.

Scoring precision is a function of what is measured and the skill needed to make the measurement. As a general rule, high scoring precision is easier to obtain when the products of performance are being measured with mechanical tools that require minimal skill on the part of the assessor. For example, measurements of physical attributes such as height and weight tend to produce consistent results because these attributes remain constant across short time periods, and it is easy to accurately read the scores from a scale or ruler. Other examples of objective scores are distance, time, number of repetitions, and number of times a target is hit. In all these examples, what is measured can be clearly seen and scored or else measured with a device such as a tape measure or stopwatch that is easy to use.

All tests require some degree of practice before they can be administered reliably. As the nature of the attribute being measured becomes more dependent

Case Study 2
Do You Know What You Are Measuring?

One day Mr. Frazier assesses his students to see how many curl-ups they can perform in one minute outside on the hard ground when the temperature is 94 degrees Fahrenheit (34 °C). The next day he assesses them inside on the same skill using mats in an air-conditioned gym. Do you think this change in conditions could affect their performance? To achieve high reliability, all the assessment conditions must be explicitly stated and followed. If an assessment instrument does not have explicit procedures, then teachers administering the test must record exactly what they do so they can follow the same procedures and replicate the same conditions on subsequent administrations.

on the skill of the person administering the assessment, more attention must be placed on training to produce high reliability. For example, administering the batting assessment in figure 4.1 requires knowing the components to observe, where to stand when observing, and in what order to observe the components, as well as skill in being able to judge when the components are being performed correctly. To achieve high reliability with these types of measures requires that the administration instructions be very specific and that the assessor be trained to an established competency level before using the instrument.

The third factor that can adversely affect reliability is **student performance variability**. All assessments assume that when students are assessed they are fully attending to the task at hand, they understand exactly what they are expected to do on the task, and they give the task their best effort. These issues can be summarized as the **ACE behaviors**: attention, comprehension, and effort. Ideally, these factors should be addressed in the administration procedures. However, even when they are well addressed in the procedures, judging whether they are met still depends on the skill of the assessor. In other words, the physical educator must assess these prerequisite behaviors whenever he or she conducts an assessment. If a student is distracted (i.e., attention problem), appears confused (i.e., comprehension problem), or just appears to be going through the motions (i.e., effort problem), this information should be recorded along with the actual assessment score. When these behaviors appear to adversely affect performance, then this information is considered when the actual assessment score is interpreted. Figure 4.2 shows a score sheet for skill level 1 of the batting objective defined in figure 4.1. Note that three columns are provided to rate the student's ACE behaviors, and each behavior is rated on a simple three-point scale (a = above average, b = average, c = below average).

Attention and comprehension problems can frequently be addressed by providing the students with extra practice trials, as long as this process does not negatively affect the validity of the item. Although recording ACE behaviors and providing extra practice can control for some of the obvious potential sources of error, clearly any number of other factors such as sleep, nutrition, mood, or motivation can influence the consistency of a student's performance on an assessment. This is particularly true for motor skills, where there is natural variation in ability. Consider this situation: Mr. Stevens wants to determine his students' proficiency at shooting basketball free throws. How many attempts should he give them to get an accurate measurement of their ability? What would be the effect of giving each student only one attempt, or at the other extreme, giving each student 100 attempts? Clearly, one attempt is too few and could be adversely affected by luck. A poorly skilled student could just get lucky on this one attempt, and a highly skilled student could be unlucky. On the other hand, 100 attempts could be adversely affected by factors such as fatigue and boredom.

Given this information, let's say Mr. Stevens decides to use 10 attempts. Will this give a consistent measurement of the students' ability? Have you ever taken 10 free throw attempts one day and hit 8 out of 10, then the next day hit only 2 out of 10? What do these scores indicate? Were you just lucky on the first day? Did you forget how to shoot free throws from one day to the next? What these results probably indicate is that getting an accurate measurement

ABC SCHOOL DISTRICT CLASS PERFORMANCE SCORE SHEET: BATTING

Teacher: _____

Start date: _____

Class: _____

Mastery criterion: _____

Grade level: _____

End date: _____

Scoring rubric: 0 = not present
1 = emerging but needs work
2 = demonstrates correct pattern consistently

ACE ratings: a = above average
b = average
c = below average

Students	Grip bat (1)	Stand sideways (2)	Swing bat forward (3)	Shift weight (4)	Contact center of ball (5)	Follow through (6)	Smooth integration (7)	Attention (A)	Comprehension (C)	Effort (E)	Comments	Evaluation values A	B	C	D	E	F

Directions: _____

Administrative considerations: _____

Reflections: _____

Figure 4.2   Sample Everyone Can! score sheet with ACE behaviors.

From Horvat, M., Kelly, L.E., Block, M.E., and Croce, R., Developmental and adapted physical activity assessment, 2nd ed. (Champaign, IL: Human Kinetics, 2019). Reprinted, by permission, from L.E. Kelly and V.J. Melograno, 2004, *Developing the physical education curriculum: An achievement-based approach* (Champaign, IL: Human Kinetics), 334.

of performance on many motor skills requires multiple attempts per trial across multiple trials. The number of trials and the number of attempts per trial are functions of the complexity of the skill being assessed and the amount of performance variation. For components of fundamental motor skills, demonstrating consistency on two out of three or three out of five trials may be sufficient. For other objectives, such as affective behaviors of cooperation or sportsmanship, it may be appropriate to take several measurements a day across two or three weeks.

Remember, the goal of assessing is to obtain an accurate measurement of a student's ability. Under ideal conditions, you should probably err on the side of providing more attempts and trials. Unfortunately, in reality, a balance must be achieved between what may be ideal and what is practical given the amount of time available to conduct the assessment. The goal, then, is to determine the minimum number of attempts and trials needed to get an accurate and consistent performance. These values will probably need to be adjusted to match the developmental level of the students being assessed. As a general rule, variability tends to be higher with younger students and during the early phases of skill acquisition; it tends to decrease as age increases and during the later stages of skill acquisition.

CONTROLLING AND MEASURING RELIABILITY

Fortunately, many of the threats to reliability can be controlled via training and systematic documentation. As discussed already, threats from administrative procedures can be minimized by identifying any potential problems and then recording how these are addressed so the assessment can be repeated under consistent conditions. Scoring threats can be addressed through training and establishing minimum competency levels before assessments are conducted. The most challenging source of error to control for is student performance variability, since this is not under the direct control of the teacher but is controlled by the student. These threats can be minimized by assessing the ACE behaviors and adjusting the number of attempts and trials to the student's developmental level. Three methods of evaluating reliability are described here to assist teachers in evaluating the reliability of their measures. It is important to note that when teachers evaluate commercially available tests, they should consult the administration manuals for information on how the reliability was determined and the strength of the correlations reported.

Test–Retest

When an assessment instrument is created, it is customary to test for reliability and report a value between 0 and 1. The simplest way to test reliability is the test–retest method, in which an instrument is administered twice to the same group of students and then a correlation, or degree of agreement, between the results is calculated. Of course care must be taken to make sure the time interval between the two evaluations is appropriate and that no instruction or training is provided between evaluations.

Test–retest reliability can be computed by calculating a **Pearson product-moment correlation**. One of the limitations of this method is that if multiple trials are involved, these data must be reduced to one score per student for each assessment. This could be done, for example, by averaging the student's scores for three trials and then using the average as the final score for the correlation. Although this technique is commonly used and does provide a general indication of overall reliability, calculating an **intraclass correlation coefficient** is the most appropriate method for calculating reliability when motor performance tests involve two or more trials. The advantage of using the intraclass correlation method is that it uses all the data that have been collected and allows for the variance to be examined from three sources: students, trials, and the interaction of students by trials.

Alternate Form and Split Half

Two other methods for testing reliability are **alternate form** and **split half**. These techniques are most commonly used with written tests. For the alternate-form method, two equivalent forms of the test are created. They are both then administered to the same students, who are divided into two groups. The order for the forms is randomly assigned to each group. For example, the first group of students might take form B and then form A, and the other group form A and then form B. After the students finish the tests, a correlation is calculated between their scores on forms A and B. An advantage of this method is that it yields two tests; using alternate forms within a single class can address issues such as cheating. The downside is that twice as many good questions must be created, which requires more development time. A second technique that addresses the issue of test development time is the split-half method. In this case, a single test is administered to one group of students and then divided into two forms, typically by the odd and even items. Two scores are calculated for each student. These scores are then correlated to produce a reliability correlation. The obvious advantage of this technique is that it requires only one version of the test and one group of students.

OBJECTIVITY

Objectivity is a special type of reliability. Reliability as discussed previously focuses on the consistency of the results obtained by the same assessor across multiple administrations. This is commonly referred to as **intrarater reliability**. Objectivity is an indication of the reliability between two administrations of a test to the same group of students by different teachers. This is referred to as **interrater reliability**. Objectivity is affected by the same factors that influence reliability: administration procedures, scoring precision, and student performance variability. As a general rule, high intrarater reliability is easier to achieve than high interrater reliability. Theoretically, if the administration procedures for a test are well defined, two comparably trained physical educators should be able to review the instructions, practice their administration, and then administer the test to the same group of students and get the same results. The objectivity of the test is determined by totaling the number of agreements (i.e., items both raters gave the same score), dividing this sum by the total number of items on the test, and finally multiplying this number by 100. For example, if a motor skills test involves a total of 20 ratings, and the two teachers agree on 16 of the ratings, their objectivity is 80 percent:

$$(16/20) \times 100 = 80\%$$

One way to increase objectivity is to control the competency of the teachers using a given assessment tool. This can be done by creating or using a training video containing clips of a wide variety of students performing the skill being assessed. The clips are divided into two pools. One pool is used by the teachers to learn and develop their assessing skills; the other pool is used to test their degree of competency. The higher the competency level demonstrated by the teachers, the greater their measurement reliability and objectivity. Scoring of competitive gymnastics, figure skating, and diving at the Olympic level illustrates that, with extensive training, high objectivity can be achieved when measuring extremely complex motor skills performed at high speed and involving subjective judgments.

NORMS

Many commercially available assessment instruments provide norms to help teachers interpret how their students are performing compared with other students that have taken the same assessment. It is important to understand that *norms* does not mean normal. **Norms** are a description of how a sample of students performs on a test in relation to the students in the **normative sample**. The norms may be organized around any number of relevant factors. Simple norms can be organized around gender, grade, or age. In these cases, the values reported in the norm table represent the average score for the students in the normative sample reported by gender, grade, or age.

Table 4.1 shows the percentage of students demonstrating mastery of each of the seven components of a criterion-referenced instrument assessing batting. This chart provides normative data by gender (i.e., males) and age (i.e., 6 to 12). The values in the table indicate the percentage of males at each age that have demonstrated mastery of each component. For example, 88 percent of the eight-year-old males demonstrated the correct grip, and 66 percent of the males at age 10 were demonstrating the correct weight transfer. More sophisticated normative tables use values such as percentiles, z scores, and T scores. Before any norms are used, it is important to determine three things:

1. Are the norms appropriate?
2. Are they up to date?
3. Is enough information provided to judge?

The appropriateness of a set of norms is a function of how similar the students in the normative sample are to the students being assessed and of the decision the teacher wants to make. For example, Ms. Fong teaches elementary physical education twice a week to her second-grade class, and she wants to evaluate how their performance on locomotor skills compares with others to see if her teaching is effective. She finds a set of norms for locomotor skills

Table 4.1 Percentage of Students Demonstrating Mastery of Batting

Component	Age 6	Age 7	Age 8	Age 9	Age 10	Age 11	Age 12
Grip	79	84	88	89	90	94	97
Side orientation	64	76	81	85	87	92	96
Bat position	67	77	84	88	90	94	98
Rotation	54	59	67	72	79	85	92
Weight transfer	47	49	52	58	66	73	81
Follow-through	44	46	49	57	61	69	78
Smooth integration	34	35	42	47	53	62	69

Note: Normative data for males.

from another state and compares her students to these norms. Overall, her students are just below the means on the norms for all the skills. What does this mean? Is she a poor teacher? Are the students in her classes developmentally delayed? What if the norms were created using students that received physical education five times a week, taught by physical education specialists, and all students with disabilities were removed? Now how would you evaluate Ms. Fong's performance? Considering that she has several students with disabilities in her classes and 60 percent less instructional time (two times a week versus five times a week), the fact that her students are performing only slightly below the means of the norms might indicate that her instruction is very effective. The point is that you need to know the characteristics of the students used to create the norms so that you know what you are comparing your scores against. Clearly, the larger and more representative the sample used to create the norms, the more useful they are for comparisons.

When creating norms, the challenge is to maximize representativeness while balancing costs. For example, if you were creating norms for a new test, ideally you would like to include representative data on a variety of factors, such as school district size (above 10,000 versus below 10,000), geographic region (Northeast, Southeast, Midwest, Northwest, Southwest), age (5 to 12), gender (male or female), and special education status (developmentally delayed, orthopedically impaired, sensory impaired, nondisabled), to name just a few. Let's say you want at least 30 students for each comparative norm. To control representativeness for just these five factors and to have 30 students for each norm, you would need 19,200 individuals in your sample (two school district sizes × five regions × eight ages × two genders × four special education categories × 30 students). If it costs $25 to assess each student in the normative sample, you would need a budget of $480,000 to create your norms. This example illustrates how costly it can be to develop norms based on large representative samples. As a result, many physical fitness and motor skills tests have norms based on smaller, less representative samples. This does not mean these norms are useless. What it does mean is that you must understand the limitations of the norms when you use them to interpret student performance.

It is also important that norms be up to date. Because creating norms is so expensive, it is not uncommon for norms to sometimes be 15 or 20 years old. Since performance is reflective of the programs students participate in, and since the programs reflect the values and societal trends of the times, it is important to know when the norms were created.

To judge the appropriateness and timeliness of the norms for any given assessment, the physical educator must have access to the procedures used to create the norms. You might logically expect that this information would be provided with the tests, but this is not always the case. A compromise is frequently made between how much information is presented in order to reduce costs and make the test appear more user-friendly. It is not uncommon for a test to include a brief summary of the procedures and then refer the reader to another source, such as an article published in a research journal. It is important to track down this information and review it to determine the characteristics of the students used to create the norms and the administrative procedures and conditions of the norm data collection. In terms of the characteristics of the students in the norm sample, relevant factors include the size of the sample, how the students were selected, its representativeness, and its overall diversity. For example, a sample composed of students who volunteered for the assessment should be viewed with more caution than a sample that was randomly selected from all the students in a school.

A variety of issues should be considered when reviewing the procedures and conditions used to collect normative data. For example, who collected the data? Was it collected by the students' regular teacher, or did outside assessors come in and collect the data? How was motivation controlled for (i.e., what was done to elicit the students' best performance)? When were the data collected? Was it at the start or end of the school year? Had the students just completed a unit involving these skills? Can you see how issues such as these could affect performance? Not all these factors can be controlled, but they can be defined so that this information can be used by the test administrators in the interpretation of the results.

What You Need to Know

Key Terms

ACE behaviors
administration procedures
alternate form
concurrent validity
construct validity
content validity
criterion (predictive) validity
face (logical) validity
interrater reliability
intraclass correlation coefficient
intrarater reliability
normative sample

norms
objectivity
Pearson product-moment correlation
reliability
scoring precision
split half
student performance variability
test–retest reliability
validity

Key Concepts

1. You should know the five types of validity and be able to explain how each applies to assessment instruments in physical education.
2. You should know the three major factors that affect reliability of assessment instruments in physical education.
3. You should understand the relationship between validity, reliability, and objectivity and the importance of each of these factors when selecting an assessment instrument.
4. You should know the ACE behaviors and how they interact with student variability and reliability during assessment.

Review Questions

1. What is face validity, and why is this the most common type of validity reported for physical education assessment instruments?
2. What are some ways to improve the objectivity of an assessment instrument in physical education?
3. What factors should you consider when evaluating the norms provided with an assessment instrument or when you develop your own norms?
4. Explain how common threats to reliability of physical education assessment instruments can be controlled.

Chapter 5

Selecting and Administering Tests

Collecting accurate assessment data is challenging because several factors interact with each other. Initially, you need to determine the type of decision required and what information is necessary to make that decision. Next, you need to select and competently administer a valid and reliable instrument designed to collect this information. Finally, you must interpret the test results to make an appropriate decision such as what LRE placement will help various students achieve their APE program goals.

Although the focus of assessment is on evaluating one or more aspects of physical or motor performance, teachers must also consider the total student when conducting and interpreting assessment performance. Chapter 3 focuses on various information sources, such as school records and key personnel who should be consulted to get to know the students before they are assessed. The ACE factors of attention, comprehension, and effort are introduced in chapter 4 as a method of focusing a teacher's attention on how students respond during the assessment. Chapter 4 also discusses factors relating to reliability and validity.

Case Study 1

Matching the Assessment Tool to the Assessment Decision

Mr. Simon has three students with disabilities in one of his fourth-grade physical education classes. He is about to start a new unit that focuses on the overhand throw. He decides to preassess the class so he can plan his instruction according to the needs of these three students, and also to determine whether this class placement is the most appropriate setting for them. Mr. Simon reviews his test and measurement textbook and finds a simple assessment for throwing that can be administered to a group of students. The test, which involves averaging three throws for distance, has face validity for ages 4 through 12. He administers the assessment to his class and compares their scores with the norms provided with the test. The results indicate that the class overall is performing at the 53rd percentile. One of the three students with disabilities is performing above the class mean, while the other two students are among the lower-performing students in the class.

Mr. Simon concludes that the assessment results clearly indicate the class needs to work on throwing. However, having spent one class period conducting the assessment and another two hours interpreting the results, he is a bit perplexed about how to actually use this information to plan his instruction. He could form instructional groups based on how far the students can throw, but he realizes he does not have any information on why they are throwing so poorly. For example, is it because they do not know the correct throwing pattern? Or is it because they are weak and need to work on strength? In regard to the students with disabilities, one student appears to be in the right placement since she is throwing as well as half the other students in the class, but it seems that this may not be the best placement for the other two students.

Mr. Simon needs to make two decisions: an instructional decision regarding the overhand throw and a placement decision to determine whether this class is appropriate for his students with disabilities. His problem is that he used a **norm-referenced instrument** that measured the outcome, or product, of throwing performance. What he needed in this situation was a **criterion-referenced instrument** (CRI) to evaluate how the students were actually performing the throw. Had he collected this information, he would have known which components of the throw the students had mastered and which ones still needed work. He could have then used this information to plan his instruction. The criterion-referenced assessment information could have also been used to determine any unique needs the students with disabilities have on the throw objective and how these needs can be accommodated within the class. Teachers learn that they should use assessment to guide their decision making in physical education, but when they actually try to use it, some do not find the assessment results useful and subsequently stop assessing. The assessment process is not the problem; the problem is not knowing how to select the appropriate assessment tool to match the decision that needs to be made.

The purpose of this chapter is to provide a set of rules that can be used to select the appropriate assessment instrument to match the decision to be made. It also provides a basic set of rules that should guide the administration of any assessment.

Assessment is a dynamic process by which teachers make informed decisions, and it can be broken into the following six steps.

- Step 1: Identify the type of decision that needs to be made.
- Step 2: Understand the unique attributes and needs of the student.
- Step 3: Identify the dimensions of physical education that need to be evaluated.
- Step 4: Select or create an appropriate assessment instrument to match the decision to be made.
- Step 5: Learn and administer the instrument so that valid and reliable data are collected.
- Step 6: Interpret the assessment data collected and make an appropriate decision.

STEP 1: Identify the Type of Decision That Needs to Be Made

Chapter 2 explains that physical educators are called on to make decisions in four categories: qualification, curriculum, placement, and instruction. In reality, the first decision to be made in the assessment process is which of these four types of decisions you are being asked to make.

Qualification Decisions

The focus of **qualification decisions** is to determine whether a student's performance warrants special consideration. Qualification decisions are typically made by a school committee commonly referred to as the admission, review, and dismissal (ARD) committee. Depending on the size of the school district and the availability of adapted physical educators, the educators may be sitting members on this committee or invited when needed by the committee to evaluate students. This committee is charged with evaluating all students who are referred for special education consideration and for reevaluating students every three years after they have qualified for special education.

Qualification decisions in physical education can range from formal to informal. Formal qualification decisions typically involve individually evaluating students using clearly defined measures and testing conditions and then interpreting the results based on clearly defined criteria. The awarding of fitness awards in physical education is a common example of a qualification decision. To receive the Presidential Youth Fitness Award, students must score in the healthy fitness zone on five of the six fitness categories. The test and administration procedures for evaluating each category are clearly defined. For example, the powerful PACER test is used to measure aerobic capacity.

The results are interpreted by comparing the scores achieved against the healthy fitness zone score for their age and gender. Students who meet or exceed the criteria for five of the six fitness categories measured by the award qualify for recognition. In adapted physical education, the most common qualification decisions are determining if students are eligible for special education as described in chapter 2. In this situation, students are evaluated under clearly defined procedures using established evaluation criteria. The results must meet the criteria for qualifying for one of 13 special education labels in IDEA.

Two critical elements come into play when making a qualification decision: (1) There must be established eligibility criteria, and (2) the assessment instrument used must provide comparative standards such as norms. To qualify for special education, students must meet professionally established criteria as measured by two or more valid instruments. For physical education, the criteria for qualifying for services and the assessment instruments that are appropriate to use are less universally defined. This is in part because of the breadth of the content covered in physical education and the diversity of abilities exhibited by students with disabilities. For example, a 12-minute run for distance may be a valid measure of cardiorespiratory endurance for a student with a learning disability or hearing impairment, but it would not be valid for a student with spastic cerebral palsy or spina bifida.

Qualification decisions can also be less formal. In these situations, the goal is often quickly **screening** a large number of students to identify anyone having problems and in need of more formal evaluation. For example, it is common practice in many areas for physical educators to screen all their upper elementary grade students during class for scoliosis. If students are observed to have unequal shoulder and hip heights along with a gradual C curve in the spine, they are referred to a specialist for further evaluation (see chapter 8 for more information on posture screening). A teacher might also screen students in class using a checklist similar to the example provided in figure 5.1. A student found to be significantly inadequate on a predetermined number of items set by the school would then be referred for a more formal assessment and possibly for special education consideration.

Curriculum Decisions

After students have been identified and found to qualify for services, the next step is to determine their physical education needs. Adapted physical educators should always be involved in **curriculum decisions**. The purpose of physical education is to provide all students with the necessary physical and motor skills to participate in a variety of lifetime recreational sports activities that can develop and maintain their fitness and allow them to live healthy and productive lives. For the majority of students with mild and moderate disabilities, it is reasonable to assume that with appropriate accommodations and instructional modifications, the general physical education curriculum goals would be appropriate or would require only minor modifications. Unfortunately, this important consideration is frequently overlooked when making placement decisions for students with disabilities. The problem is that the amount of time allocated for physical education is usually predetermined. That is, school personnel do not determine students' physical education needs,

INITIAL OBSERVATION AND REFERRAL FORM

Child's name: _____   Evaluator: _____

School: _____   Date: _____

Use this form when first observing a child with a disability who has been referred for adapted physical education. Rate each item based on how the child compares with other students in his or her physical education class.

	Adequate	Needs improvement	Significantly inadequate	Not observed
Physical fitness				
Performs activities that require upper-body strength (e.g., push-ups, throwing, chest passes)	☐	☐	☐	☐
Performs activities that require lower-body strength (e.g., running, hopping, kicking)	☐	☐	☐	☐
Performs activities that require flexibility (e.g., stretching, bending, tumbling)	☐	☐	☐	☐
Performs activities that require endurance (e.g., mile run, games that involve endurance)	☐	☐	☐	☐
Body composition (e.g., child's weight and general appearance)	☐	☐	☐	☐
Gross motor skills				
Performs nonlocomotor skills (e.g., twisting, turning, balancing, bending)	☐	☐	☐	☐
Moves safely around environment (e.g., dodging, space awareness, directions)	☐	☐	☐	☐
Uses physical education equipment (e.g., balls, bats, scooters)	☐	☐	☐	☐
Performs locomotor skills (e.g., running, jumping, galloping, hopping, skipping)	☐	☐	☐	☐
Performs manipulative skills (e.g., throwing, catching, kicking, striking)	☐	☐	☐	☐
Performs dance skills (e.g., rhythm, patterns, creative)	☐	☐	☐	☐
Plays low-organized games (e.g., dodgeball, relays, tag, teacher-developed games)	☐	☐	☐	☐
Sports skills (e.g., throwing in softball, kicking in soccer, serving in volleyball, hitting a tennis ball)	☐	☐	☐	☐
Plays organized sports (e.g., basketball, soccer)	☐	☐	☐	☐
Transition to and from physical education				
Enters without interruption	☐	☐	☐	☐
Sits in assigned area	☐	☐	☐	☐
Stops playing with equipment when asked	☐	☐	☐	☐
Lines up to leave when asked	☐	☐	☐	☐
Responding to teacher				
Remains quiet when teacher is talking	☐	☐	☐	☐
Follows directions in a timely manner during warm-up	☐	☐	☐	☐

Figure 5.1 Block's initial observation and referral screening form.

(continued)

	Adequate	Needs improvement	Significantly inadequate	Not observed
Responding to teacher				
Follows directions in a timely manner during skill focus	☐	☐	☐	☐
Follows directions in a timely manner during games	☐	☐	☐	☐
Accepts feedback from teacher	☐	☐	☐	☐
Uses positive or appropriate language	☐	☐	☐	☐
Relating to peers and equipment				
Works cooperatively with a partner when asked (e.g., shares, takes turns)	☐	☐	☐	☐
Works cooperatively as a member of a group when asked	☐	☐	☐	☐
Uses positive or appropriate comments with peers	☐	☐	☐	☐
Seeks social interactions with peers	☐	☐	☐	☐
Displays sportsmanship by avoiding conflict with others	☐	☐	☐	☐
Uses equipment appropriately	☐	☐	☐	☐
Effort and self-acceptance				
Quickly begins the activity once instructed	☐	☐	☐	☐
Continues to participate independently throughout activity	☐	☐	☐	☐
Adapts to new tasks and changes	☐	☐	☐	☐
Strives to succeed and is motivated to learn	☐	☐	☐	☐
Accepts his or her own skill whether successful or improving	☐	☐	☐	☐
Cognitive abilities				
Understands nonverbal directions	☐	☐	☐	☐
Understands verbal directions	☐	☐	☐	☐
Processes multistep cues	☐	☐	☐	☐
Attends to instructions	☐	☐	☐	☐

Comments regarding fitness or motor skills:_____

_____

Comments regarding behaviors and social or cognitive abilities: _____

_____

Figure 5.1 *(continued)*

From Horvat, M., Kelly, L.E., Block, M.E., and Croce, R., *Developmental and adapted physical activity assessment*, 2nd ed. (Champaign, IL: Human Kinetics, 2019). Reprinted, by permission, from M.E. Block, 2000, *A teacher's guide to including students with disabilities in general physical education* (Baltimore, MD: Paul H. Brookes Publishing Co.), 85-86.

calculate how much time is needed to achieve their goals, and then build that amount of instructional time into their school schedules. In most cases, students with disabilities are allocated approximately the same amount of physical education time as the other students without disabilities. Since time is fixed, this requires that curriculum adjustments be made to ensure that students with disabilities can learn and master functional lifetime leisure skills during the time allocated for physical education.

Clearly, if instructional time for physical education is relatively fixed and students are starting with delays in their physical and motor development—and are going to learn motor skills at a slower rate because of their disabilities—some adjustment must be made in the amount of content that is targeted for them to learn. It is imperative that the content of their physical education curriculum culminates in the achievement of lifetime sports skills they can use after graduation for recreation and for maintaining their fitness and health (Kelly & Melograno, 2004). If the general physical education curriculum includes 200 objectives that lead to the achievement of 10 lifetime sports skills, then a student with a disability who learns at half the rate of the students without disabilities should have a more delimited curriculum of 100 objectives that lead to the achievement of five lifetime sports activities. This delimited curriculum would then become the basis for creating the student's physical education IEP goals and instructional objectives. Figure 5.2 illustrates the relationship between the GPE and APE curricula. For most students with mild and moderate disabilities, their APE curricula is represented by the smaller triangle within the larger GPE pyramid. For students with more severe disabilities, who will work on even fewer goals and objectives, their pyramids will have less common content with the GPE curriculum.

The most efficient way of making curriculum decisions is to conduct a curriculum needs assessment (CNA) as described in chapter 2 and then use these results to determine whether students need an APE curriculum. If their PLOP is within 30 percent of the target class's performance, they should be able to participate and achieve the objectives and goals in the GPE curriculum, but they will probably require some additional APE and support to catch them up and remediate their current deficits. If they are more than 30 percent behind the

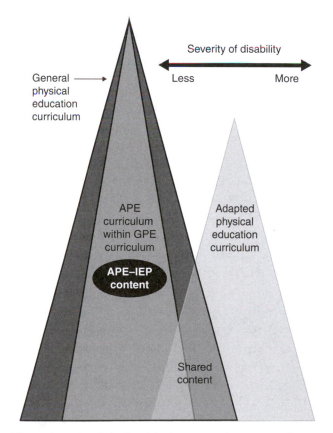

Figure 5.2 Relationship between the GPE and APE curricula.

Reprinted, by permission, from L.E. Kelly, 2011, *Designing and implementing effective adapted physical education programs* (Urbana, IL: Sagamore), 60.

Case Study 2
What Does Appropriate Placement in Physical Education Mean?

Maya was diagnosed as having autism spectrum disorder (ASD) when she was three years old. She is currently nine years old and in third grade. She likes physical education but is four-plus years behind her peers in motor skill development. Her physical education teacher reports that she can learn motor skills, but it takes her approximately three times as long to learn as the other students because of her cognitive processing problems and attention problems. What will happen to Maya if she is placed in the general physical education curriculum with no adjustments to the objectives? Odds are that by the time Maya graduates, she will not have mastered any of the lifetime sports activities in the general curriculum. In reality she will probably have the fundamental motor skill levels of a fourth or fifth grader. The problem is there is just too much content to learn and too little time. Given that Maya already has a marked delay and requires more time to learn, she will make little progress on the objectives taught in the general physical education program even when accommodations are made. By the time she starts to learn an objective, the unit will end and she will have to start working on a new objective. As a result, she will be exposed to a lot of content but will not master any of it. As she progresses through each successive grade, she will fall further and further behind and become less and less capable of learning the grade-level content because she lacks the prerequisite skills. In many cases, students like Maya eventually become frustrated with physical education and either stop trying or in some cases begin to act out.

students in the target GPE setting, an individualized APE curricula must be developed based on their unique needs. For information on how to create APE curricula, consult the Kelly (2011) reference in chapter 2 on designing and implementing effective adapted physical education programs.

Placement Decisions

The key to making appropriate **placement decisions** is determining the most appropriate and least restrictive environment in which a student's APE curriculum can be implemented and achieved. The intent of IDEA is to educate all students with disabilities in the general education environment—to the maximum extent possible—using appropriate support services to achieve their educational goals. The placement decision process starts by reviewing the objectives in the student's APE curriculum that were the products of the curriculum decision process. One of these products will be the student's elementary APE curriculum scope and sequence chart, an example of which is shown in table 5.1. Note that the complete scope and sequence chart would include all the middle school and high school objectives leading to the achievement of this student's program goals. This chart shows what objectives this student needs to work on and which ones are targeted to be mastered at each grade level. With this information in hand, the first question is determining if the GPE curriculum would be an appropriate place where the student can work on and achieve target objectives. This does not mean the objectives have to be exactly the same as the target objectives in the GPE curriculum, but they need to be compatible so that all students can participate in the same instructional activities and games with minor modifications. For example, when students in GPE are working on running, hopping, skipping, and sliding, a student with a disability might work on just the run and hop. This accommodation affords them twice as much time to work on half as many objectives, making them achievable in the GPE setting.

The key is that students with disabilities must be working on and achieving their objectives and goals. If students cannot make reasonable progress on their curriculum objectives in the GPE setting with accommodations and support services, then alternative placements must be found. A continuum of placements with corresponding support services and accommodations should be available, ranging from full-time adapted physical education to full inclusion in general physical education. Once an alternative placement is defined, it should not be viewed as a permanent placement; progress is reviewed yearly, with the possibility of modifying the alternative placement or moving students closer to a GPE placement when appropriate.

The placement decision must also evaluate and determine whether GPE is an appropriate learning environment for the student. The issues here relate to students' unique learning needs and the characteristics of the learning environment. Factors to consider are safety, the needs and attributes of the students both with and without disabilities, and potential secondary benefits of the placement. Safety concerns are relatively self-explanatory. Clearly, a student who does not possess the appropriate defensive reactions to protect herself from fast-moving objects should not be placed in a dangerous setting where she could be struck by such objects.

For students to optimally learn, they must be relaxed and comfortable in the learning environment. If a student with a disability cannot relax in his target placement, then it would not be an appropriate setting. For example, some students with autism may be overstimulated by the actions of others and subsequently unable to focus on their own learning objectives. Conversely, other students with disabilities may exhibit unusual or disruptive behaviors that distract and interfere with the learning of others in the environment. In cases where these behaviors cannot be managed by teacher aides and other support services, the placement would also be inappropriate. An ideal placement should afford students the opportunity for secondary benefits such as interacting socially with their peers, sharing common experiences, learning from their peers, and developing friendships. Since every student with a disability is unique and every class is unique, placement decisions are highly individualized. In all cases, every attempt should be made to address any minor placement issues with appropriate accommodations. However, when an appropriate learning environment cannot be attained with reasonable accommodations, then alternative placements should be created.

Table 5.1 Elementary K-5 Curriculum Scope and Sequence

Category	Objective	K	1	2	3	4	5
Locomotor patterns	1.1 Run	**					
	1.2 Gallop	**					
	1.3 Horizontal jump	- -	- -	**			
	1.4 Vertical jump		- -	**			
	1.5 Hop (on both right foot and left foot)	- -	**				
	1.6 Slide	- -	**				
	1.7 Skip		- -	- -	**		
	1.8 Leap			- -	- -	**	
Object control	2.1 Underhand roll	**					
	2.2 Bounce and dribble		- -	**			
	2.3 Underhand throw	- -	**				
	2.4 Overhand throw		- -	- -	- -	**	
	2.5 Kick		- -	- -	**		
	2.6 Punt				- -	- -	**
	2.7 Two-hand sidearm strike (baseball)		- -	- -	**		
	2.8 Catch and field			- -	- -	- -	**
	2.9 Underhand strike (volleyball serve)			- -	**		
	2.10 Chest pass (basketball)		- -	**			
	2.11 Bounce pass (basketball)		- -	- -	**		
Physical fitness	3.1 Knowledge				- -	- -	**
	3.2 Training concepts				- -	- -	**
	3.3 Terminology			- -	- -	**	
	3.4 Leg strength		- -	**			
	3.5 Flexibility		- -	**			
	3.6 Abdominal strength		- -	- -	**		
	3.7 Endurance		- -	- -	- -	**	
	3.8 Arm and shoulder strength				- -	- -	**
	3.9 Agility			- -	- -	**	
	3.10 Speed				- -	- -	**
Social	4.1 Self-discipline (control)	- -	**				
	4.2 Cooperation	- -	**				
	4.3 Fair play	- -	- -	- -	**		
	4.4 Winning and losing	- -	- -	**			
	4.5 Respecting equipment and property	**					
Body management	5.1 Nonlocomotor	**					
	5.2 Body awareness	**					
	5.3 Spatial awareness	**					
	5.4 Use of space		- -	**			
	5.5 Quality of movement	- -	- -	**			
	5.6 Relationship of body to other objects	- -	- -	- -	**		
	5.7 Basic dance patterns				- -	**	
	5.8 Forward roll					- -	**
	5.9 Rope jumping		- -	- -	**		
Game and sports skills	6.1 Following directions	**					
	6.2 Knowledge of safety and rules	- -	**				
	6.3 Member of team				- -	- -	**
	6.4 Participating in games and sports	- -	- -	- -	- -	- -	**

** indicates when the objective is to be mastered. - - indicates when instruction will begin.

Reprinted, by permission, from L.E. Kelly and V.J. Melograno, 2004, *Developing the physical education curriculum: An achievement-based approach* (Champaign, IL: Human Kinetics), 74-75.

Instructional Decisions

Once a student's placement is determined, the last type of decision that must be addressed is instructional. **Instructional decisions** involve determining what objectives are targeted for instruction, what learning and behavioral characteristics should be considered when delivering instruction, and how students should be grouped. These decisions are made almost exclusively with CRIs. Referring to table 5.1, let's assume students are scheduled to work on the skip and overhand throw objectives first. The teacher would conduct a preassessment activity that involves the students in an activity, game, or drill that features these objectives. She would then observe the students and assess which components of each objective they can already perform using a score sheet similar to figure 5.3. In addition, the teacher would observe and record the students' ACE (attention, comprehension, effort) behaviors as well as any other pertinent learning and behavioral information. She might note that Diana appears to be more of an auditory than a visual learner, José is self-conscious and does not perform as well as he can in front of some of his peers, and finally that Asha is totally distracted by Denise. The teacher interprets the recorded data to make a variety of instructional decisions such as what focal points to focus on for each skill, how to group the students, and what instructional activities to use.

Conducting instructional assessments is a relatively straightforward process. First, the physical educator needs to know what content the students are expected to learn. This information is provided in the curriculum, such as the example shown in table 5.1. Once the instructional content is targeted, the next step is identifying an assessment instrument to measure this content. Referring to table 5.1, let's assume the objective being worked on is the overhand throw. The teacher would find an assessment item to measure this objective. It is common for these assessments to be included in the curriculum materials (Kelly & Melograno, 2004). Figure 5.4 shows a sample Everyone Can! CRI for the overhand throw. Note the CRI indicates the basic administration instructions as well as the specific components that must be observed.

Although the primary focus of most instructional decisions is learning physical, motor, and cognitive objectives, it is not uncommon for students with disabilities to also have behavioral objectives. These might involve learning behaviors such as attending to a task, learning not to scream when excited, or looking at the teacher when spoken to. In all these cases, the process is the same. First, the behavior must be clearly defined in terms of what behavior is desired and in some cases what behavior is being inhibited. Next, a baseline is established that shows the current strength of the desired behavior, or how often it is exhibited. A plan is created to develop and reinforce the desired behavior and, when appropriate, to extinguish the undesired behavior. The students are then periodically observed, and the frequency of behavior is recorded to show their progress.

ABC School District Class Performance Score Sheet: Overhand Throw

Teacher: _____

Class: _____

Start date: _____

Grade level: _____

Mastery criterion: _____

End date: _____

Scoring rubric: 0 = not present
1 = emerging but needs work
2 = demonstrates correct pattern consistently

ACE ratings: a = above average
b = average
c = below average

Students	1 Nondominant side toward target	2 T position	3 Throwing arm above shoulder	4 Weight shift	5 Ball release toward target	6 Follow-through	7 Smooth integration	A Attention	C Comprehension	E Effort	Comments	Evaluation criteria A	B	C	D	E	F

Directions: _____

Administrative considerations: _____

Reflections: _____

Figure 5.3   Sample Everyone Can! CRI score sheet for the overhand throw.

From Horvat, M., Kelly, L.E., Block, M.E., and Croce, R., *Developmental and adapted physical activity assessment*, 2nd ed. (Champaign, IL: Human Kinetics, 2019). Reprinted, by permission, from L.E. Kelly and V.J. Melograno, 2004, *Developing the physical education curriculum: An achievement-based approach* (Champaign, IL: Human Kinetics), 334.

Equipment and Space Requirements:

- Use a tennis ball (2.5-inch diameter) for skill level 1. Use a softball (12-inch circumference, official weight) with a no-sting surface for skill level 2 and skill level 3.
- Use a 4-foot-square vertical target placed 2 feet off the ground (target markings may be taped to a wall).
- Throw in an outdoor field or large gymnasium at least 70 feet in length (10-foot staging area plus 60-foot throwing distance).

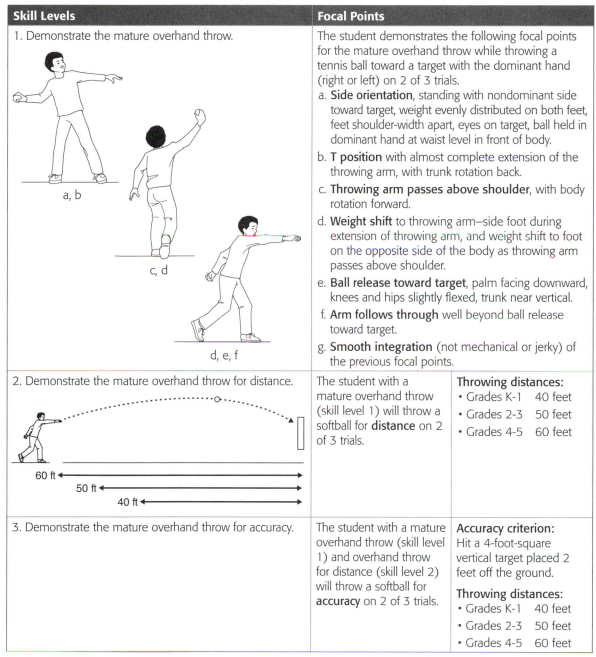

Skill Levels	Focal Points	
1. Demonstrate the mature overhand throw.	The student demonstrates the following focal points for the mature overhand throw while throwing a tennis ball toward a target with the dominant hand (right or left) on 2 of 3 trials. a. **Side orientation**, standing with nondominant side toward target, weight evenly distributed on both feet, feet shoulder-width apart, eyes on target, ball held in dominant hand at waist level in front of body. b. **T position** with almost complete extension of the throwing arm, with trunk rotation back. c. **Throwing arm passes above shoulder**, with body rotation forward. d. **Weight shift** to throwing arm–side foot during extension of throwing arm, and weight shift to foot on the opposite side of the body as throwing arm passes above shoulder. e. **Ball release toward target**, palm facing downward, knees and hips slightly flexed, trunk near vertical. f. **Arm follows through** well beyond ball release toward target. g. **Smooth integration** (not mechanical or jerky) of the previous focal points.	
2. Demonstrate the mature overhand throw for distance. 60 ft / 50 ft / 40 ft	The student with a mature overhand throw (skill level 1) will throw a softball for **distance** on 2 of 3 trials.	**Throwing distances:** • Grades K-1 40 feet • Grades 2-3 50 feet • Grades 4-5 60 feet
3. Demonstrate the mature overhand throw for accuracy.	The student with a mature overhand throw (skill level 1) and overhand throw for distance (skill level 2) will throw a softball for **accuracy** on 2 of 3 trials.	**Accuracy criterion:** Hit a 4-foot-square vertical target placed 2 feet off the ground. **Throwing distances:** • Grades K-1 40 feet • Grades 2-3 50 feet • Grades 4-5 60 feet

Reference data: A baseline distance of 60 feet is used in fast-pitch softball.

Figure 5.4   Sample Everyone Can! CRI for the overhand throw.

From Horvat, M., Kelly, L.E., Block, M.E., and Croce, R., *Developmental and adapted physical activity assessment*, 2nd ed. (Champaign, IL: Human Kinetics, 2019). Reprinted, by permission, from L.E. Kelly, J.A. Wessel, G.M. Dummer, and T. Sampson, 2010, *Everyone can* (Champaign, IL: Human Kinetics), 114. Illustrations reprinted from J. Wessel, 1976, *I CAN: Object control* (North Brook, IL: Hubbard Scientific Company), 89. By permission of J. Wessel.

STEP 2: Understand the Unique Attributes and Needs of the Student

Now that you understand what type of decision you need to make, the next step is to understand the unique needs of the student you are assessing. (This topic is addressed in chapter 3.) You cannot select or administer an assessment instrument without knowing the needs and attributes of the student. For example, what information does a physical educator need in order to select an appropriate assessment test to measure physical fitness? Would knowing just age and gender be sufficient? Or would it also be important to know that the student is nonverbal, has asthma, uses a wheelchair for mobility, is latex sensitive, and has anxiety attacks when under pressure? This is a relatively extreme example, but it illustrates the importance of knowing the attributes of the student being assessed before selecting and administering a test. In general, the students' needs and attributes should be considered in five areas:

1. Communication
2. Cognition
3. Physical and motor—limitations and assistive devices
4. Social and behavioral
5. Medical

Clearly, you must be able to communicate to the student what you want her to do during the assessment as well as understand any questions she may have during the assessment. This may involve using an interpreter for a student who is deaf, if you cannot sign, or a computerized language board for a student with a neurological condition. The bottom line is you must recognize any communication limitations in order to select an appropriate test. For example, if Mr. MacNeil wants to use a shuttle run to measure agility, he would need to explain how the test is performed, that it is important that the students run as fast as they can, and that the time does not stop until they cross the finish line. Although he may be able to communicate the basic test by demonstrating the skill, it would still be necessary to communicate some information about how the test should be performed. Once the teacher knows the students' communication abilities and the nature of the test he plans to use, he can then make any appropriate accommodations (e.g., getting an interpreter) to ensure that the test can be administered appropriately.

A student's level of cognitive functioning is closely related to the ability to communicate but has greater implications regarding test selection and administration. For students to perform adequately on a test, they must know what they should do and why they are doing it—and they must also want to do well. Many students with low cognitive abilities do not understand the concept of a test. In these cases, if what the teacher is asking them to do does not make some functional sense to them, they probably will not comply. Others may grasp the basic task but not understand the need to perform the task quickly, accurately, or to the best of their ability. The teacher must know students' level of cognitive functioning to select appropriate test items as well as to interpret their performance on the items.

Many students have physical and motor limitations as a result of their disabilities that require special consideration when selecting tests. For example, when evaluating running ability, the physical educator may need to select a test that allows some variations, such as using a wheelchair or providing guide wires for students who are blind. For students with neurological impairments, factors such as range of motion and degree of motor control can impose limits on how fast or how intensely they can move.

Although not as obvious as cognitive and communication needs, social and behavioral issues must also be considered when selecting and administering tests. An assumption underlying most assessments is that the students want to do well. In other words, there is a general social expectation that when a test is given, you should do your best. For many students with disabilities, this is not a shared social expectation. They have taken hundreds of tests and have not typically done well. As a result, their expectation may be, *Here is another test I am going to fail.* Since they do not believe they can succeed, they may underperform because they lack motivation. Other students have learning or behavioral problems that interfere with their testing ability. For example, some students may have difficulty attending to instructions, so they get incomplete information on what they are supposed to do and then perform inappropriately. It is important to know whether what you are observing and assessing is their best ability for the skill you are assessing or their best guess as to what it is they think you are assessing.

Many students with disabilities also have secondary medical conditions or take medications that can have an adverse effect on their ability to perform physical and motor skills. For example, before giving a test to measure cardiorespiratory endurance, it would be important to know if a student has a heart or respiratory condition. Other students may take medications that impose limitations on their ability to perform. For example, a student with seizures may take medication that controls his condition but has a side effect of impaired balance. Other students may need to adjust (e.g., students with diabetes) or supplement (e.g., students with asthma) their medications in preparation for certain types of tests, necessitating a thorough understanding of medical conditions and any medications.

STEP 3: Identify the Dimensions of Physical Education That Need to Be Evaluated

This step may initially seem rather odd. If you want to evaluate how well a student can catch, you would select a test that measures catching. The question becomes more complicated when you want to assess whether a student is physically educated, well skilled, or physically fit. The problem is that physical education includes a number of fundamental skill areas (e.g., locomotor skills, object control skills, body awareness, body management, posture, and fitness) as well as numerous complex motor skills, where fundamental motor skills are combined to perform team and individual sports skills. In addition, physical education also teaches a wide range of cognitive objectives, such as fitness training principles and sports rules, as well as values such as ethical play and sportsmanship. The problem is that proficiency in one area is not necessarily correlated with proficiency in another. For example, a student can be physically fit but not well skilled or well skilled but not very knowledgeable about how games and sports are played. It is important therefore to know what aspects of physical education you want to evaluate and then to pick assessment instruments that include these dimensions.

STEP 4: Select or Create an Appropriate Assessment Instrument to Match the Decision to Be Made

Most assessment instruments are selected based on very practical considerations such as how easy they are or how much time they require to administer. Although these are important issues, many other factors should also be taken into account. Table 5.2 outlines a number of questions that should be considered when selecting an assessment instrument to make different types of assessment-based decisions. The questions in the table parallel the issues addressed thus far under the first three steps of the assessment process, as well as the psychometric qualities covered in chapter 4. The common assessment-based decisions made in physical education are listed down the left side of the table, and the various factors that should be considered when selecting an assessment instrument for each decision are listed across the top. To help you read the table, each factor is briefly explained here.

- *Decision.* What decision needs to be made: qualification, curriculum, placement, or instructional?
- *Type of decision.* This column identifies the focus of the four major types of decisions. For qualification decisions, this focus is typically on either informally screening students to identify those who may have motor problems or conducting more formal evaluations to determine whether a student meets the established criteria to receive special services such as APE. In terms of curriculum, the two major decisions involve first determining how close a student's PLOP is to her target GPE placement and then, as warranted, developing an APE curriculum to address her physical education goals. For placement decisions, the subquestions focus on determining the degree of overlap between the student's APE curriculum and the target GPE content and then determining the LRE for PE where the student's learning needs can be addressed and he can achieve the content in his APE curricula. Although these questions are directly linked, they can require different assessments to be answered. For example, it may be appropriate to administer a curriculum needs assessment to evaluate a student's present level of performance when determining his physical education needs. But to determine whether these needs can be addressed in the general physical education setting, it may be appropriate to observe this student in general physical education to evaluate how he attends, behaves, and interacts in a class setting.

- *What needs to be evaluated.* This factor parallels the previous question and identifies what aspects of physical, motor, cognitive, and social behavior need to be evaluated to address the decision that needs to be made. Some of the challenges in physical education include the tremendous amount and range of content covered and the lack of comprehensive assessment instruments that measure all aspects of this content. As a result, it is frequently necessary to administer several different assessment instruments to get a comprehensive understanding of a student's abilities so that an appropriate decision can be made.

- *Reference standard needed.* What are the reference standards for the decision being made? If, for example, the decision is a determination of whether a student qualifies for special education services, then the assessment used must have normative standards. For other decisions, such as what objective to focus on during instruction, the assessment must have specific performance criteria that indicate what aspects of the skill the student being assessed can and cannot perform.

- *Type of administration.* Can the assessment be administered individually, or can it be administered to a group of students? The underlying issue is time. Although it would be ideal to individually assess every student, this is not practical in many situations. As a result, screening instruments are used to evaluate large groups of students, and then individual assessments are used to make follow-up identification and placement decisions. For instructional decisions, it is most common to select instruments that can be used with entire classes. When needed, these instruments can also be individually administered.

- *Type of data needed.* This question is closely related to the reference standard discussed previously and the type of decision that needs to be made. The issue is whether the data collected by the instrument provide information on how skills are performed (i.e., the process) or focus on the outcome of the performance. For example, does the instrument collect information on how the student threw, such as whether she stepped with the opposite foot or followed through in the intended direction of the throw, or does it just measure how far she threw the ball?

- *Equipment and space.* This is a practical consideration. Do you have the space and equipment required to administer the assessment instrument?

- *Skill to administer.* Do you have or can you develop the skills necessary to administer the instrument? This issue is addressed in more detail in step 5 of the assessment process, learn and administer the instrument.

- *Validity.* Does the instrument have **validity**? An instrument must be valid for a given student's disability.

- *Reliability.* Is the instrument reliable? **Reliability** issues can usually be addressed with training.

- *Objectivity.* **Objectivity** is an important consideration if two or more teachers will be administering a given instrument to the same students. How consistent are the results?

Table 5.2 Decision Matrix for Selecting Assessment Instruments

Decision	Type of decision	**Preliminary questions**					
		What needs to be evaluated	Reference standard needed	Type of administration	Type of data needed	Equipment and space	Skill to administer
Qualification	Informal	• General motor ability • Physical fitness • Locomotor skills • Object control skills • Body awareness • Behavior • Knowledge	Norms or criteria, but usually norms	Individual or group; usually group for screening	Product or process; usually product	Do you have the necessary equipment and space to administer the test?	Do you have the prerequisite skills to administer the test?
Qualification	Formal	• General motor ability • Physical fitness • Locomotor skills • Object control skills • Body awareness • Behavior • Knowledge	Norms	Individual	May include both process and product measures, but most focus on product measures	Do you have the necessary equipment and space to administer the test?	Do you have the prerequisite skills to administer the test? Should the test be given by an APE specialist?
Curriculum	Formal	• Physical fitness • Locomotor skills • Object control skills • Body awareness • Behavior • Knowledge • Appropriateness of GPE goals and scope and sequence	GPE grade mastery standards and school district APE qualification standard	Individual	May include both process and product measures, but most focus on process measures	Do you have the necessary equipment and space to administer the needs assessment?	Do you have the prerequisite skills to administer the needs assessment? Should the test be given by an APE specialist?
Placement	PE goals	• Present level of performance • Learning rate • Long-term physical and motor needs	Combination of NRI and CRI	Individual	Product and process, with more emphasis on process	Do you have the necessary equipment and space to administer the test?	Do you have the prerequisite skills to administer the test? Should the test be given by an APE specialist?
Placement	LRE	• Content in the GPE curriculum • Performance levels of the students in the target placements	Physical education curriculum, local norms, and performance criteria	Group	Product and process, with more emphasis on process	Normal instructional space and equipment	Do you have the prerequisite skills to administer the test?
Instructional	Content	Where the student ranks on the content targeted for instruction in the curriculum	CRI for each objective taught in the curriculum	Individual or group; usually group	Product and process, with more emphasis on process	Normal instructional space and equipment	Do you have the prerequisite skills to administer the test?

	Test selection criteria			
Validity	**Reliability**	**Objectivity**	**Norms appropriate for disability**	**Sample sources**
Is the test valid for each student's disability, age, and gender?	Is there evidence to support the test's reliability?	Is the test being administered by more than one person?	Are the norms applicable to the students being evaluated?	These tend to be commercial tests such as the New York State Posture Test. See chapters 7-10.
Is the test valid for each student's disability, age, and gender?	Is there evidence to support the test's reliability?	Is the test being administered by more than one person?	Are the norms applicable to the students being evaluated?	These tend to be commercial tests such as TGMD. See chapters 6-10.
Is the test valid for each student's disability, age, and gender?	Is there evidence to support the test's reliability?	Is the test being administered by more than one person?	Are the school's norms for mastery of the GPE curriculum up to date?	See Needs Assessment in Kelly (2011).
Is the test valid for each student's disability, age, and gender?	Is there evidence to support the test's reliability?	Is the test being administered by more than one person?	Are the norms applicable to the students being evaluated?	These can be commercial or teacher-developed tests. See chapters 6-10.
Is the test valid for the students?	Is there evidence to support the test's reliability?	Is the test being administered by more than one person?	Local norms created on the students in the program	These can be commercial or teacher-developed tests. See chapters 6-10.
Is the test valid for the students?	Is there evidence to support the test's reliability?	Is the test being administered by more than one person?	Local norms can be created for when mastery is demonstrated of the criteria for each objective	These can be commercial tests such as Everyone Can! CRIs or teacher-developed tests. See this chapter.

- *Norms appropriate for disability.* Are the norms appropriate for the student's disability? Carefully review the information provided with the assessment instrument to make sure it is appropriate for the decision and students you plan to use it with.
- *Sample sources.* The last column provides examples or sources for finding assessment instruments to match the various types of decisions made in physical education. More detail is provided on a variety of these assessment instruments in other chapters in the book. You can also find additional information on assessment instruments in many physical education elementary and secondary methods books as well as test and measurement books.

The purpose of table 5.2 is to guide you through a series of questions that will help you select the most appropriate assessment instrument for the decision you need to make. Unfortunately, in many cases when evaluating students with disabilities, there may not be a commercially available test that meets your needs. In these situations, you will need to develop your own instruments.

STEP 5: Learn and Administer the Instrument so That Valid and Reliable Data Are Collected

A critical factor in instrument selection is the training and preparation required to administer the instrument. Regardless of whether a standardized NRI or a teacher-developed CRI is being used, the tester must consider both preparation and administration of the instrument. For most NRIs, these procedures will be clearly defined in the manual and must be followed exactly in order to use the interpretative data provided. Most CRIs offer teachers a little more latitude, but certain rules must be followed to ensure the data collected are both valid and reliable. A general set of guidelines that can be applied to preparing for most assessment situations follows.

1. Review and know how to administer the instrument well enough so that you can focus your attention on the student being assessed and not on the mechanics of administering the items (e.g., reading the instructions or reviewing the performance criteria to be observed).
2. When using an instrument for the first time, plan for a few pilot tests. Practice giving the test to one of your children or a neighbor's child. These practice trials will help you internalize the procedures and will most likely identify other potential administration problems that can be addressed and prevented.
3. When possible, set up any necessary equipment in advance, and anticipate any potential problems. Be prepared with backup equipment, such as stopwatches and targets that are critical for administering a given item.
4. When using instruments that focus on the process of a skill (e.g., throwing), identify where you need to stand (how far away and at what angle) so you can see the components that need to be evaluated.

5. Choose an appropriate assessing activity or organizational format so that students are actively engaged and you are free to move as needed to conduct the assessment.

6. Develop an efficient method to accurately record the assessment data you need to collect.

7. Remove all environmental factors that may interfere with performance, such as unnecessary equipment or audience effects.

There is no substitute for good planning and preparation when assessing. Although being aware of the student's attention, comprehension, and effort during assessing will improve the validity of the data collected, teachers must also employ common sense. Here are a few simple rules you should follow when conducting an assessment.

1. *When in doubt, do not give credit.* Given the complexity and subjective nature of many of the behaviors assessed in physical education, it is not uncommon for there to be some ambiguity as to whether a student is consistently demonstrating a given motor skill or behavior pattern. Whenever there is doubt, the rule to follow is to not give the student credit for mastery of the behavior in question. If you err in this direction, the worst that can happen is you will continue work on this behavior. If the student has actually mastered the behavior in question, the worst he can experience is success and maybe a little boredom until you reassess. On the other hand, if you err in the direction of giving credit for the behavior, you will not focus any additional instruction on this behavior. If the student has not mastered this behavior, she now will potentially fail or at a minimum practice the incorrect pattern until you reassess her and catch your error.

2. *Make sure the testing conditions do not compete with or confound the performance.* If you want to assess a student's qualitative throwing performance, then the assessment task should require the student to throw the ball both hard and far. Because of space and motivation considerations, it is not uncommon for teachers to use a throwing task that requires students to throw at a small target that is relatively close. If students misinterpret the task, they may decide it is more important to hit the target than to throw hard. In this case, they may modify their throwing pattern to maximize accuracy at the expense of correct form. The end result is that the teachers get an assessment of how well the students can modify their throwing pattern to do well on an accuracy task rather than an accurate assessment of their throwing pattern.

3. *Make sure the students know what you are asking them to do.* When using NRIs, teachers usually do not have much flexibility in how the instrument is administered. However, if while administering an instrument you observe that the students appear confused by the instructions, you should question the validity of the data you collect. With most CRIs, teachers have a little more flexibility in how the items are administered. If a student appears confused, follow up and ask the student if she understands what is being requested.

4. *Be aware of any potential audience effects.* Because most assessments in physical education must be administered in a public setting, there is always

a threat that one or more environmental factors may negatively affect performance. If students know they are going to perform worse than other students, they may just dismiss the assessment and act as if they do not care. Unfortunately, if the students do not give their best effort, you do not get an accurate assessment of their ability. Therefore it is critical that assessments be conducted in such a fashion that students do not feel they are being "tested." One of the best ways to deal with test avoidance is to make assessment an ongoing process and to integrate it into natural activities in the class.

5. *Do not teach while formally assessing.* Periodically, at least at the beginning and end of units of instruction, it is important to assess students to rate them on the objectives being taught. One of the toughest things to do while formally assessing students is to not immediately use the assessment information to give instructional feedback. Again, one of the best ways to conduct this form of assessment is to observe the students in a naturalistic setting, such as a game where they are applying the skills being assessed and can be observed without the expectation of immediate feedback.

6. *Give general positive feedback.* Inevitably, students know they are being evaluated in some situations, and they will naturally look to the teacher after each performance for feedback. If you say nothing, it is possible that the students will interpret this as negative feedback and try to alter their performance. In these instances, it is probably best to give a general positive statement such as "Nice effort."

7. *Devise and use a method that allows you to record performance data as soon as possible.* Probably the single greatest complaint teachers have about assessment relates to the time involved in collecting and recording assessment data. Develop innovative ways to quickly and accurately record assessment data such as using a simple X or O scoring method or a medium like an iPad where the performance can be recorded with one or two simple touches.

8. *Be prepared.* All assessments require some amount of practice to administer efficiently. To be effective, teachers must internalize the components of the skills they are going to observe. If you need to refer to your checklist while assessing to review the components of a skill, you are not ready. It typically requires about an hour of practice to memorize the components of most motor skills and to see them accurately. After several hours of practice, you will begin to see the skill in terms of the components. At that point, instead of looking at the skill and mentally comparing the performance with the checklist, you will see the performance in terms of which components are performed correctly and incorrectly.

STEP 6: Interpret the Assessment Data Collected and Make an Appropriate Decision

The last step is interpreting the data collected throughout the assessment process and making decisions. A qualification decision typically involves looking up raw scores or a composite score in the normative tables provided with the instrument and obtaining a percentile or age-equivalent score. The teacher then compares this value to the established eligibility criteria. If the value meets or exceeds this standard, the student would be deemed eligible. For students with disabilities, this type of decision must be made to determine whether they qualify for special education services. Students are typically assessed on a number of factors such as motor skills, IQ, and adaptive behavior; they must be found to have delays greater than two standard deviations below the mean for their age and gender. Remember that test scores are only indicators that sample specific dimensions of ability. When making qualification decisions, physical educators need to look at the total student in the context of the setting and the decision they are making. When the scores do not add up or are inconsistent, do not be afraid to add a little common sense to the equation.

Curriculum decisions involve analyzing the student's PLOP and then using this information to guide two decisions. First, is the GPE curriculum appropriate for this student? This question can be addressed by administering a curriculum needs assessment that collects performance data on how the student performs on the GPE objectives that should have been mastered by her current grade level. The results of the CNA produce an overall mastery score as well as mastery scores for each year of the GPE curriculum evaluated. The student's overall mastery score is compared with the school's cutoff score, which is typically between 60 and 70 percent. Students falling below the established cutoff score are judged to be delayed enough to require a modified curriculum. When a modified curriculum is needed, the next decision is what needs to be included in this curriculum to address this student's physical education needs so she can leave school with adequate physical and motor skills to maintain her health and fitness and to participate in physical and recreational activities. The grade-level mastery results from the CNA can be used to guide the curriculum development process by identifying the student's strengths and weaknesses. The magnitude of the CNA score can also be used to estimate the degree to which the APE curriculum will need to be delimited to ensure it can be achieved in the time available in the student's program.

The process for placement decisions is similar to procedures described for curriculum decisions. The major difference is it may be appropriate to use either an NRI or a CRI test, depending on the nature of the placement decision. In GPE, a placement decision could involve whether a new student should be placed in an intermediate or advanced tennis class. To address this question, it is necessary to know the prerequisite objectives for the intermediate and advanced classes as well as what objectives are targeted for instruction in each. The new student can then be assessed on these prerequisite and target skills and his results compared with the performance levels of the students in the intermediate and advanced classes. A decision can then be made as to which class the student would be most successful in.

For students with disabilities, making placement decisions is a two-step procedure. The first step is to compare the student's APE curriculum created from her PLOP assessment data, in particular her scope and sequence of objectives, which indicates which objectives in her APE curriculum need to be mastered during each year, with the scope and sequence of objectives for the GPE curriculum. The scope and sequence charts should be compared and analyzed for the degree of overlap or the number of objectives they have in common. Although APE curricula by design will overall have fewer goals and objectives, they will frequently share many common objectives with the GPE curriculum, particularly at the elementary level. As a general rule, the greater the number of common objectives between the curricula, the better the fit and the easier it will be to successfully include a student in GPE with appropriate support services.

Sharing common objectives, however, is only part of the decision. The second part of the placement decision is evaluating whether the student can learn and achieve her objectives in GPE. To make this decision, the assessment information collected during the qualification and curriculum procedures (e.g., ACE behaviors during the CNA) can be used to judge whether this student's communication, cognitive, medical, social, and behavioral needs can also be addressed so she can learn in the GPE environment. The law requires that students be placed in the general educational setting to the maximum degree possible as long as their instructional needs can be met and they can be successful. It is therefore your responsibility to ensure that they are placed in the LRE where they can learn the content in their APE curricula.

Interpreting assessment data for instructional decisions has several dimensions. At the start of the unit, initial assessment data are used to determine the students' initial learning objectives (i.e., what focal point of the skill they each need to work on) on the content targeted for instruction. This information in turn guides a variety of decisions, such as the focus of instruction for the next class; how students should be grouped for instruction; and what games, drills, and activities should be planned. The data are also used to set target expectations (i.e., how much learning is expected) for both the students and the teacher. Students should be informed of what they have achieved in terms of content and what they need to focus on during instruction to improve. During instruction, teachers use assessment data every time they observe students and give feedback. Finally, reassessment and postassessment data are used to evaluate and make decisions regarding student progress, teacher effectiveness, the appropriateness of instructional methods, and the overall merit of the program.

What You Need to Know

Key Terms

criterion-referenced instrument
curriculum decisions
instructional decisions
norm-referenced instrument
objectivity

placement decisions
qualification decisions
reliability
screening
validity

Key Concepts

1. You should understand the six steps in the assessment process.
2. You should know the five areas of students' needs and attributes to be considered when selecting an assessment instrument in physical education.
3. You should understand the factors to be considered when selecting a physical education assessment instrument.
4. You should know the seven guidelines that ensure the assessment data you collect are both valid and reliable.

Review Questions

1. What is curriculum-based evaluation, and when is it used in physical education?
2. If during your assessment you have some doubt whether students have demonstrated mastery of a skill component, why is it recommended that you not give them credit?
3. Compare norm-referenced and criterion-referenced instruments in physical education in terms of the time needed to learn the instruments and administer them correctly.
4. What are the step-by-step procedures you would follow to determine the LRE placement for a new student with autism that is entering your school? Specifically, what instruments would you use and why?

Chapter **6**

Assessing Motor Development and Motor Skill Performance

The focus of overall development should be on relevant information regarding placement and the determination of functional capabilities of persons with disabilities. Several sources of information contribute to identifying specific developmental landmarks, reflex movements, and voluntary movements that are used for ambulation, stability, and object control. Later these movements become patterns and are used in conjunction with other movements to accomplish specific functional tasks, or are performed on an individual basis or in a competitive format as sports activities. In this chapter, the focus is on development of movement and coordination, including tests of motor development, reflexes, motor ability, perceptual-motor skills, sports skills, and balance assessments.

Motor development tests evaluate progression of typical motor functioning on a continuum. The use of developmental norms assumes that comparing the performance of a student with disabilities against norms for typical development is appropriate, and deviations from the norm are indicative of a delay or problem in development, or are associated with a physical or cognitive

Case Study 1
Determining Qualification for Special Education Services

Mr. Warren was recently hired as the first adapted physical education specialist for Curry County Public Schools. Mr. Warren was told by the county's director of special education that he would need to determine which students with disabilities have significant gross motor delays and thus qualify for adapted physical education services. The school district is relatively small, with only 3,000 students in all grades. However, 12 percent of those 3,000 receive special education services through Curry County Public Schools. There is no way Mr. Warren can service all 360. Fortunately, most of those 360 don't have significant motor delays and do not need adapted physical education services, but how can Mr. Warren efficiently and accurately determine which students have significant gross motor delays and thus qualify for his services?

disability. Developmental scores, including age and grade equivalents, compare performances across age or grade peer groups and can detect potential movement dysfunctions. These data are useful in clinical case studies, initial motor development screening, and longitudinal research on motor development. The use of a developmental approach assumes that all people progress through the same series of motor development tasks, although they may encounter landmarks at various time intervals in the developmental process.

It is important that teachers quickly determine which students qualify for their special education services. Once it has been established that a student has a significant gross motor delay, the cause of the delay should be established in order to focus on program intervention. For example, a student with a neurological condition may still encounter some primitive reflex activity that affects or disrupts movement. Likewise, lack of strength or the presence of a sensory impairment may also affect motor functioning. With the assistance of physical and occupational therapists (and perhaps a neurologist), the teacher can identify these limitations, determine what might be causing the delay, and develop a program plan to guide intervention.

REFLEXES AND REFLEX TESTS

Infantile reflexes are involuntary subcortical movement reactions exhibited after sensory stimulation such as head movement, light, touch, and sound. The primary purpose of **reflex movements** is for infant protection and survival and to stimulate the central nervous and muscle systems (Haywood & Getchell, 2014; Payne & Isaacs, 2016). Most reflexes appear in infancy (and some even during late prenatal development), and these reflexes usually are inhibited or disappear by six months of age in typically developing children. For example, an infant's strong grasp reflex (i.e., grasping onto anything after stimulation to the palm of the hand) is enjoyable for a parent during the infant's first few months of life. However, by six months, the grasp reflex should all but disappear, allowing the child to demonstrate more voluntary grasping and releasing abilities.

Infantile reflexes can be divided into three categories: postural (symmetric and asymmetric tonic neck, tonic labyrinthine, positive support), primitive (grasp, Moro, suck/swallow, rooting, Babinski), and locomotor (stepping, crawling, swimming) (Haywood & Getchell, 2014) (see table 6.1).

Reflexes that persist can be a sign of neurological problems and may ultimately make it difficult for a child to demonstrate coordinated voluntary movement (Burger & Louw, 2009; Futagi, Yanagihara, Mogami, Ikeda, & Suzuki, 2013; Payne & Isaacs, 2016). For example, the **asymmetrical tonic neck reflex** (ATNR) can be stimulated by turning the infant's head to one side. The face-side extremities will extend, while extremities on the other side will flex. This reflex is common in infants up to six months, but the reflex is usually subtle in most normally developing infants and does not appear every time the child's head is turned to the side. On the other hand, in infants with neurological damage (such as cerebral palsy), the ATNR may be very strong when the child's head is turned, may appear every time the child is stimulated around the head, and may persist well into early childhood (and even later childhood in students with severe neurological damage). Infants with persistent ATNR will have difficulty exploring their bodies with their hands, bringing their hands to midline, and rolling over; students with persistent ATNR will have difficulty with movements that require symmetry, such as walking and using two hands together.

In addition, certain reactions or responses appear during later infancy and early childhood. These responses include **righting reactions** (keeping one's head in line with the body), **balance reactions** (keeping oneself from falling over when balance is lost), and **protective reactions** (putting arms or legs out to prevent injury during a fall). These responses, which are controlled cortically and thus reflect higher neurological development, remain throughout the life span; they provide righting or protective reactions that allow the infant to assume some movement control and coordinate various body positions, such as lifting the head and turning the body (Barnes, Crutchfield, Heriza, & Herdman, 1990). For example, if a child is standing and is pushed forward, she might tilt her head away from the direction of the push in order to maintain balance (righting reaction). If the push is hard enough that the child feels she may fall, she may put her arms and even one leg out in an effort to maintain balance (balance reaction). And if the push is hard enough that the child actually falls, then she will put her arms out to break the fall (protective reaction). If these responses do not develop, such skills as sitting, standing, and walking will be delayed or may not appear at all because of the child's inability to maintain balance in response to changes in the center of gravity (Zafeiriou, 2004; Zafeiriou, Tsikoulas, Kremenopoulos, & Kontopoulos, 1998) (see table 6.2).

Reflex assessments are not commonly performed in most schools unless it is clear that a student has persistent neurological problems such as cerebral palsy or a head injury. However, awareness of persistent reflex behaviors is imperative to understand if the reflex is detracting from a student's motor development and performance. For example, the teacher can avoid movements that initiate a reflex (such as turning the head, which stimulates the ATNR)

Table 6.1   Select Reflexes

Reflex or reaction	Stimulus	Response	Persistence
Primitive reflexes			
Grasping (palmar and plantar) reflex	Apply pressure to palm of hand or hyperextend wrist Stroke the sole of foot	Flexion of fingers to grasp, then extension to release Toes contract around object stroking foot	In hand, causes difficulty in releasing objects, in throwing and striking, and in reception of tactile stimuli
Moro reflex	Change head position; drop backward in a sitting position	Extension of arms and legs, fingers spread, then flexion of arms; addition of arms across chest	Interferes with ability to sit unsupported and to perform locomotor patterns or sports skills with sudden movements (e.g., abduction of arms and legs during gymnastics interferes with balance)
Suck/swallow reflex	Touch face above or below lips	Sucking motion followed by swallowing motion	Lack of response prevents normal intake of food Persistence interferes with ability to eat regular food
Rooting reflex	Touch cheek close to lips	Rotates head toward stimulation	Cannot align head with neck when body is turned Impedes segmental rolling
Babinski reflex	Stroke sole of foot from heel to toes	Toes extend	Persistence after 6 months suggests neurological damage
Locomotor reflexes			
Stepping reflex	Support infant upright and gently place feet on flat surface	Walking pattern in legs (alternating steps)	Interferes with voluntary movement Persistence after 6 months suggests neurological damage
Crawling reflex	With infant prone on flat surface, gently push against soles of one foot or both feet alternately	Crawling pattern in arms and legs	Interferes with voluntary movement Persistence after 6 months suggests neurological damage
Swimming reflex	With infant in prone position, place over or in water	Swimming movement of arms and legs	Interferes with voluntary movement Persistence after 6 months suggests neurological damage
Postural reflexes			
Asymmetrical tonic neck reflex	Turn or laterally flex the head	Increased extension on chin side, with accompanying flexion of limbs on head side	Difficulty in rolling because of extended arm Interferes with holding the head in midline, resulting in problems with tracking and fixating on objects Evident in catching and throwing when one elbow is bent while the other extends because head position rotates or tilts to track a ball
Symmetrical tonic neck reflex	Flex or extend the head and neck	With head flexion, flexion of arms and upper extremities, with extension of the legs Backward extension of head results in extension of arms and flexion of legs	Prevents creeping because head controls position of arms and legs Retention prohibits infants from flexing and extending legs in creeping patterns Also interferes with catching, kicking, and throwing since changes in head position affect muscle tone and reciprocation of muscle groups

Table 6.1 *(continued)*

Reflex or reaction	Stimulus	Response	Persistence
	Postural reflexes		
Tonic labyrinthine (prone and supine) reflex	Stimulate vestibular apparatus by tilting or changing head position	In prone position, increased flexion in the limbs; in supine position, extension occurs in limbs	Affects muscle tone and ability to move body segments independently into various positions, such as propping the body up in a support position before crawling or rolling
Positive support reflex	Touch balls of the feet to a firm surface in an upright position	Extension of the legs to support weight in a standing position	Disruption of muscle tone needed to support weight or adduction and internal rotation of the hips, interfering with standing and locomotion

Data from Haywood 2014.

Table 6.2 Selected Equilibrium Responses

Reflex or reaction	Stimulus	Response	Persistence
	Righting reactions		
Labyrinthine righting	Limit vision or tilt body in various directions	Head will move to maintain upright position	Unable to reorient head in proper body alignment and position Interferes with head control in movement
Optic righting	Tilt body in various directions	Head will move to maintain upright position	Unable to reorient head in proper body alignment and body posture
	Balance reactions		
Postural fixation	Apply external force to body when base of support is stable	Curving of spine and extension of arms or legs toward force in order to maintain balance	Lack of support to prevent body from falling Clumsiness and awkwardness resulting in loss of balance, muscle tone, and falling
Tilting reaction	Displace center of gravity by tilting or moving support surface	Protective extension and muscle tone on downward side Upward side has curvature of trunk and extension of extremities	Lack of support to prevent body from falling Clumsiness and awkwardness resulting in loss of balance, muscle tone, and falling
	Other reactions		
Protective reactions	Rapidly lower infant forward, to the side or backward	Extension of legs and arms to protect self from fall	Lack of support to prevent injury from fall

and implement strategies (such as strengthening neck muscles) that can help the student avoid some reflex actions. For students with disabilities, it is best to have a physical therapist identify the level of reflex functioning, determine whether these reflexes are affecting the student's development, and then provide appropriate tasks to facilitate reflex inhibition.

Scoring of reflexes is generally subjective, using a scoring key to denote absence or changes in the movement. Scoring may range from 0 (normal) to 1 (decreased), 2 (absent), 3 (exaggerated), or 4 (sustained). Equilibrium, tilting, and protective responses are evaluated by equilibrium platforms or therapy balls to assess **tilting reactions** and the infants' adjustments to maintain balance.

Primitive Reflex Profile

Capute, Palmer, Shapiro, Wachtel, Ross, and Accardo (1984) developed an instrument that quantifiably assesses primitive reflex behaviors (asymmetrical tonic neck, symmetrical tonic neck, and the Moro reflex). Primitive reflexes were selected because their role in the development of typical functioning makes them the most indicative of atypical development. The scale, which follows, employs a five-point classification scoring system, not only to observe typical and atypical movement responses but also to note the strength of the reflex. To quantify the reflex, the following scores are assigned:

0 = absent

1 = small change in tone

2 = physically present and visible

3 = noticeable strength and force

4 = strong

MOTOR DEVELOPMENT TESTS

A major premise in **motor development** is that certain behaviors emerge through maturational processes and then develop through learning and practice. Problems may interfere with this process, resulting in failure to achieve appropriate **developmental landmarks** or motor milestones. For example, watching a child develop the ability to creep on his hands and knees is a visible change from the child's previous ability to simply crawl on his belly. Factors that have led to this change in motor behavior might include increased strength, postural control, and ability to coordinate the limbs for movement; understanding of his body; and awareness and desire to explore his surroundings. In terms of assessment, most motor development tests examine the visible changes, or motor milestones, a child achieves from birth to around six years of age (depending on the specific test) as opposed to the processes that underlie the development of these milestones. Most motor development tests also include accompanying age norms describing when most children should achieve a particular milestone. The following is a list of typical motor behaviors found in most motor development tests, along with estimated ages when children are expected to achieve these behaviors:

Estimated Age	Motor Behavior
2 to 3 months	Lifts head from floor when placed in prone position
4 to 5 months	Reaches for and grasps rattle
5 to 6 months	Sits independently
6 to 7 months	Rolls over
7 to 8 months	Crawls on belly
9 to 10 months	Creeps on hands and knees
10 to 11 months	Stands independently for a few seconds
11 to 12 months	Takes first independent steps
1-1/2 to 2 years	Fast walk in attempt to run
2 to 2-1/2 years	Jumps so both feet are off the ground at same time
2-1/2 to 3 years	Basic gallop with one foot leading other
3 to 3-1/2 years	Catches (scoops) playground ball when ball is tossed to child
3-1/2 to 4 years	Basic hop on one foot
4 to 5 years	Throws ball overhand and hits target in two out of three trials
4 to 6 years	Basic skipping pattern

Motor development is often divided into two categories: gross motor development and fine motor development. **Gross motor skills**, which make up gross motor development, refer to skills controlled by large muscles or muscle groups, such as the muscles in the legs (locomotor patterns) and in the trunk and arms (object control skills). **Fine motor skills**, which make up fine motor development, refer to skills controlled by smaller muscles or muscle groups, such as movements with the hands (grasping and releasing, cutting with scissors, stringing beads, holding a crayon, drawing) (Payne & Isaacs, 2016; Gallahue, Ozmun & Goodaway, 2012). Adapted and general physical educators as well as physical therapists are more concerned with gross motor development, while special education and classroom teachers as well as occupational therapists tend to be more concerned with fine motor development. Early identification and intervention are critical in order for students with disabilities to develop to their fullest potential (Bricker, Capt, Johnson, Pretti-Frontczak, Waddell, & Straka, 2002; Cowden & Torrey, 2007).

The most effective way to determine whether students experience motor delays and require motor intervention programs is to screen students using a test that measures motor development and then compare the results with what is typically expected during development. Such tools are known as developmental tests. Developmental tests tend to be standardized, with very clear directions and criteria. These instruments also tend to be norm referenced, allowing a teacher to compare the development of the student she is testing with a sample of similar-aged students. For example, a student who is five years old might score at a three-year-old's motor level on a developmental test. The teacher would know that the student has a two-year motor delay in overall development and would clearly qualify for early intervention services.

Developmental tests tend to examine the acquisition of motor milestones such as the appearance of reflexes, sitting posture, creeping, crawling, rolling over, standing, walking, jumping, and balance (Burton & Miller, 1998; Cowden & Torrey, 2007; Moodie, Daneri, Goldhagen, Halle, Green, & LaMonte, 2014). With few exceptions, test items are graded as pass or fail based on whether or not a subject can accomplish a particular milestone. The pass or fail format and clear criteria (e.g., can the subject stand on one foot for three seconds) make these tests easy to administer, but unfortunately, they do not generally examine the quality of movement patterns except for a few select items (e.g., walking up stairs alternating feet, throwing overhand versus underhand).

The study of typical development and the creation of norms for when infants and toddlers should achieve certain motor milestones form the basis of most motor development tests (Burton & Miller, 1998; Moodie, Daneri, Goldhagen, Halle, Green, & LaMonte, 2014). In this context, the development of the central nervous system during infancy and early childhood proceeds in a normal hierarchical pattern that can be seen in the appearance of certain motor milestones. The appearance of these milestones at certain times indicates normal development, while delays in their appearance might indicate potential problems in development (Payne & Isaacs, 2016). For the physical education teacher, being able to identify potential problems that interfere with development will facilitate intervention and program planning based on individual needs. Therefore, the students in case study 1 can be assessed to identify problem areas that lead to placement decisions and an intervention plan. Several of the common tests used to assess developmental landmarks are outlined in this section.

Peabody Developmental Motor Scales 2 (PDMS-2)

The Peabody Developmental Motor Scales 2 (PDMS-2) assesses fine and gross motor skills from birth to seven years of age (Folio & Fewell, 2000). Like other global developmental tests, the PDMS-2 is standardized and norm referenced. But the PDMS-2 focuses solely on motor development, with gross motor and fine motor subsections. The gross motor subsection has 151 items divided into four categories: reflexes, stationary, locomotion, and object manipulation. The fine motor section, which is popular with occupational therapists, has 98 items divided into two categories: grasping and visual-motor integration (Folio & Fewell, 2000). The PDMS-2 is included in a sample write-up in appendix A.

All items on the PDMS-2 are scored on a three-point scale. A score of 2 indicates passing at the set criteria for the test item; a score of 1 indicates the subject shows a clear resemblance to the skill but cannot perform the skill to the set criteria; and a score of 0 indicates the subject cannot or will not attempt the item, or the attempt does not show the skill is even emerging (Folio & Fewell, 2000). For example, when scoring the item in which the subject stands for five seconds on one foot with the nonstanding leg held parallel to the ground, the subject would receive a 0 if he could not stand on one foot at all or only very briefly. But if he stood on one foot for two or three seconds with hands on hips part of the time, or perhaps keeping his leg not quite parallel to the floor, then he would receive a score of 1. And finally, if the subject could stand on one foot for five seconds using the criteria set in the item, he would receive a score of 2. This three-point scoring system is more sensitive than the simple two-point pass or fail measure typically used in most developmental tests. The examiner can give credit to students whose skills might be emerging but who have not quite mastered them.

As noted earlier, the gross motor portion of the PDMS-2 is divided into four categories. Scores from all the categories can be combined to calculate an overall gross motor age, which can then be used to determine whether a student is on age level or delayed. More important, these categories can be calculated separately, allowing a teacher to determine whether a student has strengths or weaknesses in particular motor areas. For example, a student might have good locomotor and stationary skills but score poorly on object manipulation. This indicates that his motor problems revolve around eye–hand coordination or upper-body coordination. By identifying submotor areas where a student has problems, the teacher can create a more focused intervention program (see table 6.3 for a sample of items from the locomotor subarea).

Because this test is widely accepted in early intervention and is easy to use, it is recommended for infants and toddlers with disabilities (Cowden & Torrey, 2007). Folio and Fewell (2000) indicate that the PDMS-2 does not include norms for students with disabilities but provides vital information that is valid and useful for identifying developmental needs. The performance of students with physical disabilities may be compromised on the PDMS-2, but the test is still recommended. The accompanying curriculum is also helpful in early movement analysis and program planning.

Table 6.3 Sample Items in the Locomotor Section of the Peabody Developmental Motor Scales 2

Item	Age in months	Item name	Highest scoring criteria (2 points)
47	21-22	Walking sideways	Walks sideways 10 ft (3 m) with same foot leading
48	21-22	Walking line	Walks with 1 foot on line for 6 ft (2 m)
49	23-24	Jumping forward	Jumps forward 4 in. (10 cm), maintaining balance
50	23-24	Jumping up	Jumps up 2 in. (5 cm) with feet together
51	23-24	Jumping down	Jumps down without assistance from 7 in. (17.5 cm)
52	23-24	Walking up stairs	Walks up 4 steps without support (1 or both feet on step is okay)
53	25-26	Walking down stairs	Walks down 4 steps without support (1 or both feet on step is okay)
54	25-26	Walking backward	Walks backward 10 ft (3 m) without heels touching toes

From M.R. Folio and R.R. Fewell, 2000, *Peabody developmental motor scales,* 2nd ed. (Austin, TX: Pro-Ed).

Brigance Inventory of Early Development III (IED-III)

Another functional test that provides useful information on motor development is the Brigance IED-III Standardized (IED-III) (Brigance & French, 2013), a criterion-referenced (curricular objectives directly related to instruction) and norm-referenced (age benchmarks) developmental test for children from birth to 7 years, 11 months of age. The IED-III helps early childhood educators assess key school readiness skills; identify each student's specific strengths and needs; plan individualized instruction based on assessment results; and monitor student progress. The inventory contains 55 norm-referenced assessment items standardized in 2012 using a sample population representative of the United States in terms of race and ethnicity, sex, socioeconomic status, and geographic location. Summative normative scores include standard scores, percentiles, and age equivalents, which can be used as supporting identification of special needs. The inventory has strong test–retest and interrater reliability as well as content, construct, and criterion-related validity. No special training is required to administer the IED-III. However, the manual recommends that the examiner be very familiar with directions and scoring procedures, practice administering the tool to a student so there is no pause between items, master following directions for each item, and understand how to accurately record responses on the scoring sheet (Brigance & French, 2013).

The IED-III is a global developmental test covering a broad range of areas, including the following domains, which align to early learning standards and Common Core State Standards:

- Physical development (preambulatory, gross motor, and fine motor)
- Language development (receptive language and expressive language)
- Literacy
- Mathematics and science
- Daily living
- Social and emotional development

Scores are recorded as pass or fail for specific items. As long as the student is successful, she can proceed until the highest item is completed correctly.

Of most interest to the adapted physical educators and physical therapists are the motor subsections and the social-emotional subsections on the Brigance IED-III. Gross motor skills include infant developmental milestones, standing, walking, skipping, galloping, jumping, hopping, stair climbing, rolling, throwing, and catching. Fine motor skills include basic grasping and releasing, building a tower with blocks, visual-motor skills, and writing and drawing skills. Social and emotional development subsections include relationships with adults, play and relationships with peers, motivation and self-confidence, and prosocial skills and behaviors.

A nice feature of the Brigance IED-III is the comprehensive skill sequence presented for each developmental area. This skill sequence includes all the items on the Brigance, including milestone skills as well as other secondary items, along with the expected age when these skills appear in normally developing students. The skill sequence can easily be used to chart developmental progress as well as to estimate the developmental level of a student. This method is recommended when testing students with more significant delays and disabilities. Teachers can also choose to use the accompanying developmental record book, which focuses on primary milestones that are appropriate for most students.

In both types of assessments, the examiner reviews the list of developmental items and determines an entry level for assessment (a subjective rating of where the student ranks developmentally). She then engages the student in play, encouraging him to demonstrate the behaviors on the test. The examiner circles the items the student can demonstrate and underlines the items the student cannot demonstrate. The manual suggests a color-coding system for tracking progress. After the first round of assessment, use a regular black-lead pencil to circle items that have been mastered and a blue pencil to underline items (simply underline the item number) targeted for immediate instruction. After completing the second assessment, use a blue pencil to circle all items mastered during this second marking period. Then use a red pencil to underline items targeted for immediate instruction in the next marking period. After completing the third assessment, use a red pencil to circle all items mastered during this marking period. This type of color-coded marking record allows teachers and therapists to easily note the student's level when he started the program, skills targeted for instruction after each assessment, and skills mastered between the first and second and then second and third marking periods. Since each task on the Brigance has a developmental age associated with it, it is also easier for the examiner to interpret the results of the Brigance in terms of developmental norms and whether or not the student has a developmental delay.

Developmental Assessment of Young Children, Second Edition (DAYC-2)

The Developmental Assessment of Young Children, Second Edition, is used to identify delays from birth through 5 years, 11 months. Authors of DAYC-2 report three major purposes:

1. Identifying children who are significantly below their peers in cognitive, communicative, social-emotional, physical, or adaptive behavior abilities
2. Monitoring children's progress in special intervention programs
3. Researching studying abilities in young students (Voress & Maddox, 2013).

Domains assessed include cognition, communication, social-emotional development, physical development, and adaptive behavior. Each domain reflects an area mentioned for young students in IDEA. The domains can be assessed independently (e.g., the adapted physical educator may be interested only in the physical domain), or all five domains can be assessed when measuring general development. Data can be collected through observation, interview of caregivers, and direct assessment. The DAYC-2 may be used in arena assessment so that each discipline can use the evaluation tool independently (Voress & Maddox, 2013). No special training is required to administer and score the DAYC-2. The developers suggest qualified examiners are likely to be early childhood specialists, school psychologists, diagnosticians, speech-language pathologists, physical therapists, occupational therapists, or other professionals who have some formal training in assessment and early childhood development.

The DAYC-2 was normed on a national sample of 1,832 children between 2009 and 2011. According to the manual, characteristics of the normative sample approximate the 2010 census (Voress & Maddox, 2013). Standard scores, percentile ranks, and age equivalents are provided for each domain and for overall general development if all five domains are tested. Validity and reliability were good, and validity studies, including studies of the test's sensitivity and specificity, are now included in the test manual.

Ages and Stages Questionnaires, Third Edition (ASQ-3)

The Ages and Stages Questionnaires, Third Edition (ASQ-3), is a developmental screening system for children from 1 to 66 months of age. There are 21 separate age-specific questionnaires, each containing 30 items, completed by parents or primary caregivers of young children. The questionnaires can identify children who are in need of further assessment to determine whether they are eligible for early intervention or early childhood special education services.

The third edition (published in 2009) features new two- and nine-month questionnaires, expanded administration windows, and new standardization. The new norms were based on 15,138 children and their families, representative of the U.S. population in geography, in ethnicity, and across socioeconomic groups (Squires, Twombly, Bricker, & Potter, 2009).

The ASQ-3 questionnaires are completed by parents using a three-point scoring system: yes (10 points), sometimes (5 points), or not yet (0 points). Scoring is based on whether the child exhibits certain skills or behaviors within five areas: communication, gross motor, fine motor, problem solving, and personal-social. There is also an additional section where parents can report any concerns they have about their child (Squires, Twombly, Bricker, & Potter, 2009). Sample gross motor items from the 16-month questionnaire in the ASQ-3 are as follows:

1. Does your child stand up in the middle of the floor by himself and take several steps forward?
2. Does your child climb onto furniture or other large objects, such as large climbing blocks?
3. Does your child bend over or squat to pick up an object from the floor and then stand up again without any support?
4. Does your child move around by walking, rather than crawling on her hands and knees?
5. Does your child walk well and seldom fall?
6. Does your child climb on an object such as a chair to reach something he wants (e.g., to get a toy on a counter or to "help" you in the kitchen)?

The ASQ-3 has strong reliability, validity, and discriminative sensitivity. It is not necessary to have a professional background or technical training to complete or score the ASQ-3. It was developed as a parent-completed screening tool, and having parents and caregivers complete the questionnaires is the preferred method. The manual does suggest that all ASQ-3 users become familiar with the information in the manual, with a particular emphasis on administering the questionnaires.

Assessment, Evaluation, and Programming System (AEPS) for Infants and Children

The Assessment, Evaluation, and Programming System (AEPS) is an activity-based instrument that links assessment, intervention, and evaluation for children with disabilities or those at risk for developmental delays (Bricker, Capt, Johnson, Pretti-Frontczak, Waddell, & Straka, 2002). The updated second edition assesses and monitors six developmental areas in children from birth to six years of age:

1. Fine motor
2. Adaptive
3. Gross motor
4. Social communication
5. Cognitive
6. Social

According to the AEPS test manual (Bricker, Capt, Johnson, Pretti-Frontczak, Waddell, & Straka, 2002), each developmental area is subdivided into a progression of skills (including strands of general skill areas) and goals for specific skills, as well as instructional objectives that are task analyzed and designed to meet overall goals. Scoring on each item is based on 0 (does not pass), 1 (inconsistent performance), or 2 (passes consistently). Specific comments are also used in what Bricker and colleagues term qualifying notes to emphasize performance scores.

The gross motor domain measures skill acquisition in the following four strands (Bricker, Capt, Johnson, Pretti-Frontczak, Waddell, & Straka, 2002, 89):

1. Moving body parts independently of each other and positioning the body in supine and prone positions to facilitate movement and locomotion
2. Maintaining balance and moving in a balanced sitting position
3. Maintaining balance and moving in an upright position
4. Using coordinated actions while moving

The teacher selects items from each of the four strands that have specific objectives. For example, in strand A (balance and mobility), goal 1 is to run while avoiding obstacles, and goal 2 is to alternate feet while walking up and down stairs. The teacher can then score the item (0, 1, or 2) and add a qualifying note, such as "assistance provided" or "adaptation needed."

This test is highly recommended for teachers of young students—especially since the assessment is linked to activities—as well as for developing the IEP and individualized family service plan (IFSP).

Gross Motor Function Measure (GMFM)

The Gross Motor Function Measure (GMFM) is the most common functional test used by physical therapists and other rehabilitation specialists to measure gross motor functioning in children with cerebral palsy (CP) (Alotaibi, Long, Kennedy, & Bavishi, 2014). The first version of the GMFM was known as the GMFM-88, and the most recent version is the GMFM-66 (Russell, Rosenbaum, Avery, & Lane, 2002, 2000). Both versions are criterion-referenced tools that measure present-level gross motor function as well as change over time in children with disabilities from ages five months to 16 years (Alotaibi, Long, Kennedy, & Bavishi, 2014; Josenby, Jarnio, Gummesson, & Nordmark, 2009; Jooyeon, 2014; Russell, Rosenbaum, Avery, & Lane, 2002).

Test items on the GMFM-88 are grouped into five dimensions reflecting developmental gross motor milestones: lying and rolling (17 items); sitting (20 items); crawling and kneeling (14 items); standing (13 items); and walking, running, and jumping (24 items) (see figure 6.1 for select items on the GMFM). Outcome scores measure how much of an activity a subject can accomplish (function) rather than how well the activity is performed. Items are scored on four-point ordinal scales (0 = cannot initiate; 1 = initiates; 2 = partially completes item; 3 = completes item independently). Any item that has been omitted or the subject is unable, or unwilling, to attempt is scored as 0. The subject is allowed a maximum of three trials on each item. Percentage scores are calculated within each dimension and averaged to obtain a total score that ranges from 0 to 100. Scores can then be used to determine GMFCS, which is a five-point rating of severity of motor function. Higher scores indicate better gross motor functional capacity (Russell, Rosenbaum, Avery, & Lane, 2002). Although specialist training is not required to administer the tool, the authors recommend that administrators become familiar with the GMFM administration guidelines and scoring procedures.

The GMFM-88 reliability values range from 0.87 to 0.99.9. The 66-item GMFM was developed using Rasch analysis in an attempt to improve the interpretability and clinical usefulness of the earlier measure. Sixty-six of the original 88 items were retained and represent the unidimensional construct of gross motor ability (Russell, Rosenbaum, Avery, & Lane, 2002). The GMFM-66 provides detailed information on the level of difficulty of each item, thereby providing much more information to assist with goal setting. The items are administered in the same way as with the GMFM-88. The Gross Motor Ability Estimator (GMAE), a computer program, is used to convert individual scores into an interval-level scoring system. Test–retest reliability for the GMFM-66 is high, with an intraclass correlation coefficient of 0.99 (Russell, Rosenbaum, Avery, & Lane, 2002).

The GMFM is used by a variety of rehabilitation specialists for clinical and research purposes to measure change over time along with the effectiveness of interventions to effect change (Alotaibi, Long, Kennedy, & Bavishi, 2014). The standardized measures provide objective information in an easy-to-un-

SAMPLE ITEM FROM THE GROSS MOTOR FUNCTION MEASURE (GMFM)

Item B: SITTING

18. Supine, hands grasped by examiner: pulls self to sitting with head control

19. Supine: rolls to R side, attains sitting

20. Supine: rolls to L side, attains sitting

21. Sit on mat, supported at thorax by therapist: lifts head upright, maintains 3 seconds

22. Sit on mat, supported at thorax by therapist: lifts head midline, maintains 10 seconds

23. Sit on mat, arm(s) propping: maintains, 5 seconds

Figure 6.1   Select items from the GMFM, a criterion-referenced tool that measures present-level gross motor function as well as change over time in children with disabilities from 5 months to 16 years of age.

From Horvat, M., Kelly, L.E., Block, M.E., and Croce, R., *Developmental and adapted physical activity assessment*, 2nd ed. (Champaign, IL: Human Kinetics, 2019).

derstand format. Adapted physical educators and school-based therapists can use the GMFM to get a basic profile and baseline of movement capabilities of students with multiple severe disabilities and to guide development of appropriate IEP objectives within the motor domain.

FUNDAMENTAL MOTOR PATTERN TESTS

A subcategory of motor development is the development of **fundamental motor patterns**, or movement patterns necessary, or fundamental, for participation in sports. For example, soccer players need to run and kick; softball players need to throw and catch; and basketball players need to dribble, shoot, and catch. Students who do not develop mastery of these fundamental motor patterns will be unable to successfully and effectively participate in sports in middle and high school (or as adults) (Payne & Isaacs, 2016).

Fundamental motor skills are usually divided into two categories: locomotor skills and object control skills. Typical locomotor skills that are taught and mastered in elementary school include the run, gallop, jump, slide, hop, and skip. Typical object control skills include the throw, catch, two-hand sidearm strike (like a baseball strike), one-hand sidearm strike (like a forehand shot in tennis), kick, punt, soccer dribble, and basketball dribble. Although many preschool-aged children can demonstrate rudimentary patterns of these skills, it is not until elementary school (and even middle school) that most students are expected to master many of these patterns. Unlike tests of early motor development that examine whether or not a child has reached a particular motor milestone without concern for the pattern, tests of fundamental motor patterns focus on how the subject performs the skill. In other words, what does the subject's movement pattern, or qualitative aspects of the pattern, look like when he is throwing a ball? Tests of fundamental motor patterns identify differences in the development of various qualitative aspects of the patterns.

As students reach elementary school and early childhood (5 to 10 years), developmental tests may no longer be appropriate. Motor milestones seen in infancy and early childhood follow a fairly set developmental course, both in terms of the sequence of skills (i.e., the order in which they develop) and when these skills appear. Because of a variety of factors such as interest level, culture, socioeconomic status, youth sports participation, and gender, the development of movement patterns at the elementary-aged level is much more variable, both in sequence and time of appearance (Payne & Isaacs, 2016). For example, some students might acquire a fairly skilled throwing pattern by age six because they practice at home or compete in youth sports programs, while students with disabilities may not have the opportunities to practice or learn specific skills.

Most tests of fundamental motor patterns are criterion-referenced instruments based on observational assessment. That is, the focus of the test is to determine whether or not a student displays the prescribed pattern for a motor skill without regard to the student's age. It is clearly anticipated that younger elementary-aged students may not be developmentally ready to master some of these skills (e.g., they do not have the upper-body strength or coordination to demonstrate mastery of the overhand throw). Nevertheless, a teacher can determine how close a student is to achieving mastery of various fundamental movement patterns and gauge whether a student is delayed by comparing her performance to that of others in the school.

Tests of fundamental motor patterns tend to focus on the qualitative aspects of each skill (what the skill looks like) rather than on the outcome of the skill (how many times a student catches or hits a ball or how far a student throws a ball). When examining the qualitative aspects of a motor skill, two models tend to be followed. The component model assesses various developmental levels of a particular skill. This can be done by examining whole-body move-

Case Study 2
Next Steps After Assessment

Peter, a seven-year-old second grader, has been referred by his parents for an adapted physical education evaluation. The adapted physical education teacher asks him to perform various locomotor and object control skills, noting that he has mastered most of the locomotor patterns—with the exception of skipping—but has not mastered any of the object control skills. Although mastering object control skills is not necessarily typical for second-grade students, this student is not even close to mastering many of these skills. During testing, Peter does not attempt to step when throwing, and he allows the ball to hit his chest rather than try to use his hands to catch it.

In comparison to the rest of the students in his second-grade class, Peter is less advanced. The teacher can provide some extra opportunities for him to practice, or if the problem persists, recommend neurological screening, sensory screening, or placement in adapted physical education.

ment (e.g., the throwing pattern is at an initial, elementary, or mature level [Gallahue & Ozmun, 2006]) or the development of each component of the skill.

With the component model, the physical educator examines the various developmental levels of the arm action, trunk action, and leg action of a movement such as the overhand throw. For example, the leg component of the overhand throw could be broken into four developmental levels: no step, stepping with same-side foot (same side as throwing hand), short step with opposite foot, and long step with opposite foot (Haywood & Getchell, 2009). Each component of the throw (e.g., arm action, trunk action) is broken down into similar developmental levels. When a student is tested, the examiner notes which level the student displays for each component. This model allows an APE specialist to determine the student's current pattern and then target and determine a logical progression for the next step in instruction. For example, a student who is not stepping at all would not be taught how to take a long step when throwing. Rather, a teacher might want to focus on intermediate-level instruction of leg action for the overhand throw, such as shifting weight and taking a short step. On the downside, the level of detail in this model requires a keen eye and a fair amount of time to watch and classify developmental components of each skill.

In the second model (master only model), the overhand throw is broken down into qualitative components, but only the most skillful level (mastery) is outlined for assessment. For example, the components of a skillful overhand throw might include the following:

1. Initiates windup with downward movement of hand and arm
2. Rotates hips and shoulders to a point where the nonthrowing side faces the target
3. Transfers weight by stepping with the foot opposite the throwing hand
4. Follows through beyond ball release diagonally across body toward nonpreferred side

With this as the target for mastery, the examiner simply watches the subject's performance and marks yes if the subject displays mastery of a component and no if the subject does not. The advantage of this model is it provides a simpler and quicker way to qualitatively screen students' fundamental motor skills, which is particularly important when screening several students. The teacher still has the ability to clearly determine which components a student has not yet mastered and thus should be targeted for instruction.

Test of Gross Motor Development 3 (TGMD-3)

The Test of Gross Motor Development 3 (TGMD-3) is an individually administered norm- and criterion-referenced test that measures the gross motor functioning of children 3 to 10 years of age. This is one of the few tests that examine qualitative components of fundamental motor skills based on a normative component. This normative component allows teachers to quickly and more accurately determine whether a student has delayed fundamental motor patterns compared with other students of the same age.

The TGMD-3 contains 13 gross motor patterns frequently taught to students in preschool and elementary school. Six locomotor subitems include the run, gallop, hop, skip, horizontal jump, and slide (the TGMD-2 also included the leap). The seven ball skills subtest (previously titled object control in the TGMD-2) measures the two-hand strike, stationary dribble, catch, kick, overhand throw, underhand throw (which replaces the underhand roll in the TGMD-2), and the one-hand tennis-like strike (new for TGMD-3). Also new with the TGMD-3 is that any skill requiring a specific number of repetitions has been standardized to four. An example is the stationary bounce, which requires four bounces.

Each skill has been broken down into three to five components. The following shows a sample of how a locomotor and a ball skill subitem are broken down on the TGMD-3:

Horizontal Jump

1. Preparatory movement includes flexion of both knees, with arms extended behind the body.
2. Extends arms forcefully forward and upward, reaching full extension above the head.
3. Takes off and lands on both feet simultaneously.
4. Brings arms downward during landing.

Two-Hand Strike

1. Dominant hand grips bat above nondominant hand.
2. Nondominant side of body faces the tosser, feet parallel.
3. Rotates hips and shoulders during swing.
4. Transfers body weight to front foot.
5. Bat contacts ball.

The examiner analyzes the fundamental motor skills on the TGMD-3 to determine whether a component is present (1) or not present (0). Results are then tallied across two trials and totaled for locomotor and object control subtests. Finally, each subtest score is compared with a normative sample for analysis. Results can be presented in two easy ways for parents and teachers to understand. The first is to present a percentile ranking comparing a student's score with other students of the same age. For example, eight-year-old Chandra scores 32 on the locomotor portion of the TGMD-3. This puts her at the fifth percentile, which means 95 percent of the students Chandra's age would be expected to perform better than she does on locomotor development. Such a low percentile ranking would most likely qualify her for adapted physical education. Another way to present results is to calculate a developmental motor age, or age equivalent. A subject who scores 32 on the locomotor portion of the TGMD-3 would have an age equivalent of 5 years, 3 months. This means Chandra has a delay of more than two years and thus would likely qualify for APE services.

The TGMD-3 is straightforward and easy to administer. This instrument is helpful in identifying areas of motor weakness and allows the APE specialist to translate the test results to IEP goals as well as specific targets for instruction. For these reasons, the TGMD-3 is one of the most popular motor tests used by adapted physical educators and is highly recommended. See appendix B for a sample write-up using the TGMD-3.

Everyone Can!

Everyone Can!: Skill Development and Assessment in Elementary Physical Education is a book and website package that addresses the needs of all elementary-aged students. This includes skilled students who are ready for more challenging activities, those who are developmentally on age level, those who have not yet mastered the essential skills but have no disability, and finally students with disabilities that may affect motor performance (Kelly, Wessel, Dummer, & Sampson, 2010). Specifically regarding assessment, Everyone Can! offers 70 curriculum-embedded assessment items and 140 score sheets. The program is aligned with standards from SHAPE America and the Adapted Physical Education National Standards (APENS).

The online resource materials are organized on two levels. The assessments, assessing activities, accommodations for individuals with disabilities, score sheets, and posters are designed around the objectives, with one of each of these resources provided for each of the 70 objectives in the model K-5 program. The remaining instructional resources are organized around the focal points and skill levels within each objective. These include instruction activities for the teacher, station cards, and games.

The 70 elementary objectives, including fundamental locomotor and ball skill patterns, have been broken into teachable components and then organized into a criterion-referenced assessment instrument. Each objective is divided into three skill levels. The first skill level defines the most skillful pattern by breaking skills into essential components, or focal points, needed to perform the overall skill. Students must demonstrate all focal points of an objective on two out of three trials to earn mastery at skill level 1. Although skill level 1 emphasizes the basic pattern of the skill, skill levels 2 and 3 focus on the application of the skill. To illustrate, skill level 1 for the hop focuses on the mechanics of a mature hop, while skill levels 2 and 3 focus on changing speeds and changing directions of the mature hop (Kelly, Wessel, Dummer, & Sampson, 2010). Figure 6.2 presents an assessment item for the mature hop.

The advantage of Everyone Can! is the seamless interconnection between preassessment, instructional activities and games, and monitoring of progress. The 70 Everyone Can! objectives are typically found in elementary physical education programs. As a result, assessment directs the physical educator to the students' present level, which in turn guides the physical educator on what to teach. The teacher then selects Everyone Can! activities to help students master specific components. Finally, postassessment allows the physical educator to determine whether the program was effective in helping students master objectives (Kelly, Wessel, Dummer, & Sampson, 2010).

MOTOR ABILITY TESTS

When testing students with disabilities to determine whether they qualify for services, motor abilities should be considered. **Motor abilities** are general

Equipment and Space Requirements:

- Students wear gym shoes or running shoes.
- Use cones, tape, or jump ropes to mark the start and finish lines of a 20-foot (6-m) straight-away course in an indoor gymnasium or outdoor track or playground (skill level 2) and 20-foot (6-m) course with two 180° turns (skill level 3).

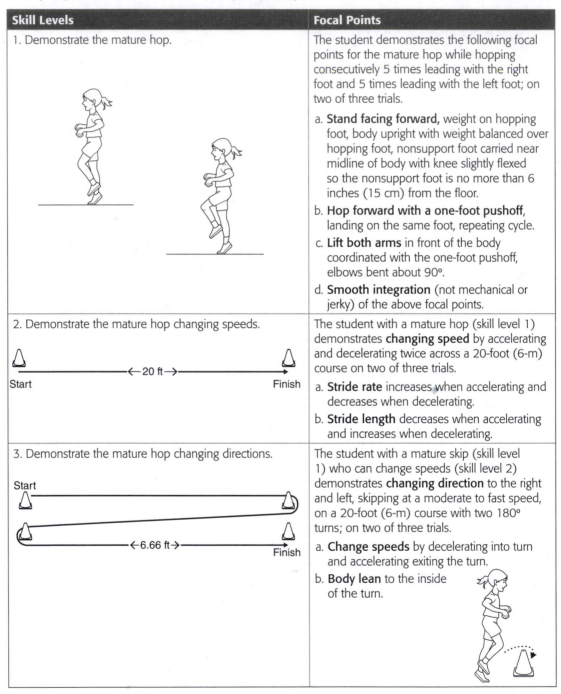

Skill Levels	Focal Points
1. Demonstrate the mature hop.	The student demonstrates the following focal points for the mature hop while hopping consecutively 5 times leading with the right foot and 5 times leading with the left foot; on two of three trials. a. **Stand facing forward,** weight on hopping foot, body upright with weight balanced over hopping foot, nonsupport foot carried near midline of body with knee slightly flexed so the nonsupport foot is no more than 6 inches (15 cm) from the floor. b. **Hop forward with a one-foot pushoff,** landing on the same foot, repeating cycle. c. **Lift both arms** in front of the body coordinated with the one-foot pushoff, elbows bent about 90°. d. **Smooth integration** (not mechanical or jerky) of the above focal points.
2. Demonstrate the mature hop changing speeds.	The student with a mature hop (skill level 1) demonstrates **changing speed** by accelerating and decelerating twice across a 20-foot (6-m) course on two of three trials. a. **Stride rate** increases when accelerating and decreases when decelerating. b. **Stride length** decreases when accelerating and increases when decelerating.
3. Demonstrate the mature hop changing directions.	The student with a mature skip (skill level 1) who can change speeds (skill level 2) demonstrates **changing direction** to the right and left, skipping at a moderate to fast speed, on a 20-foot (6-m) course with two 180° turns; on two of three trials. a. **Change speeds** by decelerating into turn and accelerating exiting the turn. b. **Body lean** to the inside of the turn.

Figure 6.2 Everyone Can! assessment for the mature hop.

From Horvat, M., Kelly, L.E., Block, M.E., and Croce, R., *Developmental and adapted physical activity assessment*, 2nd ed. (Champaign, IL: Human Kinetics, 2019). Reprinted, by permission, from L.E. Kelly, J.A. Wessel, G.M. Dummer, and T. Sampson, 2010, *Everyone can!* (Champaign, IL: Human Kinetics). Illustrations reprinted from J. Wessel, 1976, *I CAN: Object control* (North Brook, IL: Hubbard Scientific Company), 89. By permission of J. Wessel.

capacities or characteristics that are related to the ability to perform motor skills such as running, jumping, throwing, or catching. These capacities or traits are assumed to be fairly stable and not easily changed with short amounts of practice or experience. In other words, each student possesses a certain level of balance and speed and coordination that is difficult to change. In addition, these motor abilities directly relate to a student's ability to perform locomotor and object control skills. For example, a student needs a certain level of dynamic balance (a motor ability) to successfully hop and skip (motor skills). Similarly, a student needs a certain amount of eye–hand coordination to be able to catch.

Motor ability assessments tend to include items not commonly seen or practiced by students, such as stringing beads (manual dexterity), jumping while clapping the hands (general coordination), catching a tennis ball with one hand (eye–hand coordination), and standing on a balance beam (static balance). Unlike motor milestones and fundamental motor skills, tests of motor abilities provide a glimpse into why a student might be struggling with motor skill development. For example, Ricardo does not step when throwing, striking, or receiving a ball. Although it is clear that he has not mastered these fundamental skills, why he is missing these particular components is left to speculation. With a test of motor ability, a subtest of balance might indicate that he has trouble with both static and dynamic balance. Now by examining the missing qualitative components of throwing, catching, and striking along with the information that Ricardo has some underlying balance problems, the adapted physical education teacher can make a stronger case that the student's balance problems are why he is unable to step when performing these fundamental motor patterns.

Motor abilities include balance, postural control, agility, bilateral coordination (using two hands together), eye–hand and eye–foot coordination, and dexterity (fine motor skills), as well as specific types of strength and flexibility that are needed for successful motor skill performance. Each of these motor abilities is tested with relatively novel tests. For example, in the Bruininks-Oseretsky Test of Motor Proficiency (Bruininks & Bruininks, 2005), eye–hand coordination and speed are measured by having the student sort cards that feature either a blue circle or red square. The challenge for the student is to sort as many cards as possible, correctly, in 15 seconds or less. A student who scores well on such a test item is assumed to have good eye–hand coordination and speed, which in turn suggests she should perform well in skills requiring that type of motor ability, such as returning a serve in tennis or hitting a pitched ball in softball.

One of the strengths of motor ability tests is that they tend to be highly standardized, with clear administrative directions that increase reliability and are easy for an examiner to follow. Another strength is that they are usually norm referenced, allowing comparison with students of similar ages. As noted earlier, norm comparisons help the teacher quickly determine whether a student is performing at her developmental age level or is delayed in comparison to her peers. In addition, results such as percentile rank or developmental motor age are easily communicated to parents and other teachers.

Bruininks-Oseretsky Test of Motor Proficiency 2 (BOT-2)

Of the various motor ability tests, the Bruininks-Oseretsky Test of Motor Proficiency (BOT) was one of the most widely used in adapted physical education. The current version, the BOT-2, is an individually administered norm-referenced test that assesses the motor functioning of children and adults from 4 to 21 years of age. The complete battery for this version has 53 items divided into eight subtests: fine motor precision, fine motor integration, manual dexterity, upper-limb coordination, bilateral coordination, balance, running speed and agility, and strength. The long form takes about 60 minutes to administer and generates either a battery composite score or a composite score for one of the four motor areas (fine motor control, manual coordination, body coordination, and strength and agility). The short form of the BOT-2 consists of 14 items, with at least one item taken from each of the eight subtests. The short form is often used to quickly screen a subject to see if further testing is required. It takes about 15 to 20 minutes to administer and also yields a composite score. Scoring varies from item to item, including drawing a number of objects, number of repetitions, or time required to complete a task.

After tallying the raw scores on the BOT-2, teachers can analyze the results in several ways. The easiest way is to convert the raw data to points for percentile rankings and age equivalents. Norm tables are provided so the examiner can locate percentile rankings and age equivalents for the total test, battery composite, or motor composite. Norms are also available separately for the short-form composite score, as well as each test item. This allows the examiner to determine whether a student has deficits (or strengths) in a particular motor area. In addition, the BOT-2 provides percentile rankings and age equivalents for each subtest in the motor areas. For example, the teacher would be able to determine whether a student is on age level or significantly behind her peers on each of the four motor composites, allowing the teacher to pinpoint delays and instructional needs.

The BOT-2 was standardized on a representative sample of 1,520 individuals from 4 to 21 years of age. The original version was one of the first motor tests to be developed from stringent standardization procedures. Test–retest reliability coefficients for the long form and the short form are generally high but need to be replicated. Validity data presented in the test manual are considered to be measures of content and construct validity. These results support the use of the test to screen students for motor difficulties. However, the test does contain scores that are compared with the normative sample for developmental coordination disorder (ages 4 to 15, $n = 50$), mild to moderate intellectual disability (ages 5 to 12, $n = 66$), and autism spectrum disorder (ASD) (ages 4 to 20, $n = 45$). The BOT-2 is an appropriate assessment of motor ability, but further study is needed to determine whether the revisions are appropriate for individuals with disabilities.

In addition, the motor skills inventory (MSI) and the accompanying motor development curriculum for students developed by Werder and Bruininks (1988) can be used to give a criterion-based assessment on a pass (+) or fail (–) basis. Werder and Bruininks indicate that the BOT can be administered at the beginning and end of a program, with the MSI administered more frequently throughout the year for periodic assessments of each skill to document progress. See appendix C for a sample write-up of the Bruininks-Oseretsky Test of Motor Proficiency 2.

Movement Assessment Battery for Children, Second Edition (Movement ABC-2)

The Movement Assessment Battery for Children (MABC), is a validated, norm-referenced, and product-oriented motor assessment developed as a screening tool to identify children at risk of developmental coordination disorder (Henderson, Sugden, & Barnett, 2007). The MABC-2 is an updated version of the MABC, which itself was a revised version of the Test of Motor Impairment (TOMI). The TOMI and MABC had norms for children aged 4 to 12; however, the MABC-2 has an expanded range of between 3 and 16 years of age. Updated normative data for the MABC-2 included 1,172 subjects from Britain and Northern Ireland aged 3 to 16, stratified for geographic region, population density, social class, and race or ethnicity (Cools, De Martelaer, Samaey, & Andries, 2009).

Items on the MABC-2 focus on the product of movement such as time taken to complete a task or number of successful trials. The assessment has two parts: an individually administered test requiring the subject to perform a series of motor tasks and a checklist to be administered by a parent or teacher who is familiar with the subject's functioning. The latest version also includes a companion manual that describes an ecological approach on intervention for students with movement difficulties (Henderson, Sugden, & Barnett, 2007). Other notable differences in the revised edition include changing the bicycle test item into a drawing trial and changing rolling a ball into a goal to throwing a beanbag onto a mat. These changes have been made to increase correspondence, sensitivity, and consistency between test items of the different age bands (Cools, De Martelaer, Samaey, & Andries, 2009).

Major categories assessed include

- manual dexterity items such as threading nuts on bolts, shifting pegs by rows, turning pegs, making cutouts, and other fine motor items;
- ball skills including throwing beanbags and balls, catching a bounced ball, catching off a wall with one hand, and hitting a target; and
- static and dynamic balance items such as using balance boards, beam walking, jumping over a cord, and clapping.

Henderson and colleagues (2007) indicate that task requirements in each level are identical but vary slightly with each age band. In addition, for each age band a qualitative observation is available to note variables that relate to the subject's behavior during testing, such as concentration, confidence, posture, and control. The number of age bands was reduced from four to three categories (age band 1 = 3 to 6 years, age band 2 = 7 to 10 years, and age band 3 = 11 to 16 years) in the revised MABC-2 compared with the original MABC.

Items are scored at the age level of the subject based on, for example, the number of seconds to complete a trial or the number of catches executed out of 10 attempts. If a subject does not start a task, the score is recorded as a failed attempt (F), inappropriate for the subject (I), or a refusal to attempt a task (R). A shorter version (the Movement ABC Checklist) provides an opportunity to screen and monitor students on a daily basis; it includes 48 questions in four sections, with responses from 0 (very well) to 3 (not close). The following sections detail movement over what Henderson and colleagues (2007) refer to as more complex interactions:

Section 1   The child is stationary and the environment is stable.
Section 2   The child is moving and the environment is stable.
Section 3   The child is stationary and the environment is changing.
Section 4   The child is moving and the environment is changing.
Section 5   Behaviors related to physical activity.

Section 5 of the checklist provides behavioral information that may influence performance and movement competence on sections 1 to 4 (Henderson, Sugden, & Barnett, 2007). For example, section 5 is used to interpret or consider whether a behavior or environment may contribute to an inappropriate response.

The first four sections are then scored to determine whether students are at risk (15% of the population) or have definite movement problems (5% of the population). Behavior factors from section 5 are ranked high, medium, or low as contributing factors to the student's performance.

MABC-2 is particularly popular among clinicians and therapists for identifying students with developmental coordination disorder and autism (e.g., Clark, Getchell, Smiley-Oyen, & Whitall, 2005; Darsaklis, Snider, Majnemer, & Mazer, 2013; Logan & Getchell, 2010; Stins, Emck, de Vries, Doop, & Beek, 2015; Ting, 2013).

SPORTS SKILLS TESTS

Sports skills are simply those skills required in specific sports. Most sports require some object control skills (e.g., throwing and catching) and locomotor skills (e.g., running and sliding). For example, to be successful in football, a player needs to be able to throw and catch (and in some cases, kick and punt) as well as run, slide, or gallop (when backing up to play defense to cover a receiver) and jump (to catch or knock down a high ball). Sports skills are specific to each sport, although many sports share some similar skills. Catching, for example, is common to basketball, baseball, and lacrosse. However, a basketball player catches a ball with two hands, a baseball player catches a ball with a glove, and a lacrosse player catches a ball with a lacrosse stick. Skill assessment should therefore be specific to the sport a student is playing or may play in the future.

As students reach middle school and beyond, the focus of physical education and recreation turns to individual and team sports and physical fitness. (Physical fitness testing is covered in chapter 7.) Sports skills testing becomes the most appropriate form of assessment for middle- and high-school-aged youngsters. This type of testing can have multiple purposes. First, a student with suspected motor problems could be compared with peers in his class or school on various sports skills to determine whether he is delayed. For example, Ms. Beals could test a student on the basic skills needed to play sports that are popular in a particular community—say volleyball, basketball, and soccer. She could test all the students in each grade on skills within these sports to create a norm sample. Then she could compare how well the targeted student did in relation to his peers on these sports skills.

Ms. Beals might find that 90 percent of students in ninth grade can demonstrate the basic skills in each of the selected sports. However, the targeted student has mastered only 20 percent of the sports skills tested. This might be enough of a delay to indicate that he qualifies for adapted physical education. See appendix D for a sample write-up using tests of sports skills.

Another use of skill testing is determining which sports skills a student with disabilities has interest in learning and has the potential to learn. In other words, a student who has already qualified for APE services could be tested on skills in several different individual and team sports to gauge the student's abilities and interest in particular sports. Results might indicate that a high schooler with Down syndrome has some well-developed basketball skills and seems to enjoy the sport. Goals could then be created that might eventually allow this student to play in a community basketball league, a special basketball program such as Special Olympics, or even just in the driveway of his group home when he comes home from work.

Finally, sports skills testing can be used to guide the development of IEP objectives and lesson plans. For the individual in the previous example, the APE specialist could create and administer a qualitative basketball skills test to determine exactly what skill components this student can perform well and what components need to be targeted for instruction. For example, the following qualitative breakdown of shooting indicates that the target of instruction should be coordinating his shooting action and his follow-through.

Shooting

Yes   Eyes on basket, feet shoulder-width apart, knees flexed

Yes   Marked flexion of knees before shooting

Yes   Shooting hand under ball with fingers apart; ball held slightly off center of forehead, shooting-hand side; elbow directly under ball, pointed down; nondominant hand on side of ball

No   Coordinated extension of knees, hips, and ankles while flexing wrist and fingers to guide ball on release

No   Follow-through with the shooting hand remaining briefly in the release position toward basket

Special Olympics Sports Skills Assessment

Special Olympics provides sports skill guides that contain skills tests for each sport they offer. These criterion-referenced tests break down skills into progressions of competency rather than into component parts, as the TGMD or other qualitative tests do. A nice feature of the Special Olympics skills assessments is the inclusion of a knowledge component (understanding of the rules) and a social component (participation). Although these components are basic, they do indicate how much a student understands the game and how to play it. Each item on the test is graded as a pass, or successful (score of 1), or a fail, or unsuccessful (score of 0). A scoring mechanism allows the coach or examiner to tally the scores from each item of the test to get a total score. This total score can be used to group athletes and to chart progress (Special Olympics, 2016). Figure 6.3 shows the basketball skills assessment. Note that the Special Olympics Alaska Functional Performance Test was developed to quantify performance and overall health of Special Olympics athletes and can also be used to record sports performance.

Teacher-Developed Sports Skills Assessment

It is often easier and more realistic for the adapted physical education teacher to create a sports skills checklist that breaks down various sports skills into components. This could be done independently or with the help of other teachers in the school district. By working together, adapted physical education teachers can ensure the test is valid and useful for all teachers in the district. In addition, many teachers are also coaches who have expertise in sports and games. Skills can be broken into four or five components or into even more detail. Figure 6.4 provides an example of a volleyball skills test that was created by the physical education staff of a school district.

A sports skills test can also take the form of a rubric that contains specific criteria or standards to evaluate performance and progress, providing the teacher or therapist with detailed guidelines for making scoring decisions (Block, Lieberman, & Connor-Kuntz, 1998). Rubrics are part of the **authentic assessment** model, which involves measuring performance in real-world settings on functional skills that a student needs in order to be successful in physical education, recreation, and community sports (Block, Lieberman, & Connor-Kuntz, 1998). For example, Ms. Anderson wants to assess 12-year-old John's present level of baseball skills so she can better prepare him to play on a Challenger Baseball team in the community. Instead of using a standardized test such as the Bruininks-Oseretsky Test or even the Test of Gross Motor Development, she can create a simple rubric for baseball. The rubric can include important skills such as running the bases, fielding (see figure 6.5 for an example), hitting a ball off a tee, and throwing to a teammate. Ms. Anderson can create the rubric in such a way that John's present level as well as progress toward higher-level skills can be recorded.

This type of rubric assessment can be easily translated into goals for this student as they relate to baseball. John, who has ASD, tested at a "Minor Leaguer: A Ball" level. Recall from figure 6.5 that this means he reacts to the ball if provided verbal cues, pays attention to the batter about 50 percent of the time with verbal reminders, and is involved in self-stimulatory behaviors or may not be in proper position 50 percent of the time. Our logical goal for

SPECIAL OLYMPICS BASKETBALL SKILLS ASSESSMENT CARD (continued)

Athlete's name _____   Date: _____

Coach's name _____   Date: _____

Instructions

1. Use tool at the beginning of the training/competition season to establish a basis of the athlete's starting skill level.
2. Have the athlete perform the skill several times.
3. If the athlete performs the skill correctly three out of five times, check the box next to the skill to indicate that the skill has been accomplished.
4. Program assessment sessions into your program.
5. Athletes may accomplish skills in any order. Athletes have accomplished this list when **all possible items** have been achieved.

Dribbling

- ☐ Attempts to dribble a basketball in any manner.
- ☐ Dribbles the ball in any manner at least three bounces in a row.
- ☐ Dribbles the ball with one hand more than three bounces in a row while standing in one place.
- ☐ Dribbles the ball with the opposite hand more than three bounces in a row while standing in one place.
- ☐ Dribbles the ball with one hand, then the other hand, three bounces in a row each, without stopping and while standing still.
- ☐ Dribbles the ball with one hand while walking forward 10 steps.
- ☐ Dribbles the ball with one hand while running forward 20 steps.
- ☐ Dribbles the ball with either hand while moving in any direction (forward, backward, or sideways).

Passing

- ☐ Attempts to pass a basketball.
- ☐ Passes the ball in any manner and in any direction.
- ☐ Passes the ball in any manner to an intended target.
- ☐ Makes a two-hand chest pass in any direction.
- ☐ Makes a two-hand chest pass to an intended target.
- ☐ Makes a bounce pass to an intended target.
- ☐ Makes a two-hand overhead pass to an intended target.
- ☐ Makes a lob pass to an intended target.
- ☐ Makes a baseball pass to an intended target.
- ☐ Participates in team passing drills.

Catching

- ☐ Attempts to catch a basketball in any manner.
- ☐ Catches the ball in any manner.
- ☐ Catches a bounce pass in arms and chest.
- ☐ Catches a bounce pass with hands only.
- ☐ Catches a chest pass in arms and chest.
- ☐ Catches a chest pass with hands only.
- ☐ Attempts to catch a pass in any manner while moving.
- ☐ Catches a pass in any manner while moving.
- ☐ Catches a pass with hands only, while moving.

Figure 6.3   This criterion-referenced test breaks down skills into progressions of competency rather than into component parts, as the TGMD or other qualitative tests do.

(continued)

Shooting

- ☐ Attempts to shoot a basketball toward the basket.
- ☐ Hits the backboard with a one-hand set shot.
- ☐ Makes a basket with a one-hand set shot.
- ☐ Hits the backboard on a layup.
- ☐ Makes a basket on a layup.
- ☐ Hits the backboard with a jump shot.
- ☐ Makes a basket with a jump shot.

Rebounding

- ☐ Attempts to catch in any manner a basketball that is tossed into the air.
- ☐ Catches a ball that is tossed into the air.
- ☐ Attempts to catch in any manner a ball that rebounds off the backboard.
- ☐ Tracks the ball as it is shot at the basket.
- ☐ Turns to face the basket and takes ready position for rebounding.
- ☐ Catches in any manner the ball after it rebounds off the backboard and bounces once on the floor.
- ☐ Catches the ball with hands only, after it rebounds off the backboard and bounces once on the floor.
- ☐ Catches the ball in the air with hands only after it rebounds off the backboard.
- ☐ Participates in team rebounding drills.

Team Play

- ☐ Attempts to participate in team play skills.
- ☐ Participates in any manner in an offensive team play drill.
- ☐ Participates in any manner in a defensive team play drill.
- ☐ Demonstrates knowledge of fundamentals of offensive team play.
- ☐ Demonstrates knowledge of fundamentals of defensive team play.

Participation

- ☐ Attempts to participate in a basketball training program.
- ☐ Participates in any manner in a basketball training program.
- ☐ Participates upon own initiative in a basketball training program.
- ☐ Practices basketball skills a minimum of three days a week.
- ☐ Takes part in team activities.
- ☐ Demonstrates knowledge of the basic rules of basketball.

Figure 6.3 *(continued)*

From Horvat, M., Kelly, L.E., Block, M.E., and Croce, R., *Developmental and adapted physical activity assessment*, 2nd ed. (Champaign, IL: Human Kinetics, 2019). Reprinted, by permission, from D. Lenox and R. Murphy, 2007, *Special Olympics basketball coaching guide*. Available: http://digitalguides.specialolympics.org/basketball

Underhand Serve

- ☐ Preparatory position: face net, feet shoulder-width apart; 45° forward trunk lean; hold ball in nondominant hand, with arm extended across body at waist height in front of serving arm.
- ☐ Hold serving arm straight; pendular swing back at least 45° to initiate serve; then bring serving arm forward with pendular arm motion.
- ☐ Stride forward with opposite foot in concert with forward motion of striking arm.
- ☐ Heel of striking hand strikes center of ball held at or below waist height in line with back foot and in front of serving foot.

Overhead Pass

- ☐ Preparatory position: face oncoming ball, feet (set) staggered shoulder-width apart, knees slightly bent, arms and hands hanging by knees; eyes are on ball.
- ☐ Move to get under ball, with head tilted back, legs flexed; move hands to just above forehead.
- ☐ Hand position: palms out, fingers apart and slightly bent.
- ☐ Upon contact, keep head in tilted position, eyes focused on ball; hyperextend wrists and flex fingers to form a diamond or triangle to absorb force of the ball.
- ☐ Extend knees and arms upward on follow-through.
- ☐ Pass ball to above net height.

Forearm Pass

- ☐ Ready position: face ball, feet shoulder-width apart, knees slightly bent; arms hang below waist and extend in front of body, palms facing up.
- ☐ Preparatory hand position: one hand placed in the other hand, with thumb of lower hand placed across fingers of upper hand, forearms together.
- ☐ Eyes are on ball.
- ☐ Move to meet ball by transferring weight forward, arms together, knees bent.
- ☐ Contact ball with flat side of forearms.
- ☐ Upon contact, extend knees to raise the arms upward.
- ☐ Complete pass standing straight up, arms parallel to floor; hands stay together throughout the entire motion.
- ☐ Pass ball to a height of at least 8 ft (2.5 m) to stationary teammate.

Figure 6.4 Checklist showing skills broken down into four simple components (underhand serve) and into more detailed components (six for the overhead pass, eight for the forearm pass).

From Horvat, M., Kelly, L.E., Block, M.E., and Croce, R., *Developmental and adapted physical activity assessment*, 2nd ed. (Champaign, IL: Human Kinetics, 2019). From Albemarle County Public Schools, 1995, *Albemarle County Middle School physical education curriculum*.

RUBRIC FOR FIELDING A GROUND BALL

Little Leaguer

- ☐ Does not react to ball, even with verbal cues
- ☐ Pays attention to batter 25 percent of the time or less, even with verbal cues
- ☐ Involved in self-stimulatory behavior or may not stay in proper position 75 percent of the time or more

Minor Leaguer: A Ball

- ☐ Reacts to ball if provided verbal cue
- ☐ Pays attention to batter 50 percent of the time with verbal reminders
- ☐ Involved in self-stimulatory behavior or may not stay in proper position 50 percent of the time

Minor Leaguer: AA Ball

- ☐ Reacts to ball (looks at ball) and will walk to retrieve ball if given verbal reminder
- ☐ Pays attention to batter 75 percent of the time and needs only occasional verbal reminders
- ☐ Displays appropriate waiting behavior 75 percent of the time, with occasional verbal reminders

Minor Leaguer: AAA Ball

- ☐ Reacts to ball and walks to retrieve hit ball independently four out of five trials
- ☐ Pays attention to batter independently four out of five trials but may not display ready position
- ☐ Displays appropriate waiting behavior independently four out of five trials but may not cheer teammates

Major Leaguer

- ☐ Reacts to ball independently by quickly walking or running to where ball was hit
- ☐ Pays attention to batter and displays ready position
- ☐ Displays appropriate waiting behavior, including proper positioning and cheering on batter or teammates

Note: Category names (minor leaguer, major leaguer) are made up and can be anything from colors to numbers to letters to names of teams.

Figure 6.5   A teacher-created rubric is an alternative to a standardized test.

From Horvat, M., Kelly, L.E., Block, M.E., and Croce, R., *Developmental and adapted physical activity assessment*, 2nd ed. (Champaign, IL: Human Kinetics, 2019).

this student is to get him to the next level on the rubric, Minor Leaguer: AA Ball. So, his IEP might read as follows:

Goal: John will show significant improvement in fielding skills as noted by mastery of the following objectives:

Objective 1: John will react to ball (looks at ball) and will walk to retrieve ball within five seconds of a verbal cue in three out of four trials.

Objective 2: John will pay attention to the batter (watches batter) 75 percent of the time, independently, with only one verbal reminder during a batter's turn at the plate, in three out of four trials.

Objective 3: John will display appropriate waiting behavior (stands in correct position, does not walk around field, does not exhibit any self-stimulatory behaviors) 75 percent of the time, with one to three verbal reminders in a five-minute period, in three out of four trials.

Notice how easy it is to set appropriate, achievable, and meaningful IEP goals when rubrics are created. Finally, when assessing John on the rubric, Ms. Anderson could make this a truly authentic assessment by assessing him while he plays modified games of tee ball in physical education or by watching him while playing a game of Challenger Baseball over the weekend.

What You Need to Know

Key Terms

asymmetrical tonic neck reflex	motor abilities
authentic assessment	motor development
balance reactions	protective reactions
developmental landmarks	reflex movements
fine motor skills	righting reactions
fundamental motor patterns	sports skills
gross motor skills	tilting reactions

Key Concepts

1. You should understand the differences between reflex assessments, developmental assessments, and tests of motor behavior. Describe when each test is appropriate.
2. You should be able to use tests of motor development, behavior, and sports skills to develop an instructional plan. If specific tests do not fit your population, how would you create a rubric for a specific sports skill?
3. You should be familiar with testing protocols, scoring, and safety procedures for various assessments. Practice administering tests to students of various ages or disabilities and describing their performance. What would be usable to develop their instructional programs?

Review Questions

1. For students who are lacking motor skills, would you develop a home program or pair the student with a peer for additional practice?
2. If a student continues to have difficulty with balance in class, would you recommend this student for additional testing? What test would you recommend?
3. What testing or modifications are needed for students with perceptual impairments?

Chapter 7

Assessing Physical Function

Among the major goals of physical activity—including adapted physical education—is providing all individuals with the opportunity and desire to lead physically active and independent lifestyles. We want to emphasize the importance of physical function for many tasks that are needed in community- and work-related settings. Clearly, physical function is essential to achieve these goals. One could argue that physical function is *the* great facilitator for enjoying activity and increasing the independent functional abilities of persons with disabilities. Physical functioning generally facilitates development and translates to independence in the community and work-related settings.

Achieving and maintaining a functional level of fitness through activity should become a lifelong goal for all individuals and is especially important for all adapted physical education and rehabilitation programs. For this to occur, adequate assessments should be utilized to determine specific levels of physical function and performance and to determine the effects of intervention programs designed to develop and maintain overall health and physical function. For example, Marty is a participant in your high school physical education class. What fitness capabilities does he require to finish school and prepare for a job at the local supermarket? If Marty participates in sports, he may want to increase aerobic capacity, strength, or power to what is specific to his sport. Finally, moving about, rising from a chair, going up and down stairs, propelling a wheelchair, carrying groceries, and throwing a ball are all tasks that require a functional level of physical fitness. This chapter is devoted to determining the level of functioning for all individuals. It defines and discusses the components of physical function as well as the specifics of test items and batteries.

Always proceed with caution in making generalizations about persons with disabilities. People with disabilities, *as a group*, typically do not demonstrate functional levels of performance that are inherent in nondisabled counterparts. Historically, many factors have prevented persons with disabilities from achieving an optimal level of health.

A major factor that often limits potential among persons with disabilities is underexpectations on the part of others, including parents, teachers, coaches, and potential employers. The focus on the disability undermines goals or the ability to achieve and can be transmitted consciously or subconsciously and learned by persons with disabilities. Limited experience with play or physical activity may be a result of anxious or overprotective parents, but in some cases, opportunities for students to participate and engage in physical activities are restricted. These limitations often result in a lack of activity in populations with disabilities.

Individuals with disabilities may comprehend that others perceive them as being limited, which may contribute to low self-esteem. Perhaps one of the most viable avenues to improved self-esteem is maintaining parameters of physical function that promote a positive, active lifestyle that stresses independence and achieving success. Physical function and performance means being active, and being active is positive and healthy; it generalizes to independent living and integration in community- and work-related settings. The net result can be a sense of feeling good that promotes positive self-esteem, self-reliance, and functional performance. Further, enhanced physical function that promotes an active lifestyle emphasizes achievements rather than what cannot be accomplished.

PHYSICAL FUNCTION AND PERFORMANCE

Although there is widespread consensus that physical function is important (and, therefore, should be assessed), the components that make up **physical fitness** are more open to debate. Historically, the components have been divided into two major categories: (1) physical (i.e., health-related) function and (2) **motor performance**. Current interest in *health-related fitness* addresses attributes that facilitate day-to-day function and health maintenance (e.g., muscular strength and endurance, flexibility, cardiorespiratory endurance, and body composition) as well as health components as they relate to function, especially for persons with disabilities. In this context, *functional fitness* is being able to accomplish daily living tasks such as lifting, stretching, or moving to promote overall function and independence. The components of health-related and functional fitness are the major focus of this chapter, while elements of motor functioning, such as balance, are included in chapter 8.

MULTIDIMENSIONALITY OF PHYSICAL FUNCTION: Implications for Selecting Test Items

Physical function is multidimensional, and it is required for many developmental, health-related, performance-related, and work-related tasks. In addition, various components of physical function tend to exist exclusively of one another. This mutual exclusivity requires that teachers use different test items (i.e., items representative of each proficiency) to measure task-specific performance with respect to each component. For example, if Ms. Rogers wants to measure how many times Chris can lift a weighted box and stack it on a table, she needs to measure the strength and endurance of his upper body. Likewise, when measuring any given component, more than one test item may be necessary to ensure that proficiency has been thoroughly addressed. When measuring strength, for example, arm strength is not necessarily predictive of trunk or leg strength. For the sake of thoroughness, teachers should administer test items that make valid assessments of strength in each specific muscle group that is deemed relevant and, more important, task specific.

Since the components of physical function tend to be mutually exclusive, each should be addressed separately to adequately document function or health as seen in FitnessGram. Teachers may also want to test both sides of the body and develop a combination, or composite, score to give a representation of upper-body or lower-body strength. This will also identify problems with

Case Study 1
Work Productivity Challenges

Ron is a 17-year-old boy with Down syndrome who is scheduled to graduate from high school in two years and successfully work at a local supermarket. The teacher knows several things about the situation:

- Ron will need to stay on the job for a minimum of five hours.
- Most of his tasks will involve lifting, stacking, and carrying items.
- He is sedentary and seldom participates in any physical activity.

For Ron to be successful, the teacher needs to analyze the functional fitness requirements of his job. The job-specific tasks require a minimal amount of strength to lift, carry, and place objects such as boxes in a specific location. Therefore, the teacher needs to assess Ron's muscular strength in the muscle groups required to initiate task movements in the upper and lower extremities. Flexibility should also be documented to determine whether he can perform the specific movement necessary to complete his tasks. Next, she needs to gauge his endurance, or ability to repeat the movements on a continual basis. Since Ron is sedentary, the teacher may recommend a physical activity program that emphasizes strength and conditioning to improve his overall functioning.

symmetry and enable the teacher or coach to focus on specific muscle groups targeted in the intervention process. This was evident in research by Smail and Horvat (2006, 2009), who identified improvements in lower-extremity functioning among individuals with intellectual disabilities.

COMPONENTS OF PHYSICAL FUNCTION

Muscular strength and endurance, power, flexibility, cardiorespiratory endurance, and body composition are all measurable aspects of functional performance. This section describes these components and provides examples of how each is assessed.

Muscular Strength and Endurance

Muscular strength and muscular endurance are separate entities that can significantly increase the functional capabilities of persons with disabilities. These components correlate highly with self-sufficiency, job performance, and work productivity (Croce & Horvat, 1992; Zetts, Horvat, & Langone, 1995; Smail and Horvat, 2009). However, the link between strength and endurance often blurs, in part because of how these proficiencies are often measured. **Muscular strength** is defined as maximal muscular exertion of relatively brief duration; it is generally measured by the amount of force a person can exert in a single maximal effort. **Muscular endurance** is defined as submaximal exertion that extends over a relatively long period of time. Where muscular strength involves a brief, all-out effort, muscular endurance involves a submaximal, extended effort.

For individuals who rely on their physical skills, such as strength and endurance, to perform job-related tasks, enhanced physical capabilities can make a significant contribution to their overall health and vocational and social development, as well as the ability to participate in sports. For Ron in case

Case Study 2
Symmetry and Function

Glenn is a 10-year-old fifth grader with spastic hemiplegia affecting the left side of his body. He tends to favor his left side and initiates all his action with the right side. He is hesitant when walking up and down stairs, leading with the right side and then moving his left leg to the same step. How can his physical education teacher assess Glenn to discover why his gait pattern is affected in this manner? His teacher must determine the strength discrepancy between the two sides of the body. He can assess and compare the affected side with the nonaffected side and base his treatment on strengthening both sides of the body. He can also analyze Glenn's gait to see if strength is affecting his ability to maintain balance and initiate movements (see chapter 8 for posture, gait, and balance assessments). After the assessment, the teacher is aware of Glenn's strengths and weaknesses and can provide a conditioning program for him that includes range of motion (ROM) exercises, strength exercises, and specific movements to facilitate his gait.

study 1, the development of strength and endurance is a priority to accomplish work-related tasks. Likewise, lack of strength may interfere with the ability to throw a ball, walk up and down stairs, jump, or repeat a swimming stroke across the pool. Therefore, it is imperative that teachers accurately and reliably ascertain performance levels of strength and endurance and more important how they relate to specific functions in students with disabilities such as lifting a weight or jumping.

Upper-Body Muscular Strength and Endurance Assessments

Several methods are available to assess the strength and endurance performance of persons with disabilities. In laboratory settings, cable tensiometers, free weights, and isokinetic devices can be used to assess muscular strength. However, these tests are impractical in field-based settings or when many people must be tested in a short time.

To accommodate these situations, more economical and practical tests must often be employed. For example, upper-extremity assessments in field-based settings commonly use push-ups, pull-ups, or some modification of these tests (see figure 7.1). The most commonly used field-based tests for the lower

Figure 7.1 The modified pull-up is one modification that can be done for the upper-extremity strength and endurance assessment.

extremities are the long jump and vertical jump. Although some researchers consider these tests to be measures of power, each of these field-based tests is considered a relative measure of strength.

In individuals with disabilities, strength and endurance measures, such as the pull-up, often result in zero scores or, at best, inaccurate indicators of actual strength or functional capability. Body size and weight can also restrict or strongly influence physical performance. To offset these problems, researchers have attempted to minimize the effect of body weight and to eliminate zero scores in upper-body measures by developing modified pull-up tests or by using the flexed arm hang.

Field-based tests are widely variable in comparing students with disabilities. Variations based on levels of strength, body structure, and the rate and extent of growth at different developmental stages are available. Although most of these tests are not specific enough to isolate individual muscles, they do test groups of muscles that work synergistically (Horvat, Croce, & Roswal, 1993).

A major problem in using these items is that the relative functional level of the person with the disability determines whether strength or endurance is being measured. Strength can be measured more purely by using one or more of a number of devices that measure force exerted in pounds or kilograms. Examples of such devices include cable tensiometers, hand-grip dynamometers, and back and leg dynamometers. These tools enable measurement of single all-out efforts. In other settings, physical educators can determine one-repetition maximum (1RM) using a universal gym, bench press, forearm curl, or latissimus dorsi pull-down and convert it to a composite strength score. Endurance tests using 50 percent of the person's 1RM values or 50 percent of 6RM for younger students can also provide a composite endurance score for the total number of repetitions (Fleck & Kraemer, 2014).

When interpreting strength measures, a factor to consider is the force exerted in relation to body weight. For example, if a 125-pound (57 kg) person applies a given amount of leg strength to a leg dynamometer, and another person weighing 100 pounds (45 kg) applies the same force, the second person would be judged the stronger. When assessing strength, teachers must look beyond raw strength and interpret strength measures in terms of strength per pound or kilogram of body weight. Some people may have inert body weight from sitting in a wheelchair, and comparisons can be made across muscle groups or from an upper- or lower-body composite score. Among various functional components, muscular strength correlates highly with motor skill development.

Strength can be measured (and developed) isotonically, isokinetically, and isometrically. When measuring isometric strength, it is important that repeated assessments of the same person or between individuals occur at precisely the same point (i.e., degree of angle at the joint) in each person's range of motion. This is critical because strength within the same muscle or muscle group differs, often dramatically, when measured at different points throughout the muscle's or muscle group's range of motion. When measuring strength isotonically or isokinetically, examiners must ensure that subjects repeatedly exert force through the same range of motion. Typically, the best standardization procedure is to have each person exert force through the entire ROM. Getting someone with a disability to exert force through an entire range, particularly when considering fatigue or lack of motivation or attention, is sometimes difficult. In addition, some persons with low levels of strength will respond by producing their peak strength at angles that are not normally advantageous. If that can be determined, it is important to plan the intervention to develop strength across a full range of motion.

A more accurate test and one that uses current technology is the Myotest Pro. This wireless device provides a quantitative assessment of performance over a range of components. It is adaptable to school and athletic programs. For example, the device can be clipped onto a bar or attached to a belt at the waist. The Myotest Pro offers several preprogrammed tests, including a 1RM for the squat or bench press. Jumping can include the vertical jump, half squat, and various other jumps including plyometrics. The Counter Movement Jump (CMJ) test also presents repetitions, jump height, power, force, and velocity.

The bench press protocol provides repetitions, load, speed, force, and power. The Myotest clips to the bar and allows you to program the number of repetitions and load to be lifted. The instrumentation is easy to follow and presents data that can be compared against later performances. This device can detect training gains over time, which is extremely helpful. Another device that uses current technology, has similar results, and is useful in a school or therapy setting is the Tendo Power and Speed Analyzer. The Tendo unit can be programmed for velocity, movement, and speed as well as for estimating 1RM, all of which are important for tracking physical performance.

Isometric Strength and Endurance Assessments

We recommend handheld dynamometry as a reliable and objective measure of functional **isometric strength (stationary maximum force)**. Isometric strength involves a maximal voluntary contraction performed at a specific joint angle against an unyielding resistance. Handheld dynamometers quantify peak force output when manually testing various muscles (Aufsesser, Horvat, & Croce, 1996). Instead of applying a graded subjective rating of 0 (no contraction) to 5 (full movement and resistance), which occurs when manually testing a particular muscle or muscle group (Kendall, McCreary, Provance, Rogers, & Romani, 2005; Reese, 2012), handheld dynamometers provide a quantifiable measurement of muscle force, usually in kilograms of force, or Newtons. This essentially eliminates the subjective and often unreliable values obtained from standard muscle testing.

Extensive research supports the reliability and objectivity of handheld dynamometry with nondisabled adults, nondisabled students, and persons with neuromuscular disorders (Aufsesser, Horvat, & Croce, 1996; Horvat, McManis, & Seagraves, 1992). In addition, this research has been extended to investigate the reliability and objectivity of handheld dynamometry in persons with disabilities (Aufsesser, Horvat, & Austin, 2003; Horvat, Croce, and Roswal, 1993; Smail and Horvat, 2009).

Handheld dynamometers quantify isometric muscle strength and measure forces between 0 and 199.9 kilograms (440.7 lb) or forces exerted in fractions of a pound. Each unit is placed between the tester's hand and the subject's limb. Muscle force is determined by either a make or break test procedure. In a *make* test procedure, the examiner holds the dynamometer stationary while the tested individual exerts a maximum effort against the device. This contrasts with a *break* test procedure, where the tester exerts a force against the tested person's limb segment until the tested person's effort is overcome

Figure 7.2 A hand-grip dynamometer is used to examine hand and arm strength.

and the limb segment gives or breaks. Horvat and Croce (1995) recommend the make test as a more efficient procedure for students and persons with disabilities.

When using the handheld dynamometer on persons with disabilities, the adapted physical educator should familiarize the subjects with the testing protocol, test positions, and instrumentation to minimize effects of practice efforts on test performance (Croce & Horvat, 1992). The tester should place subjects in the appropriate testing positions and allow practice trials with the instrument until they are able to perform the testing protocol on cue. Test positions for measuring strength are commonly based on those outlined by Kendall and colleagues (2005) or by manufacturers of the testing devices.

According to Horvat, Croce, & Roswal (1993), to ensure consistency in testing, the tester should use consistent body joint and dynamometer positioning, stabilize movements, give consistent verbal feedback to subjects during data acquisition, provide the opportunity for subjects to visualize tested body parts, and place the dynamometer perpendicular to the limb segment on which it is applied. The final point ensures that the measured force against the instrument is maximal. The testing procedure requires minimal experience with handheld dynamometry (i.e., less than 5 hours of practical experience).

An important aspect of muscle testing is the versatility of measuring several muscle groups on both sides of the body; the sum of several muscle groups; or a composite strength score that can address overall functional ability. Clinically, muscle testing has been used to evaluate pre- and posttest performance on strength measures of high school youths with intellectual disabilities and has been used to determine work capacities by correlating strength measures with work performance (Seagraves, Horvat, Franklin, & Jones, 2004). In this context, it is recommended to use handheld dynamometers for the ease and versatility of accessing numerous muscle groups in a relatively short time. In addition, the strength composite can yield an overall level of strength rather than strength in one extremity.

Another tool for measuring static strength is the hand-grip dynamometer (figure 7.2). The subject grips the appropriate apparatus and squeezes as hard as possible to elicit maximal force. The dynamometer measures forces between 0 and 100 kilograms (up to 220 lb) and usually has an adjustable handle to accommodate hand size differences. Corbin, Welk, and Corbin

(2012) provide norms for hand-grip isometric strength in young adults 18 to 30 years of age. The Brockport Physical Fitness Test (BPFT) uses a dominant grip-strength procedure, and similar scores can be obtained with a back and leg dynamometer or cable tensiometer to record arm lifts, arm presses, or back lifts. Back and leg dynamometers use a platform while the participant flexes at the knees, grips a hand bar, and exerts force with a pulling motion. Scores are generally recorded as peak force in pounds and converted to kilograms. Endurance can also be assessed by sequencing a grip dynamometer as hard as possible for 60 seconds and comparing the initial force with the force executed at 60 seconds (Heyward & Gibson, 2014). Although the hand-grip dynamometer has been used extensively, it measures a specific component of strength (grip strength) that does not generalize to the larger muscles in the body.

Dynamic Strength and Endurance Assessments

The ability to apply force in a maximal or near-maximal contraction is known as **dynamic strength**. Strength in this context is used to lift oneself off the ground into a wheelchair or to transfer from a wheelchair to an automobile seat. Endurance relates to performing an activity for an extended time such as throwing a baseball, pushing a wheelchair, or lifting and stacking boxes in a work setting.

To measure absolute strength, the greatest amount of weight lifted for a specific exercise in one complete repetition (1RM) can be documented. For absolute endurance, a specific weight can be selected for multiple repetitions—for example, 80 and 35 pounds (36 and 16 kg) for males and females, respectively, in the YMCA bench press (figure 7.3) and 40 pounds (18 kg) for men and 25 pounds (11 kg) for women in the YMCA curl test (Golding, 2000).

For younger students and schools without bench press equipment, the flexed arm hang or isometric push-up can be substituted. To perform the push-up, the student holds his body in the up position (arms extended) of the push-up for as long as he can. For the flexed arm hang, the student grasps the bar with an overhand grip, chin over the bar, and holds this position for as long as possible. The BPFT uses the isometric push-up, pull-up, modified pull-up, dumbbell curl, reverse curl, and trunk lift as measures of strength and endurance. Further, the BPFT recommends the wheelchair ramp test or 40-meter push/walk as alternatives for strength testing. Another task that is often used in clinical settings, the seated push-up, requires the participant to lift the body 12 inches (30 cm) for a maximum of 20 seconds. This assessment is very useful because the movement is similar to the functional skills needed to accommodate transfers.

Scoring for 1RM tests commonly documents the maximal amount of weight lifted, while absolute endurance records the number of repetitions or time maintained in a particular position. Other endurance tests can utilize a percentage of repetition maximum to document the number of repetitions completed during various tasks such as the bench press, curls, and lat pull-downs. The versatility of repetition maximum tests is useful for persons who use a wheelchair or who have limited function or deficiency in some muscle groups.

Figure 7.3 The bench press can be used to measure absolute strength or endurance.

Lower-Extremity Muscular Strength and Endurance Assessments

Isometric, isokinetic, and weight training equipment can be used to measure strength in the lower extremities. A 1RM strength test for the leg press or leg extension can determine maximal values of weight lifted or moved. For individuals with disabilities, it may be advantageous to use manual muscle testing (Horvat, Croce, & Roswal, 1993) or a percentage of the repetition maximum to document the number of repetitions for the leg press, leg curl, or leg extension. In persons with weakened extremities, the ability to lift and move the leg may be indicative of the level of function that is present, providing a baseline for developing the instructional program. For example, in case study 2, Glenn demonstrates a strength discrepancy between the right and left sides of the body that ultimately affects his gait. After determining his level of functioning, the teacher can develop a program plan emphasizing exercises that can remediate the discrepancy. Another recommended test is the 30-second chair sit-to-stand, which consists of counting the number of times a person can rise from a sitting to a standing position without using the arms. The test has proven to correlate very well with lower-extremity strength in persons with visual impairments and is highly recommended for other populations (Horvat, Ray, Nocera, & Croce, 2006; Rikli & Jones, 2013; Mason, Horvat & Nocera, 2016).

Abdominal Strength and Endurance Assessments

The most common test to measure the strength and endurance of the abdominal region is the sit-up, or curl-up, with the hands placed in a variety of positions. In the BPFT battery, the modified curl-up is used; the hands slide along the thighs until the fingertips contact the knees (Winnick & Short, 2014). The YMCA uses a half-sit-up test, or abdominal crunch, designed to keep the back flat and negate the hip flexors. The total number of repetitions or the number completed within 60 seconds can be recorded. In the Physical Best test battery, the subject places the hands on the chest and flexes the knees to eliminate as much of the hip flexors as possible. A less complex and more functional assessment is a plank, which requires the performer to hold the position for 30 to 60 seconds with toes and arms in contact with the supporting surface (figure 7.4). This component also provides stability and is helpful in maintaining posture.

Figure 7.4 Abdominal and core strength assessment.

Power

Power, or explosive strength, is a combination of muscular strength and speed. It is demonstrated when muscles contract rapidly to overcome significant resistance. Power is called for in such skills as throwing, kicking, running (specifically accelerating), jumping, hopping, and leaping.

Power should be assessed in both the lower and upper extremities. In the lower extremities, the standing long jump and vertical jump are common assessment tools. In this context, especially with increasing technology, rapid responses are now available with devices like the Myotest Pro and Tendo Power and Speed Analyzer. In addition to assessing strength, both devices provide the power analysis that is used in many sports and functional tasks.

Lower-Extremity Power Assessments

Because the standing long jump and vertical jump require speed and strength for maximum performance, these measures are extremely helpful to document explosive strength, although the movements do also require coordination.

Vertical jumping may provide a more valid measure of power than the long jump because the former requires less skill. The long jump clearly calls on speed and power but also requires that the subject execute optimal forward body lean, with foot placement in front of the body, to jump the maximum possible distance.

The vertical jump may be less difficult to execute than the long jump (in terms of skill), but it often cannot be scored with the same precision. Vertical jump scoring usually requires that the subject raise the arm and mark the wall at the highest point immediately before jumping, then mark the wall again at the apex of the jump. Occasionally, height of the prejump chalk mark will be more valid than the apex mark. Although the tester can ensure that the prejump chalk mark is indicative of the person's highest reach, less control is evident when documenting where the chalk mark is made at the apex of the jump. Conceivably, a score can be invalid because the mark was made before or after the true apex had been reached. Furthermore, the tester can do little beyond visual or verbal prompting to ensure the subject is reaching as high as possible when she marks the apex of her jump. One possible solution is to eliminate measurement dependent on reach. Alternatively, the tester may mark the wall to indicate the subject's standing height, then mark the wall at a point equivalent to the height of the person's head at the apex of the jump. This method is limited by the tester's ability not only to accurately judge where the apex mark should be placed but also to avoid the jumper. A wall-mounted vertical jump tester or long jump tester can be used. The Vertec is a vertical jump apparatus used by many college and professional teams to measure vertical jump by noting the specific vanes that move during the jump.

Upper-Extremity Power Assessments

Upper-extremity power measures may be particularly appropriate among persons with significantly limited lower-extremity function. Although not originally designed for persons with disabilities, the medicine ball throw has proven adaptable for students sitting in a wheelchair. Upper-extremity power can be measured unilaterally by putting a relatively heavy object such as a shot or bilaterally by imparting velocity to a medicine ball in chest-pass fashion.

Figure 7.5 Upper-extremity power assessment.

Depending on the person's ability, the weight or selection of the object may vary. The Special Olympics Alaska Functional Performance Test uses a seated two-hand three-kilogram medicine ball throw to assess upper-extremity power.

The medicine ball chest pass can be administered with the person seated in a chair (the chair's legs are secured to the ground). Securing the chair ensures that it does not move during force application. Alternatively, the chair's back can be placed against a wall (see figure 7.5). Using both hands, the subject holds the medicine ball to the chest and then pushes or releases the ball as aggressively as possible. Upper-extremity power can be determined by measuring distance between the ball's release and landing points. Another version of the medicine ball chest pass is performed by sitting on the floor with the back against a wall and pushing the medicine ball with both hands.

Flexibility

Flexibility is defined as the ability to move the body and its parts through a wide range of motion without stress. A muscle that is not flexible can heighten the likelihood of strain, not only at attachment sites but also in the muscle itself. Lack of flexibility can lead to decreased strength and loss of functional capabilities.

When measuring flexibility, individual differences in threshold of discomfort must be recognized to ensure that testing does not put a subject at undue risk of muscle strain. Perception of discomfort is very subjective and unique to every person. Recognizing this threshold is particularly critical if the test subject is limited by muscle disease. For example, a person with Duchenne muscular dystrophy may be more susceptible to muscle strain during testing because of a lower level of muscular strength than someone whose relative inflexibility is not a function of underlying muscle disease.

Flexibility is important for a variety of reasons. Significant inflexibility places a person at a disadvantage in performing common everyday tasks. For example, reaching for an item on a high shelf or pushing a wheelchair may be difficult for individuals with contractures or spastic cerebral palsy. Discomfort and a loss of flexibility may promote a sedentary lifestyle and contribute to a cycle in which the person's sedentary lifestyle precipitates further losses of flexibility and other components of physical function.

People with disabilities, perhaps because of inopportunity or lowered expectations of themselves and from others, may not be as flexible as the general population. Flexibility, too, is a function of muscle fitness. Typically, fit muscles, provided they have been exercised through normal ranges of motion, are flexible muscles.

A number of disabilities often mitigate against flexibility. For example, spastic cerebral palsy is characterized by hypertonicity and contractures in affected muscle groups. How flexible a person with spastic cerebral palsy is at any given time may be determined, to varying degrees, by ambient temperature, level of arousal, and medication. An individual with spastic cerebral palsy who is in a warm room, calm, and taking muscle relaxants is likely to demonstrate more flexibility than if he were cold, were excited, and had neglected to take prescribed muscle-relaxing medication. Persons with Duchenne muscular dystrophy often experience decrements in flexibility owing to the dystrophic muscles' diseased state, while students with juvenile rheumatoid arthritis typically are inflexible because of joint pain that compromises movement. This pain, to the degree it discourages movement, inevitably results in some loss of range of motion.

Flexibility Assessments

Flexibility is highly specific. A tester cannot make generalizations about overall flexibility by measuring range of motion at one site only. In fact, the only valid way to determine range of motion in any joint is to specifically measure range of motion at that joint.

Many flexibility measures, even some venerable ones, may be questionable in terms of validity. Take, for example, the sit-and-reach test as a flexibility measure. At least three factors could influence the score: back flexibility, hamstring flexibility, and the ratio of arm length to leg length. It is often difficult to precisely determine the degree to which each factor has contributed. Further, the slightest flexion at the knee joint will render a sit-and-reach score invalid because the hamstrings, the major muscle group being stretched, cross the knee joint.

Flexibility scores may be reported as linear measurements or rotary measurements. Although each is efficient, linear measurements probably have greater applicability in practical settings. Typically, linear measurements require little more than some form of ruler or sit-and-reach box, in which flexibility of a particular muscle group (hamstrings) or range of motion (shoulder) is noted. Several recommended variations include the modified sit-and-reach that incorporates a finger-to-box distance to control limb-length biases, the back-saver sit-and-reach, the YMCA Flexibility Test, and the Senior Adult Flexibility Test. Each of these tests may be appropriate for persons with disabilities, not only to eliminate limb-length bias but also to circumvent problems of excessive tightness or weakness associated with certain disabilities.

Rotary measurements usually require instruments more typically seen in laboratory settings, such as flexometers (see figure 7.6) or goniometers (see figure 7.7). In addition, specific actions can be used to document movement

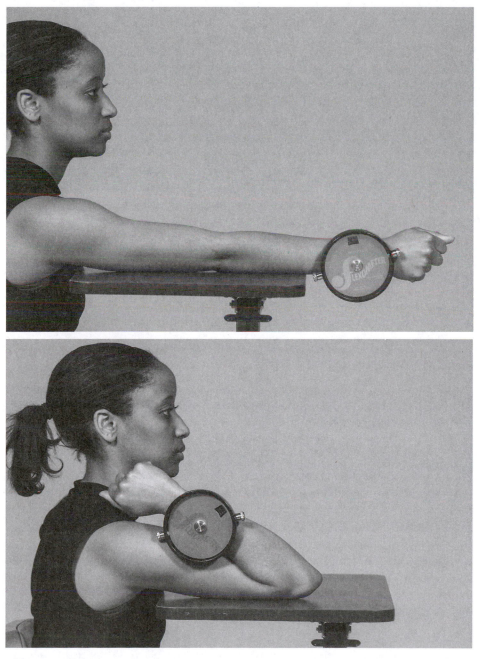

Figure 7.6   Range of motion at the elbow joint can be measured using a Leighton flexometer.

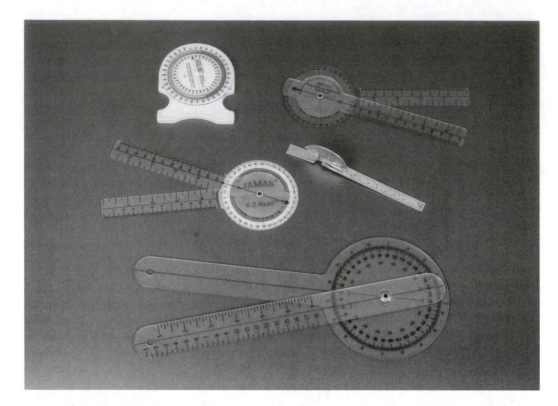

Figure 7.7   Examples of different types of goniometers used to measure range of motion.

through an arc of 0 to 180 degrees. Specific flexibility can be determined through range of motion in the extremities; rotation of the limbs; or movements in planes around the horizontal, vertical, or coronal axis (Norkin & White, 2009).

Upper-Extremity Flexibility Assessments

The Target Stretch Test includes a series of stretches through a range of motion including wrist extension, elbow extension, shoulder extension, shoulder abduction, shoulder external rotation, forearm supination, and forearm pronation. Several other measures such as the shoulder stretch and modified Thomas test, as used in the Brockport Physical Fitness Test (BPFT), can also be used to assess upper-extremity flexibility.

The BPFT measures an excellent range of flexibility using goniometers in the Target Stretch Test to estimate movement in the joint (Winnick & Short, 2014) (see figure 7.8). The positions include wrist extension, elbow extension, shoulder extension, shoulder abduction, shoulder external rotation, forearm supination, forearm pronation, and knee extension. By utilizing all the body planes, this test is useful in determining functional movement and program planning.

Lower-Extremity Flexibility Assessments

The most common test for lower-extremity flexibility is the sit-and-reach, which is included in most test batteries. Subjects sit with their heels flat against a bench or box that is 12 inches (30 cm) high and reach as far forward as possible. The farthest point reached on the fourth trial counts as the score.

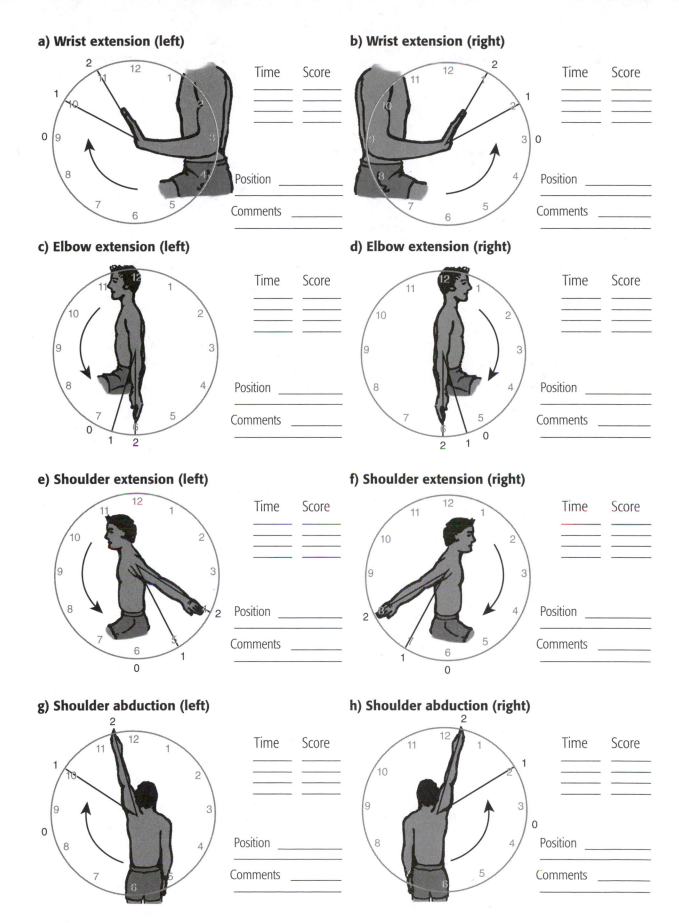

a) Wrist extension (left)

Time _____ Score _____
_____ _____
_____ _____

Position _____
Comments _____
_____

b) Wrist extension (right)

Time _____ Score _____
_____ _____
_____ _____

Position _____
Comments _____
_____

c) Elbow extension (left)

Time _____ Score _____
_____ _____
_____ _____

Position _____
Comments _____
_____

d) Elbow extension (right)

Time _____ Score _____
_____ _____
_____ _____

Position _____
Comments _____
_____

e) Shoulder extension (left)

Time _____ Score _____
_____ _____
_____ _____

Position _____
Comments _____
_____

f) Shoulder extension (right)

Time _____ Score _____
_____ _____
_____ _____

Position _____
Comments _____
_____

g) Shoulder abduction (left)

Time _____ Score _____
_____ _____
_____ _____

Position _____
Comments _____
_____

h) Shoulder abduction (right)

Time _____ Score _____
_____ _____
_____ _____

Position _____
Comments _____
_____

Figure 7.8 Target Stretch Test.

(continued)

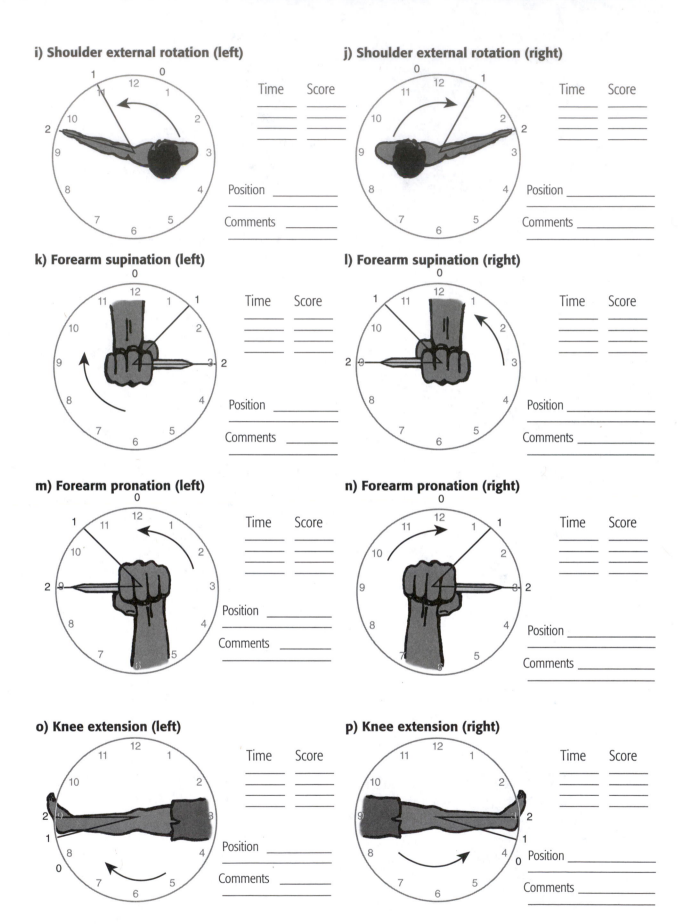

i) **Shoulder external rotation (left)**

Time _____ Score _____
_____ _____
_____ _____

Position _____
_____

Comments _____

j) **Shoulder external rotation (right)**

Time _____ Score _____
_____ _____
_____ _____

Position _____
_____

Comments _____

k) **Forearm supination (left)**

Time _____ Score _____
_____ _____
_____ _____

Position _____
_____

Comments _____

l) **Forearm supination (right)**

Time _____ Score _____
_____ _____
_____ _____

Position _____
_____

Comments _____

m) **Forearm pronation (left)**

Time _____ Score _____
_____ _____
_____ _____

Position _____
_____

Comments _____

n) **Forearm pronation (right)**

Time _____ Score _____
_____ _____
_____ _____

Position _____
_____

Comments _____

o) **Knee extension (left)**

Time _____ Score _____
_____ _____
_____ _____

Position _____
_____

Comments _____

p) **Knee extension (right)**

Time _____ Score _____
_____ _____
_____ _____

Position _____
_____

Comments _____

Figure 7.8 *(continued)*

From Horvat, M., Kelly, L.E., Block, M.E., and Croce, R., *Developmental and adapted physical activity assessment*, 2nd ed. (Champaign, IL: Human Kinetics, 2019).

Illustrations reprinted, by permission, from J. Winnick and F. Short, 2014, *Brockport physical fitness test manual: A health-related assessment for youngsters with disabilities* (Champaign, IL: Human Kinetics), 97-99.

A modified sit-and-reach test includes a sliding measurement scale. Subjects slide the scale along the top of the sit-and-reach box until the zero point of the scale is even with the fingertips (Hoeger, Hopkins, Button, & Palmer, 1990; Hui & Yuen, 2000). This finger-to-box distance establishes a zero point that accommodates limb-length variations in students and may more accurately portray the lower-limb flexibility of persons with disabilities.

Kendall and colleagues (2005) also assessed the length of the hamstrings by placing the subject's pelvis in a neutral position, anchoring the supporting leg, and lifting the other (a straight-leg raise). Normal hamstring length (70° to 80°), excessive length (110°), and short hamstring length (50°) can be detected (as shown in figure 7.9). This technique may be especially helpful for persons with disabilities because range of motion in joints may be linked to functional capabilities. For example, in paraplegia, tightness in some muscles enhances muscle function, while in quadriplegia, tightness of lower-trunk muscles aids in maintaining sitting postures by increasing trunk stability. In contrast, other persons may require flexibility to complete many functional tasks, such as transfers or dressing. The excessive flexibility in Down syndrome may result in ligament instability that affects activities of daily living and muscle development or that causes imbalances. Other functional measures of flexibility can utilize a goniometer to document range of motion in the joints or simply to document specific movements through a 180-degree range of motion during flexion and extension. In addition, rotary movement, as measured by a goniometer, can be used to measure head, arm, or leg flexibility in the frontal, horizontal, or sagittal planes (Norkin & White, 2009).

Palmer and Epler (1998) have provided illustrations of functional muscle movements, such as hip flexion, in which the person stands and places the foot of the test limb on an eight-inch (20 cm) step, then returns it to the floor.

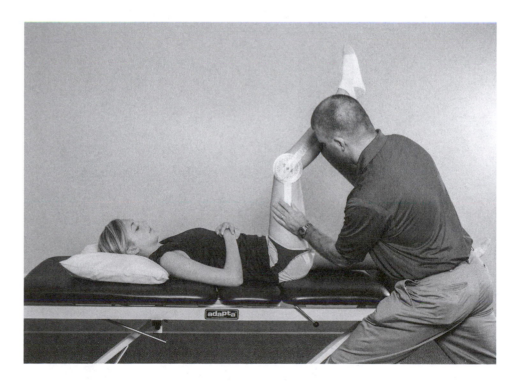

Figure 7.9   Hip flexion and hamstring length assessment.

The examiner can document the movement through the specific range needed to climb stairs or document muscle strength by the number of repetitions, from 0 (nonfunctional) to 5 (functional). The Target Stretch Test also has a lower-extremity assessment. The chair sit-and-reach used in the Special Olympics Alaska Functional Performance Test assesses flexibility and function in the lower extremity (see figure 7.10).

Cardiorespiratory Function

Many people equate fitness with the ability to effectively meet challenges requiring **cardiorespiratory endurance**. Such challenges include cycling, power walking, jogging, and swimming.

Cardiorespiratory endurance is an important component of fitness, particularly when the potential for promoting a healthy lifestyle is the primary criterion by which fitness components are judged, given its potential for reducing heart disease and obesity. Historically, the standard for measuring cardiorespiratory endurance has been maximum oxygen uptake ($\dot{V}O_2$max). However, precise measurement of $\dot{V}O_2$max requires expensive and sophisticated equipment. To evaluate $\dot{V}O_2$max in practical settings without elaborate laboratory equipment and procedures, researchers have constructed tests whose results correlate significantly with laboratory assessments of $\dot{V}O_2$max. If a field test for cardiorespiratory endurance correlates with its laboratory

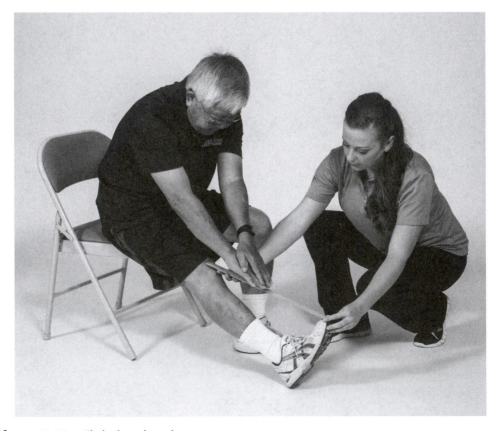

Figure 7.10   Chair sit-and-reach.

test counterpart, the field test can be assumed to validly measure cardiorespiratory endurance.

Typical cardiorespiratory endurance field tests call for the subject to run a prescribed distance (e.g., 1 or 1.5 miles [1.6 or 2.4 km]) for time or run a prescribed period of time (e.g., 9 or 12 minutes) for distance, while other measures rely on pulse recovery after a prescribed level of exertion. Some tests may rely on cadence (e.g., use of a metronome) or a CD, as in the PACER test, for standardizing workloads (see figure 7.11). Items requiring the subject to maintain cadence may be inappropriate if, for example, the person has an intellectual disability or attention-deficit/hyperactivity disorder.

When pulse counting provides the basis for determining cardiorespiratory fitness, the test administrator and test interpreter must consider a number of variables. Pulse rate for any given level of exertion can be affected by factors such as environmental temperature and the subject's level of arousal. Counting heartbeats, particularly when pulse is rapid immediately after exercise, can sometimes be difficult. While postexercise heart rate is being counted, pulse rate will be recovering toward normal. As a result, if postexercise pulse is taken over too long a period (e.g., 60 seconds), the tester will record a pulse rate lower than what was occurring at the moment exertion ceased. To remedy this problem, most postexercise pulse measures are of either 6 or 10 seconds in duration. When pulse is taken for 6 seconds, the tester need only add a zero to the number of beats counted to determine beats per minute. When pulse is taken for 10 seconds, the tester multiplies the number of beats counted by six. The major drawback of the 6-second method is that an inaccurate pulse count of only one heartbeat results in an error of 10 beats per minute.

Figure 7.11 The PACER test, one type of cardiorespiratory endurance field test.

Heart and pulse monitors can record heart rates in intervals, are more precise, and may be available in field-based settings, including the Brockport Physical Fitness Test, and in field-based studies on activity for individuals with intellectual disabilities (Lorenzi, Horvat, & Pellegrini, 2000; Horvat & Franklin, 2001). In addition, recent technology has introduced personal fitness devices such as Fitbit and Alpha Mio. Both are wrist-based monitors that allow users to input their height, weight, age, and sex and obtain a real-time heart rate during exercise that can be synced to other mobile devices for data collection.

By their very nature, most tests of cardiorespiratory endurance can be relatively time consuming. Often the number of persons needing to be tested and the degree to which those being tested can assist in their own scoring (e.g., counting heartbeats) will determine the specific measure used. Generally, in field-based settings, group tests use a timed run for distance or a 1-mile and 1.5-mile run in subjects with intellectual disabilities. The BPFT uses a 20-meter PACER, a 16-meter PACER, the Target Aerobic Movement Test (TAMT), and a 1-mile run/walk as the primary aerobic functioning measures. The PACER participants run back and forth across the distance and progressively pick up the pace, which increases each minute. The number of laps completed is recorded. The TAMT encourages participants to exercise at a recommended target heart rate using various physical activities to accommodate persons who are nonambulatory or who use supportive devices.

Alternatives to running tests include the three-minute step test and the six-minute cycle ergometer test, which have been used to test aerobic fitness with adequate results. We recommend a three-minute step test because it is brief and can be scored easily using a Mio Alpha or similar device. A smart phone or tablet app can provide visual and auditory prompts while the tester also provides verbal prompts. With heartrate technology, the tester can accurately measure heart rate (HR) max and recovery HR at various intervals. Stepping can be set at 64 or 96 steps per minute based on the population and overall fitness of the participant.

In certain cases, the person may use a wheelchair, hands, feet, or assistive device for testing, as in the TAMT. Any special circumstances relevant to mobility should be noted, and retests should be conducted under precisely the same conditions as the original. Wheelchairs, in particular, can have a significant effect on any timed test, whether the test alleges to measure cardiorespiratory endurance or speed. Wheelchair frame rigidity, weight, and state of repair are all critical factors. If there has been a change in wheelchairs or a change in the chair's state of repair between tests, test results should not be compared. Variations in the level or extent of disability may also affect remaining or functional muscle mass. For this reason, comparing scores among wheelchair users is often of limited value.

One problem inherent in cardiorespiratory endurance testing is that the person being tested may be disinclined to endure the degree of discomfort necessary to produce a valid cardiorespiratory endurance score. In such instances, the tester must determine what motivates each person; in run/walk tests in extreme cases, the tester may find herself running with and encouraging the individual(s) being tested. Obviously, in this scenario, group testing is preferred. Further, if the person administering the test is going to participate alongside the subject, that tester must be consistent with the application of motivational devices and be physically able to complete the test. Pitetti and Fernhall (2005) recommend an extensive familiarization of the testing protocol to ensure participants are comfortable with their surroundings and understand the task that is required.

Cardiorespiratory Function Assessments

One of the most difficult components of physical fitness to measure in students and persons with disabilities is cardiorespiratory endurance. The amount of time, motivation, and ability needed to generate a maximal effort is difficult to sustain, causing the measures to vary with the population assessed. Some protocols will reduce the amount to be run or walked from 900 to 600 to 300 yards (or meters). Pitetti and Fernhall (2005) provide an excellent review of measuring cardiorespiratory endurance of persons with intellectual disabilities that should be viewed as the gold standard for adapted physical education. In addition, Bar-Or (1983) has provided test data on individuals with cerebral palsy. Based on these investigations, the following field-based tests should be considered.

- *Step test*. The three-minute bench step test has been proven reliable in the Special Olympics Alaska Functional Test for individuals with intellectual disabilities. The test procedure includes monitoring HR during a step-climbing protocol onto and off of a 12-inch (30 cm) step at pace with a metronome set at 64 or 96 beats per minute. The participant can be cued verbally or visually on the pattern and completes the task for three minutes. The participant sits after completing the test, and recovery HR is recorded at the one-, three- and five-minute marks.

- *PACER*. The PACER (Progressive Aerobic Cardiovascular Endurance Run) is an aerobic-capacity test that has norms for both age and sex. The PACER is a multistage fitness test adapted from the 20-meter shuttle run published by Leger and Lambert (1982) and revised in 1988 (Leger, Mercier, Gadoury, & Lambert). Scoring the PACER requires the input of each student's height and weight. Calculation of aerobic capacity requires a score of at least 10 laps.

Body Composition

Body composition, or body fatness, refers to the percentage of total body weight that is fat. Table 7.1 shows percent body fat for children and adolescents. Minimal and average fat are dependent on age, gender, and level of activity (Heyward & Gibson, 2014). Essential fat is estimated to be approximately 8 to 12 percent for females and 3 to 5 percent for males (ACSM, 2014). Desirable levels of fatness for good health range from 10 to 20 percent in adult males and 15 to 25 percent in adult females. According to Heyward and Gibson (2014), average values of percent body fat for men and women aged 18 to 34 are 13 percent for males and 28 percent for females, with obesity greater than 20 percent body fat for men and 35 percent for women.

Table 7.1 Percentage of Body Fat in Children

	Range	Skinfold measurement (mm)	Percentage of body fat
Boys	**Triceps plus calf skinfolds**		
	Very low	0-5	0-6%
	Low	5-10	6-10%
	Optimal	10-25	10-20%
	Moderately high	25-32	20-25%
	High	32-40	25-30%
	Very high	40 or above	30% or higher
	Triceps plus subscapular skinfolds		
	Very low	0-5	0-6%
	Low	5-13	6-10%
	Optimal	13-22	10-20%
	Moderately high	22-29	20-25%
	High	29-39	25-30%
	Very high	39 or above	30% or higher
Girls	**Triceps plus calf skinfolds**		
	Very low	0-11	0-12%
	Low	11-17	12-15%
	Optimal	17-30	15-25%
	Moderately high	30-36	25-30%
	High	36-45	30-36%
	Very high	45 or above	36% or higher
	Triceps plus subscapular skinfolds		
	Very low	0-11	0-11%
	Low	11-15	11-15%
	Optimal	15-27	15-25%
	Moderately high	27-35	25-30%
	High	35-45	30-35.5%
	Very high	45 or above	35.5% or higher

A major concern is the increase in obesity and body fat in students. Because of the resultant health epidemic and tendency of obese children to become obese adults, there is renewed interest in accurately evaluating the body composition of students, including traditionally inactive students with disabilities. Because of variations in growth patterns, maturity, activity, and disability, it is important to develop accurate standards when determining body composition.

Some researchers believe that deriving percent body fat measurements from students' skinfolds may not be valid, especially since the determination of body fat varies across age ranges during development. For example, while a nine-year-old girl with a skinfold thickness of 24 millimeters may be normal at the 25th percentile for that age group, an equal thickness in a 14-year-old girl may place her at the 50th percentile. In addition, formulas for estimating percent body fat have been derived primarily from measuring adults. Concern arises over the possibility that body density and fat content relationships may differ between adults and children. A student's skinfold measurement may indicate a poor result based on equations derived from adult norms when in fact the student's percent body fat is in a healthy range for his age and level of development.

Most methods for estimating body fat are not applicable in field-based settings. In field-based settings, skinfolds typically provide an adequate estimate of body fat, while measures of body mass index (BMI) and waist-to-hip ratio are also recommended.

Taking skinfold measurements in practical settings requires that the tester become skilled in using skinfold calipers. Each measurement must be taken at the exact site specified by the test. A skinfold measurement is taken by grasping tissue to be measured with the thumb and forefinger and gently drawing the tissue away from the subject's body. At a point adjacent to the thumb–forefinger grasp of the skinfold, the tester applies the caliper (figure 7.12a-7.12b), making sure that *only* skin and adipose tissue (not muscle) is being measured. To ensure that muscle is not included in the measurement, the tester can ask the person to flex muscles directly beneath the skinfold measurement site. If the tester does not feel muscles tensing between the thumb–forefinger grasp, he may be assured that muscle will not be included in the measurement.

Body composition information for children and youth is included in most physical fitness batteries and is commonly shown as percentile rank norms rather than specific scores. Since variations in water and bone mineral content are apparent in children, specific equations have been developed (Lohman, 1982, 1986, 1987, 1992). The triceps, subscapular, and medial calf are recommended for three consecutive scores, while only the median score is recorded. This procedure is also used in the BPFT. Scoring is provided for the sum of the triceps and subscapular or triceps and calf skinfolds (table 7.1). Very little information is specific to persons with disabilities, although Heyward and Wagner (2004) provide some information on diabetes, respiratory disorders, and neuromuscular disorders. Johnson, Bulbulian, Gruber, and Sundheim (1986) developed an equation for estimating body fat of 23 athletes with spinal injuries (paraplegia), and Kelly and Rimmer (1987) developed a predictive equation for adult men with intellectual disabilities. In each case, the aim is to provide estimates of body fat specific to each population that could generalize to overall fitness.

Body Composition Assessments

Measuring body composition is difficult in school-based settings and more specifically in persons with disabilities. Students' water and bone mineral content varies with developmental age, and disease can cause differences in fat-free body density (Lohman, 1992). Based on the work of Lohman, several methods of estimating body composition in students have been developed, including the use of body mass index and bioelectric impedance. It is difficult

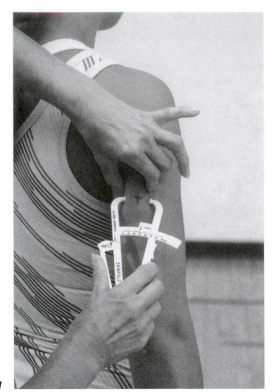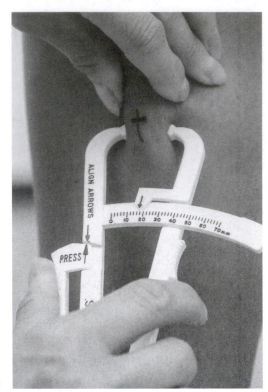

Figure 7.12   Measurement of skinfold fat: *(a)* triceps and *(b)* calf.

to find a specific test that will meet the needs of all students. The following four measures can be useful for students with disabilities. Triangulated values demonstrate a profile of body composition that can be linked to heathy functioning.

Body Mass Index

Body mass index is determined as follows:

$$\text{weight in kg/height in m}^2$$

Higher values for this index indicate higher body fatness. Lohman (1989) gives it a fair rating and indicates that research on this measure found four correlations with skinfolds. BMI should be used only when other measures are unavailable or impractical.

Skinfolds

The work of Lohman and colleagues provides a more useful measure for evaluating percent body fat in students. Body composition standards by Lohman (1987) include the sites of the triceps, subscapular, and medial calf (see table 7.1). The sum of the triceps and medial calf are used in Fitness-Gram (The Cooper Institute, 2017) and the BPFT. Another test extends this work and covers biological influences such as age, ethnicity, gender, and body composition (Heymsfield, Lohman, Wang, & Going, 2005).

Two variations that have been used for persons with disabilities include an equation for adults with intellectual disabilities (Kelly & Rimmer, 1987) using anthropometric data to estimate percent body fat. The Kelly and Rimmer equation follows:

Percent body fat = 13.545 + 0.48691649 (waist circumference in cm) – 0.52662145 (forearm circumference in cm) – 0.15504013 (height in cm) + 0.07707995 (weight in kg)

Another equation developed by Johnson and colleagues (1986) for athletes with spinal injuries (paraplegia) uses circumference, diameter, and skinfold measurements to estimate percent body fat in the following five models:

Model I (anthropometric variables):

Percent body fat = 2.271 + 0.0754 (abdomen circumference in cm) – 0.305 (weight in kg) + 0.567 (chest skinfold in mm) – 1.017 (chest diameter in cm)

Model II (diameter and length in cm):

Percent body fat = –46.601 + 3.65 (bi-iliac) + 7.75 (elbow) – 1.145 (upper-leg length) – 1.004 (lower-leg length)

Model III (circumferences in cm):

Percent body fat = –33.535 + 0.831 (abdomen) – 0.587 (calf)

Model IV (skinfolds in mm):

Percent body fat = 3.45 + 0.967 (chest) + 0.392 (calf)

Model V (abdomen circumference only):

Percent body fat = –31.804 + 0.617 (abdomen circumference)

Waist-to-Hip Ratio (WHR)

Waist-to-hip ratio (Heyward & Gibson, 2014) is an indirect measure of lower- and upper-body weight distribution. Upper-body obesity, or central adiposity, measured by WHR moderately relates to risk factors associated with cardiovascular and metabolic diseases in men and women. Young adults with WHR values in excess of 0.94 for men and 0.82 for women are at high risk for adverse health consequences. To calculate WHR, divide waist circumference (in centimeters) by hip circumference (in centimeters). A similar ratio can be obtained using weight and height, in which the measurement of the waist is compared against the height of the individual.

Bioelectrical Impedance Analysis (BIA)

Heyward and Gibson (2014) define bioelectrical impedance (BIA) analysis as "a rapid, noninvasive, and relatively inexpensive method for evaluating body composition in field settings. With this method, a low-level electrical current is passed through the client's body, and the impedance (Z), or opposition to the flow of current, is measured with a BIA analyzer" (see figure 7.13). The Tanita and Omron analyzers estimate percent body fat and fat-free mass using proprietary equations developed by the manufacturers.

Triangulation Results

Triangulation of the four measures shows that outcome measures in every case indicate a higher level of body fat. Instead of relying on one measure, the teacher can take the four measures and provide a profile of overall health and physical function.

A SAMPLING OF TEST BATTERIES

This section introduces a representative sample of fitness test batteries. Physical educators must show good judgment when selecting tests because some have been more carefully constructed than others. Teachers must not assume that a test—simply because it has been published and is in use—is valid, reliable, and objective. Instruments should reflect the population they were developed to assess. Teachers can use the featured tests to accurately assess many individuals. In addition, previous sections document test items for individuals with disabilities. Some tests are not designed for all students or can't be used for all students. It is imperative that teachers gather information and use it to develop their instructional plans.

Tests presented here are not necessarily being recommended. Rather, they are offered with comments and constructive criticisms for the potential user's

Figure 7.13   Handheld bioelectrical impedance analysis device.

Case Study 3
Evaluating Athletes and Training

Ashley is coaching a group of athletes with disabilities and is trying to determine what events they are suited for and also whether her training program is increasing their performance.

Ashley should base her tests on the specific components needed to perform the events. Muscular strength, speed, and power are common components of most sports skills. She can use a number of tests to measure strength in several muscle groups, such as bench presses or a manual muscle tester; measure flexibility with a sit-and-reach or modified Thomas test; and measure power with the vertical jump. With these assessments, Ashley can document strength, flexibility, and power to plan her training and periodically assess the progress of her athletes.

consideration. Whether *any* test is selected for use must be determined by the test's technical adequacy, the tester's competence, the information desired, and the characteristics of the person to be tested.

Teachers should select items based on the information required to develop their program plans. Since many test batteries do not represent the variety of populations encountered in adapted physical education, it is recommended that physical educators select test items that are specific to the age and task requirements of their students. By doing so, teachers can assess students who need instruction to facilitate motor development, control body composition, promote flexibility, or develop strength and endurance needed in work-related settings.

FitnessGram/ActivityGram

Based on the extensive research of many people, FitnessGram was developed as a comprehensive assessment battery for students (Plowman & Meredith, 2013). In addition to the Brockport Physical Fitness Test (Winnick & Short, 2014), the manual offers guidelines for modifying FitnessGram test items or selecting alternative items, as needed, to meet assessment needs of students with disabilities. The manual also includes curricula specific for persons with disabilities whose fitness needs may not be met in mainstream settings, as well as safety and measurement guidelines. The updated fourth edition contains health-related test items that assess cardiorespiratory fitness, muscular strength and endurance, flexibility, and body composition. In this context, the components of health-related fitness are associated with criterion-referenced standards that are consistent with good health (Plowman & Meredith, 2013). In addition, FitnessGram provides a summation of individual performance on each segment of the test that can quantify the performance on physical activity measures. Teachers and parents can then use these data as guides for program planning and performance goals.

The Healthy Fitness Zone components were established from standards based on potential risks for health problems (Plowman & Meredith, 2013). Each fitness component was analyzed to determine standards that can be used as a criterion measure or potential indicator of health problems. Students in the Healthy Fitness Zone have a small risk for health problems. The Needs Improvement Zone demonstrates a high risk for problems and a need for intervention (see figure 7.14). The next level, Needs Improvement-Health Risk, reflects the potential for future health difficulties. Students in this intermediate zone can move into a healthy zone by reducing unhealthy behavior and increasing exercise.

Alternative items for measuring aerobic capacity include submaximal assessments for some persons with respiratory and heart-related disabilities. Swimming, hand cycling, propelling a wheelchair, and walking are recommended as alternative items for persons with limited mobility. Alternative body composition measures should take into consideration that certain disabilities may preclude taking skinfolds. In this case, body composition can be assessed on an individual basis, with the person becoming his own norm. Alternative ways to test muscular strength, endurance, and flexibility include any valid test item that is within the student's capabilities. For example, when testing persons with motor limitations, the teacher can eliminate timing limits on test items or allow more trials for each criterion. Because FitnessGram items are incorporated into the assessment facet of the Physical Best FitnessGram program, the assessment part of this package may not be useful for placement purposes. Generally, criteria for placement in a modified program require a specific score (e.g., two standard deviations below the mean) on a norm-referenced test.

Brockport Physical Fitness Test (BPFT)

The Brockport Physical Fitness Test (Winnick & Short, 2014) is a criterion-referenced test of health-related fitness for persons aged 10 to 17 with intellectual disabilities, cerebral palsy, spinal cord injury, and visual impairment, as well as for individuals without disabilities. Twenty-seven test items were drawn from FitnessGram to provide the tester flexibility in personalizing the test for various students (Winnick & Short, 2014). Healthy zone criteria are not provided, but developers recommend reducing the general standards by 10 percent for students with intellectual disabilities (Winnick & Short, 2014, p. 14). For individuals with varying levels and types of disability, it is extremely difficult to control variability in functioning. Use function tasks that are specific to everyday functioning for overall health and sports performance.

Functional Movement Screen (FMS)

The Functional Movement Screen (FMS) identifies limitations along with right- and left-side imbalances in basic levels of movement. Such imbalances can distort motor learning, movement perception, body awareness, and movement mechanics. Individuals learn to adapt their movement patterns and are every bit as efficient as they potentially could be if these imbalances were corrected.

FitnessGram Student Report

FITNESSGRAM®

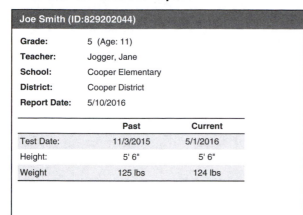

Joe Smith (ID:829202044)

Grade: 5 (Age: 11)
Teacher: Jogger, Jane
School: Cooper Elementary
District: Cooper District
Report Date: 5/10/2016

	Past	Current
Test Date:	11/3/2015	5/1/2016
Height:	5' 6"	5' 6"
Weight	125 lbs	124 lbs

Aerobic Capacity

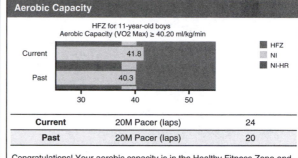

Current	20M Pacer (laps)	24
Past	20M Pacer (laps)	20

Congratulations! Your aerobic capacity is in the Healthy Fitness Zone and you are physically active most days. To maintain health and fitness, continue to participate in physical activities for at least 60 minutes each day. Keep your Body Mass Index (BMI) in the Healthy Fitness Zone.

Musculoskeletal Fitness

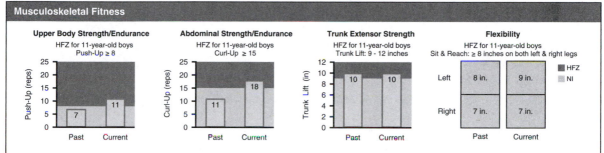

Your abdominal, trunk, and upper-body strength are all in the Healthy Fitness Zone. To maintain your fitness, be sure that your strength-training activities include exercises for all of these areas. Strength activities should be done at least 3 days per week.
In addition to aerobic and muscle-strengthening activities, it is important to perform stretching exercises to maintain or improve flexibility and some weight-bearing activity (e.g. running, hopping, jumping or dancing) to ensure good bone health at least 3 days per week.

Body Composition

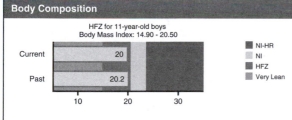

Good news! Your body composition is in the Healthy Fitness Zone. To maintain this healthy level of body composition, remember to:
-Be active for at least 60 minutes every day.
-Limit screen time to less than 2 hours a day.
-Make healthy food choices including fresh fruits and vegetables.
-Limit fried foods, foods with added sugars and sugary drinks.

Physical Activity

Reported Activity/Past 7 Days	Days	Goal
Aerobic activity for a total of 60 minutes or more	7	7
Muscle strengthening activity	3	3
Bone strengthening activity	2	3

To be healthy and fit, it is important to do some physical activity for a total of 60 minutes or more daily. Aerobic exercise is good for your heart and body composition. Muscular and bone-strengthening exercises are good for your muscles and joints.Congratulations! You are doing aerobic activity most or all days and muscular-strengthening exercises. Add some bone-strengthening exercises to improve your overall fitness.

HFZ: Healthy Fitness Zone; NI: Needs Improvement; NI-HR: Needs Improvement - Health Risk

Cooper Institute·
WELL. INTO THE FUTURE.

FitnessGram.net

A PROGRAM OF Play60 THE NFL MOVEMENT FOR AN ACTIVE GENERATION

Figure 7.14 Sample FitnessGram report.

Reprinted, by permission, from The Cooper Institute, 2017, *FitnessGram administration manual: The journey to MyHealthyZone,* 5th ed. (Champaign, IL: Human Kinetics).

The purpose of the screen is not to make a diagnosis but to identify limitations in an individual's movement patterns.

The FMS provides a seven-point screen to assess the total body. The seven basic movement patterns observed are as follows: (1) deep squat, (2) hurdle step, (3) in-line lunge, (4) shoulder mobility, (5) active straight-leg raise, (6) trunk stability push-up, and (7) rotary stability. Each individual is given three attempts to perform each movement pattern. The best of the three attempts is scored. If an individual performs the movement perfectly on the first attempt, then the tester should move on to the next test. A score is recorded for both the left and right sides of the body, and the lower of the two scores is counted toward the total. Descriptions and verbal instructions are provided in the FMS manual for each exercise.

The scores for the FMS range from 0 to 3. A score of 0 is given if at any time the individual experiences pain during testing. The tester should stop that particular portion of the screen and move to the next test. A score of 1 is given if the person is unable to complete the movement pattern or is unable to get into position to perform the movement. A score of 2 is given if the person is able to complete the movement pattern but compensates in some way to fully complete the movement. A score of 3 is given if the person performs the movement correctly without any compensation.

The FMS does require the use of certain equipment. A two-by-six-foot (0.6 m by 1.8 m) board is used to compensate for the deep squat. It is also used during the in-line lunge, active straight-leg raise, and rotary stability test for reliability. A five-foot (1.5 m) dowel is used for the deep squat, in-line lunge, hurdle step, and active straight-leg raise. The dowel increases reliability, improves scoring, and makes the test more functional. In the hurdle step, a hurdle allows for body-relative testing and improved scoring. A tape measure is needed to measure the distances in the shoulder mobility test and in-line lunge. All attachments to evaluate movements are provided along with the two-by-six-foot board.

Special Olympics Alaska Functional Performance Test (AFPT)

The Special Olympics Alaska Functional Performance Test (AFPT) was developed to quantify the performance of Special Olympics athletes in Alaska, with the goal of determining whether programming efforts were improving the performance, function, and overall health of the participants. Special Olympics Alaska has a facility that includes a full-size basketball court, a running track, and resistance training and cardiorespiratory training areas that are unique to this organization. Horvat, Roswal, Fallaize, and Croce developed the AFPT for active participants at the center. The reliability and validity were determined in Anchorage with 50 participants. Exercising and competing at the facility enhanced overall function in activities of daily living as well as increased performance for athletic competition. This approach is important for individuals with disabilities to not only increase their independence in daily living activities but also to be able to perform at a high level in Special Olympics competition.

Each of the tasks measures a specific component, and the tasks are taken from a variety of sources (table 7.2). It is important to determine whether the level of function is similar to what is needed in the student's everyday environment and how training will improve performance. The standards being developed are similar to the Healthy Fitness Zone espoused by FitnessGram.

CONCLUSION

An analysis of physical function and a subsequent needs analysis give teachers or members of the motor performance team (MPT) a profile of the participants' capabilities. If an individual is deficient in lower-extremity strength and it is affecting gait, the teacher or therapist can select specific strength exercises

Table 7.2 Components of Special Olympics Alaska Functional Performance Test

Assessment	Component	Origin	Function
Chair sit-and-reach	Flexibility Lower extremity strength	Senior Fitness Test (Rikli & Jones, 2013)	Putting on shoes, socks; picking something up from the floor
Standing functional reach	Flexibility Upper-body stability	Berg Balance Scale	Preventing falls, reaching beyond base of support (may be used from a sitting position)
Calf raise	Plantar flexor strength Stability	Analysis of movement when reaching overhead	Reaching overhead and maintaining stability
Seated medicine ball push	Upper-body strength	Reliability and validity from Harris et al., 2011	Pushing against an exterior force to generate strength/power
Plank test	Core strength	Reliability and validity from Strand et al., 2014	Maintaining stability and posture
Repeated chair stands	Lower-extremity strength	Short Physical Performance Battery	Maintaining strength and stability during repeated movements
Wall push-up	Upper-extremity strength	National Institutes of Health	Arm, shoulder, and chest strength and endurance
8-foot up and go	Agility Dynamic balance	Senior Fitness Test	Ability to rise, stabilize, ambulate, and return with balance
3-minute step test	Cardiorespiratory functioning HR recovery	YMCA Step Test	HR recovery at intervals after stepping for 3 minutes

and procedures to overcome the loss of functioning or lack of development. In case study 1, the intervention was to develop and increase strength and endurance required in a work environment. In contrast, in case study 2, Glenn was deficient on his left side, which compromised his balance and gait and was rectified with an intervention program based on test results. Identifying specific needs or components of functioning may be useful in determining strategies to overcome motor deficits or help restore overall functioning for individuals with disabilities.

What You Need to Know

Key Terms

1RM	health-related fitness
body composition	isometric strength
body mass index	motor performance
cardiorespiratory endurance	muscular strength
dynamic strength	muscular endurance
flexibility	physical fitness
functional fitness	power

Key Concepts

1. You should be able to differentiate between tests for physical fitness and functional capacity that are adaptable for students with disabilities. If specific tests are not available, what assessments would be appropriate?
2. You should be able to describe the effects of a disability on physical function; likewise, you should be able to determine whether decreased functioning is due to inactivity or overprotection.
3. You should be familiar with field-based assessments and current technology as well as special considerations for testing individuals with disabilities.
4. You should be able to use physical function as a basis for developing an intervention plan or conditioning program.

Review Questions

1. What factors characterize the development of muscular strength, muscular endurance, and aerobic functioning in students? How would a disability affect this development?
2. You are preparing some Special Olympics athletes for competition in throwing and running events. What assessments would you use to develop and monitor their training programs?
3. A six-year-old student has some difficulty with standing from a sitting

position, descending stairs, and rising from the floor. What components of physical function would you assess to develop your program plan?

4. How does body composition affect movement parameters in students with Down syndrome? With visual impairments? With spina bifida? With a high percentage of body fat?

5. For students with disabilities to exert a maximal effort during testing, what motivational or prompting strategies would you use?

6. Why is core strength important, and how does it affect performance?

7. How would body weight fit into developing a physical education program?

8. Why is it important for students to be able to perform body-weight activities?

Chapter **8**

Assessing Posture, Gait, and Balance

As individuals mature in the developmental process, they develop the ability to move within the environment. After learning to crawl and creep, children develop balance and stability capabilities as well as the ability to stand and then walk. Several factors that are specific to movement—and to any dysfunction within its physical development—should be included in the assessment process.

This chapter addresses the basic components of posture, gait, balance, and stability as they relate to movement development. It identifies movement problems that require assessment, reviews specific tests, and discusses the transition from developing balance and stability to standing. The ability to maintain static and dynamic movements (balance) is analyzed, as well as the ability to recover and return to the initial or neutral position after perturbations or movement.

POSTURE

Knowledge of appropriate posture and of structural deviations that affect standing is essential for understanding movement problems and control over the center of gravity. For many persons with disabilities, posture and gait abnormalities are the direct result of their condition or deterioration in balance and **stability**. It is essential to identify specific posture or gait abnormalities before selecting an intervention program. For students with developmental disabilities, these problems become apparent early in motor development during walking, while climbing stairs, or in movement patterns.

Posture can be defined as the manner in which the body aligns itself against gravity. It is influenced by the skeletal system, ligaments, muscles, fatigue, and self-concept. Correct posture is achieved when all segments of the body are properly aligned over a base of support, with minimum stress applied to each joint. Positions that compromise the body's base of support and increase stress on joints precipitate faulty posture (Magee, 2015).

Without proper maintenance of postural muscles and the use of corrective techniques, postural deficiencies may deteriorate, possibly becoming debilitating, and either interfering with physical performance capabilities or becoming a structural deviation. Some functional causes of faulty posture include lack of muscular development, muscular imbalance, muscle contracture, pain, obesity, muscle spasms, respiratory disorders, and loss of sensory input or proprioception.

Posture encompasses more than maintaining a static position, since movement requires the body to constantly assume and change positions. As such, **postural control** involves achieving, maintaining, or restoring a state of balance during any static posture or dynamic activity. Muscles that have sufficient strength and joints that are flexible will accommodate changes in position and adapt readily to movement stresses. For the dysfunctional muscle, the ability to maintain an upright position may be affected by muscle weakness and the body's inability to accommodate stress (Magee, 2015).

The sitting position of back against the seat, feet on the floor, and thighs and back supported by the seat permits people to maintain a relaxed position while the chair provides body support. Additionally, arm rests positioned at elbow height support the arms and relax the postural muscles. Faulty sitting posture results in improper body alignment, slumping of the back and shoulders, and concentration of the majority of weight on one side of the body. Nonambulatory persons are especially susceptible to sitting postural faults and may develop complications such as pressure sores, scoliosis, and respiratory dysfunctions. The overall lack of muscular development and stability restricts appropriate physical development and, in turn, stresses joints that maintain the proper sitting posture needed to perform functional daily living tasks.

Standing posture is characterized by an erect position with an elevated head and chest, posterior-tilted pelvis, slightly curved abdomen and lower back, slightly flexed knees, and parallel feet spaced a comfortable distance apart to allow for an even weight distribution. When observing an individual from the side, a plumb line should run

1. through the ear lobe and acromion process of the shoulder;
2. through the chest, bisecting it symmetrically;
3. midway between the abdomen and back and slightly anterior to the sacrum;
4. slightly posterior to the hip joint and through the greater trochanter of the femur; and
5. slightly anterior to the knee and slightly anterior to the lateral malleolus (used as point representing the upper ankle joint).

Orthopedic impairments may apply inappropriate stress on the muscles and joints as well as affect standing posture if proper alignment or structural components are altered. If muscle development is not promoted via an intervention, the person may demonstrate posture problems including slumped shoulders, a head tilt, a protruding abdomen, spinal deviations or curves, and improper foot placement (table 8.1). The lack of feedback in sensory disorders often affects a person's ability to maintain an appropriate postural alignment.

Individual Differences in Posture

Individual differences in posture are associated with motor development, body type, and disability. Infants and students in the primary grades may exhibit a wide base of support, slightly bowed legs, and a slightly protruding abdomen, all of which are typical until sufficient strength is developed. A curvature of the spine at this developmental age does not necessarily constitute a postural defect. However, the same occurrence in adults would indicate a marked deficit or muscle weakness that may require corrective measures.

Persons with specific body types and builds are also apt to assume various postures. For example, **body types** may be classified as mesomorphic (muscular), endomorphic (round), or ectomorphic (slender), or any combination of the three. The upper torso may be predominantly classified as one body type, while the lower extremities may characterize another specific body type. The mix of body-type classifications may lead to improper posture development (e.g., a muscular chest and back coupled with a slender abdomen and lower limbs may appear as a rounded upper back). Likewise, disabilities such as spinal injuries or amputations affect the amount of available muscle mass or alter body mechanics, often leading to faulty postures.

Causes of Postural Deviations

There is no single cause of posture deficits. Postural deviations can be either functional or structural. A functional condition may be overcome through corrective exercises or kinesthetic awareness training of proper positions. **Structural deviations** occur because of abnormalities or deformities of the skeletal system resulting from disease or injury. Common structural deviations include leg-length differences, spinal anomalies, **scoliosis**, **kyphosis**, and **lordosis**. Because of the severity of structural defects, most are treated by doctors with a combination of braces, casts, surgery, and prosthetic devices. The assessment of posture and subsequent instructional programming should

Table 8.1   Common Posture Problems

Good posture	Body segment	Poor posture
Head in balance Erect head position	Head	Chin out Head tilted or rotated to side
Arms at sides, palms facing the body Shoulders level and symmetrical Scapulae flat against the rib cage	Upper back	Stiff arms, palms rotated Shoulders rounded or one shoulder higher Scapulae pulled back or far apart; scapulae prominent, standing out from the rib cage ("winged scapulae")
Trunk erect Back in good alignment	Trunk	Depressed "hollow chest" position Ribs more prominent on one side Lower ribs protruding Trunk inclined to rear
Abdomen flat	Abdomen	Abdomen protrudes or sags
Pelvis and thighs in a straight line Normal curve (neck and lower back: forward curve; upper back and spine: backward curve)	Lower back	Lordosis, or forward curvature of the lumbar spine Pelvis tilts forward Kyphosis, or rounded upper back Increased forward curve in neck, rounded upper back, and forward head Scoliosis, or lateral curve of the spine (one side: C curve; both sides: S curve)
Hips level Spine straight	Hips	One hip higher (lateral pelvic tilt) Hips rotated forward, spine slightly or markedly curved
Legs straight	Knees and legs	Knees touch when feet apart (genu valgum) Knees apart when feet touch (genu varum) Knees curve actively backward Knees bend forward Patellae face slightly inward or outward
Standing, feet straight ahead Walking, feet parallel Running, feet parallel or toeing-in	Feet	Low arch ("flat-footed") Weight on the inner side of the foot (pronation) Weight on the outer side of the foot (supination) Toeing-out Toeing-in ("pigeon-toed")

be interrelated to avoid potential problems and minimize effects of faulty posture on physical functioning.

Specific disabilities may cause a lack of proper feedback among persons with sensory impairments; fatigue among individuals who use a wheelchair; and additional complications in walking postures, such as when shifting weight or regaining balance, for persons with a prosthetic device. As a group, persons with disabilities have a greater incidence of postural defects than do the general population because muscular function and sensory feedback are essential for appropriate posture (Horvat, Kalakian, Croce, & Dahlstrom, 2011). For example, lack of sensory information may contribute to poor posture or head tilts since the available sensory feedback is not used to maintain or reinforce appropriate posture. A person with an amputation, spinal injury, or neurological disorder may place undue pressure on his postural base while sitting and may require balance changes to reestablish the center of gravity that was altered by injury or disability. Sitting upright is essential for performing functional skills, and upright posture relies on the trunk muscles for spinal stability. A deviation such as kyphosis compromises achieving the upright sitting position. Likewise, insufficient strength in the trunk muscles— often seen in persons with muscular dystrophy, spinal deviations, lower-back problems, and mechanical movement inefficiencies—may affect the ability to maintain upright posture.

Muscle tone and strength associated with posture affect posture maintenance against gravity and coordination (Cech & Martin, 2012). Normal movements such as walking and running are supported by accompanying changes in posture and movement. In contrast, abnormal tone does not utilize the automatic adjustments in posture and movement needed for the tasks of walking and running. This effect can be seen in persons with cerebral palsy, where **spasticity**, or increased muscle tone, produces varying distributions and degrees of strength that interfere with purposeful movement.

The spastic muscle may provide excessive resistance or complicate the ability to move in response to changes in posture. These complications make it essential to observe changes in tone and movement response and relate them to changes in posture. For example, leaning to one side is normally associated with the contraction of the head and neck muscles on the other side. If the normal adaptation to this change in position is disrupted (i.e., the postural reaction mechanism is absent), the result may be a fall. In normal postures, adjustments are made as corresponding muscles adapt to specific movements. In abnormal postures, adjustment is not apparent. In addition, resistance may be encountered in some body segments such as the elbow, shoulder, hip, knee, or ankle. The inability to correctly sequence the contraction and relaxation of reciprocal muscle groups impedes the ability to lift and adjust to the load. The restricting of the hips and knees limits step length and postural control, causing individuals to shorten their steps and control at the hips.

These findings are noteworthy because the ability to maintain a postural position dramatically affects the level of functional ability. Since the trunk muscles are essential for postural control in a seated position, strengthening these muscles and maintaining an appropriate position will allow functional capabilities, such as pulmonary function and position changes, to fulfill daily living needs.

Standing posture can also be affected by lower-extremity strength. For older people and those with disabilities, postural adjustments are compromised by a lack of muscular strength, which may result in falls (Shumway-Cook & Woollacott, 2001). To facilitate adequate stability and posture, physical activity should be encouraged to eliminate patterns of inactivity that may contribute to reduced physical functioning and poor postural stability.

POSTURAL ASSESSMENTS

In most cases, standing posture is assessed by means of a plumb line. Johnson (2012) provides a postural assessment guide for lateral, anterior, and posterior alignments that are benchmarks for assessing posture. See figure 8.1 for in-depth descriptions of standard alignment for comparison purposes.

These postural assessments can detect conditions that can interfere with performing activities of daily living or work-related skills (e.g., deviations of the spine or a weak lower back). They also appear in concussion protocols (see Balance Error Scoring System). Problems that result from structural, sensory, mechanical, or neurological dysfunctions may inhibit the ability to perform functional tasks. For example, upright and walking posture, with or without a prosthetic device, may be distorted after an amputation because of shifts in body weight, loss of balance, or loss of sensory feedback. Structurally, if the base of support and center of gravity are altered, movement and postural adjustment may be required to maintain an appropriate gait or sit upright in a wheelchair. Likewise, in recent spinal injuries, loss of function and subsequent time needed for various muscles to assume functions of nonwalking muscle groups contribute to difficulties in maintaining a sitting posture.

In addition, loss of sensory function may contribute to postural tilts or lead to inadequate sensory feedback. In acquired injuries, sensory function and motor memory may not be available to assume a posture or perform a specific movement. Likewise, in incomplete spinal injuries and hemiplegia, the maintenance of dysfunctional motor patterns and muscle weakness may result from sensory deficits (Cech & Martin, 2012). A resultant loss of posture may be directly related to the lack of sensory information that controls foot placement, tripping, or dragging the feet for individuals with hearing loss (Horvat, Kalakian, Croce, & Dahlstrom, 2011). In other situations, individuals may not be able to recognize or locate sensory information, such as touch or pressure, from slight to complete **agnosia**. Without appropriate feedback, the movement feels awkward or distorted, and the individual encounters difficulty maintaining stability and control.

GAIT

Developmentally, posture and balance are the parameters that affect transition from standing to movements such as walking and running. Although posture may be adequate for a person to stand, it may vary undesirably in walking or running if the person does not have adequate maturity, balance, or strength to maintain an upright posture during these activities. Forces that are generated from running may stress the postural system's ability to maintain an upright position. Since running and stair climbing use the same pattern of intralimb coordination as creeping and walking, maintaining postures during these movements requires an increase in force production that commonly presents difficulties for young children and persons with disabilities.

Because of poor development and postural instability, students with disabilities have difficulty making transitions between basic locomotor patterns and dealing with the increase in force production. The transition from being nonambulatory to moving requires adequate balance and stability before the

Standard Posterior Alignment

Head

Plumb Line
Through midline of the skull

General Observations
The head should be facing forwards with no rotation and no lateral flexion.

Shoulders

Plumb Line
Equidistant between the medial borders of the scapulae

General Observations
The height of the shoulders should be approximately level. However, the shoulder of the dominant hand may be lower than the shoulder of the non-dominant hand.

Pelvis and thigh

Plumb Line
Through the midline of the pelvis

General Observations
•The posterior superior iliac spines (PSIS) should be equidistant from the spine and be level.
•The greater trochanters of the femurs should be level.
•The buttock creases should be level and equal.

Knees and legs

Plumb Line
Between the knees

General Observations
•The legs should be straight and equidistant from the plumb line with no genu varum or genu valgum.
•Calf bulk should be equal on the left and right legs.

Neck

Plumb Line
Through midline of all cervical vertebrae

General Observations
The neck should appear straight with no lateral flexion.

Upper limbs

General Observations
•The arms should hang equidistant from the trunk, palms facing the sides of the body.
•The elbows should be level.
•The wrists should be level.

Thorax and scapulae

Plumb Line
Through midline of all thoracic vertebrae

General Observations
•The scapulae should be equidistant from the spine, the medial borders of each approximately 1.5 to 2 inches (3.8 to 5 cm) from the spine. The scapulae should lie flat against the rib cage with no anterior tilting.
•The inferior angles of the scapulae should be level, with no evidence of elevation, depression, or scapular rotation.
•Flare in the rib cage should be symmetrical left and right.

Lumbar spine

Plumb Line
Through midline of all lumbar vertebrae

General Observations
The lumbar spine should be straight with no curvature to the right or left.

Ankle and feet

Plumb Line
Between the medial malleoli

General Observations
•The lateral malleoli should be level.
•The medial malleoli should be level.
•The Achilles tendon should be vertical.
•The calcaneus should be vertical.
•The feet should be turned out slightly.

Figure 8.1 Standard posterior, lateral, and anterior alignments outline where a plumb line (shown as the vertical black line in the illustrations) should fall with respect to various parts of the body and provide general observations for when postures are said to be good, or ideal.

(continued)

Head

Plumb Line
Through the earlobe

General Observations
The head should appear positioned over the thorax—neither pushed forwards with chin out nor pulled back.

Shoulders

Plumb Line
Through the shoulder joint: specifically, through the acromion process (not shown on this illustration)

General Observations
The shoulders should be neither internally nor (in rare cases) externally rotated.

Lumbar spine

Plumb Line
Through the bodies of the lumbar vertebrae

General Observations
The lumbar spine should have a normal lordotic curve that is neither exaggerated nor flattened.

Knees and legs

Plumb Line
Slightly anterior to the knee joint

General Observations
There should be neither flexion nor hyperextension at this joint in standing.

Neck

Plumb Line
Through the bodies of most of the cervical vertebrae

General Observations
- The cervical spine should have a normal lordotic curve that is neither exaggerated nor flattened.
- There should be no deformity at the cervicothoracic junction such as a dowager's hump.

Thorax and scapulae

Plumb Line
Midway through the trunk

General Observations
- There should be a normal kyphotic curve in this region that is neither exaggerated nor flattened.
- The chest should be held comfortably upright and not excessively elevated (military posture) nor depressed.

Pelvis and thigh

Plumb Line
Through the greater trochanter of the femur

General Observations
- The pelvis should be in a neutral position. That means the anterior superior iliac spine (ASIS) is in the same vertical plane as the pubis.
- The ASIS and the PSIS should be approximately in the same plane. There should be no anterior or posterior pelvic tilt.
- Gluteal and thigh muscle bulk should appear equal on both the left and right sides.

Ankle and feet

Plumb Line
Slightly anterior to the lateral malleolus

General Observations
There should be normal dorsiflexion at the ankle.

It is important to remember that although the plumb line in the lateral view should run vertically through the earlobe and bodies of most cervical vertebrae, when being set up for use as a marker, it is positioned slightly anterior to the lateral malleolus and not against the earlobe, cervical vertebrae, acromion or other structures listed here. Remember, this is an ideal posture, showing where, ideally, the plumb line ought to bisect the body in such a way that equal portions of the body appear anterior and posterior of the plumb line.

Figure 8.1 *(continued)*

Standard Anterior Alignment

Head

Plumb Line
Through the center of the face: through the forehead, nose and chin

General Observations
The head should be facing forwards with no rotation and no lateral flexion.

Shoulders

Plumb Line
Through the manubrium, sternum and xyphoid process

General Observations
•The shoulders should be approximately level.
•The clavicles should be level.

Lumbar spine

Plumb Line
Through the umbilicus (navel)

General Observations
The umbilicus should be central, not deviated to the left or right.

Pelvis

Plumb Line
•Bisecting the pelvis
•Through the pubic symphysis

General Observations
•The ASIS should be level.
•The ASIS should be equidistant from midline.

Thighs

Plumb Line
Equidistant between thighs

General Observations
•The femurs should be straight and with no internal or external rotation.
•Thigh bulk should be equal on left and right sides.

Knees and legs

Plumb Line
•Between the medial femoral condyles of the knees
•Equidistant between the legs

General Observations
•Knees should be level.
•The patellae should face forwards and be level.
•The tibia should be straight and leg bulk should be equal on the left and right legs.

Ankle and feet

Plumb Line
Between the medial malleoli

General Observations
•Medial malleoli should be level.
•Feet should turn out from the midline.

Figure 8.1 *(continued)*

Case Study 1
Insufficient Back Flexibility

A postural screening shows that Kimberly has lumbar lordosis. She also has a tendency to slouch. Her parents have contacted the physical education teacher about possible problems and recommendations for intervention.

It is important to assess factors from the screening that may be causing Kimberly's problems. First, the teacher should determine whether Kimberly has insufficient flexibility in the back and hamstrings, which may contribute to her lordosis. She may also have a muscle imbalance, contraction, or weakness resulting from another condition. Likewise, the teacher should evaluate Kimberly's abdominal strength to look at opposing muscle groups that may exacerbate her lordosis. Her slouching may result from being taller than her peers, a growth spurt, onset of puberty, or muscle weakness. Depending on his assessment, the teacher can begin to remediate specific problems by developing a program based on the student's needs. In this case, standard alignments espoused by Johnson (2012) provide observational data from standard posterior alignment, standard lateral alignment, and standard anterior alignment. These standard alignments can be used as benchmarks to assess posture and determine how to remediate Kimberly's problem by developing a program she can perform in class, at home, or in a clinical setting with a therapist.

coordinative pattern of walking becomes apparent (Horvat, Kalakian, Croce, & Dahlstrom, 2011). A student who has difficulty developing these patterns has difficulty rotating or adjusting to changes in the environment, such as variations in terrain. If the individual does not develop a combination of strength and stability, she will not achieve independent walking or movement. Disorders that affect the ability to coordinate movement patterns, such as cerebral palsy, change basic movements. For example, the normal order of hip movements in walking is **flexion, abduction**, and **external rotation**. In students with spastic cerebral palsy, movements are flexion, **adduction**, and **internal rotation** (Sugden & Keogh, 1990).

Movement difficulties may result from some underlying neurological or muscular component that should be assessed to adequately portray the person's developmental needs. The observation that a student cannot run should be more thoroughly investigated to determine the specific components that may be interfering with or delaying development of the appropriate movement pattern. Likewise, if a student has difficulty ascending or descending stairs, a characteristic of muscular dystrophy, gait and underlying components such as strength and balance should be assessed to preserve function. Likewise an athlete recovering from a concussion should be observed to determine when he can be medically released to resume physical activity and active participation.

GAIT ASSESSMENTS

In clinical settings, a variety of gait-analysis techniques can be used to evaluate muscle functions and correlate them with gait. Most comprehensive gait assessments are conducted with electromyographs for muscle function and with force plates to record forces and torques on body segments. Although this information is beneficial, most field-based assessments rely on observational data and videotapes of gaits to detect abnormalities. These latter techniques should be sufficient for the teacher to detect problem areas in strength and posture that affect ambulation and development patterns. More important, the information generated can be incorporated in the program or instructional plan.

Functional gait patterns are observed extensively in clinical settings. Observational assessments such as those used at the Los Amigos Research and Education Institute (LAREI, 2001) direct attention to a specific body segment at a point during a **gait cycle**. For example, the tester may observe heel strike at that specific point in the cycle to determine whether normal or abnormal movements are occurring during walking.

Scoring may vary from a system of present, inconsistent, borderline, occurs throughout, absent, limited, or exaggerated gait deviations to the Rancho Los Amigos system of assessing movements of body segments in the gait cycle: ankle, foot, knee, hip, pelvis, and trunk (LAREI, 2001). The Rancho Los Amigos assessment consists of a full-body gait analysis through weight acceptance (WA), single-leg support (SLS), and single-leg advancement (SLA). This assessment, developed by Dr. Jacquelin Perry at Rancho Los Amigos National Rehabilitation Center, is the foremost instrument for observational gait analysis.

For the teacher, observation of the movement pattern is the most useful and functional way to detect gait abnormalities and conduct a gait analysis in a field-based instructional or recreational setting. It is recommended that the tester become familiar with normal gait, normal gait terminology, the normal gait cycle, and abnormal gait before applying the analysis to detect gait abnormalities.

Because observational gait analysis is subjective and requires quick decisions, the subject's patterns should be recorded on video to provide a complete analysis of the process. Recording the procedure also helps determine reliability within the observational assessment by analyzing and comparing the movement.

Normal Gait and Gait Terminology

To adequately assess deviations in gait patterns, an understanding of gait terminology (table 8.2) and the normal pattern is necessary (Magee, 2015). Developmentally, changes in gait patterns are achieved as early as two years for an advanced pattern. Pelvic rotation is usually evident at 13.8 months, knee flexion at midsupport at 16.3 months, base of support at 17 months, and heel and forefoot strike at 18.5 months (Payne & Isaacs, 2016).

Table 8.2   Gait Terminology

Term	Description
Gait cycle	Time interval or sequence of motions between two contacts of the same foot
Stride	One complete gait cycle
Step	Beginning of sequence by one limb until beginning of sequence with the contralateral limb
Stance phase	Foot is on the ground bearing weight, allowing lower leg to support body and advancement of the body over the supporting limb; makes up 60% of gait cycle and consists of 5 subphases: 1. Initial contact (heel strike) 2. Loading response (foot flat) 3. Midstance (single-leg stance) 4. Terminal stance (heel-off) 5. Preswing (toe-off)
Swing phase	Foot is moving forward and not bearing weight, allowing toes to clear floor and adjusting the leg as well as advancing the swing leg forward; makes up 40% of gait cycle and consists of 3 subphases: 1. Initial swing (acceleration) 2. Midswing 3. Terminal swing (deceleration)
Double-leg stance	Phase when parts of both feet are on the ground, making up 25% of gait cycle
Single-leg stance	Phase when one leg is on the ground, occurring twice during gait cycle and making up approximately 30% of gait cycle
Base width	Distance between opposite feet (usually 2 to 4 in. [5 to 10 cm]); varies with poor balance, loss of sensation and proprioception
Step length	Distance between successive contact points in opposite feet; varies with age, height, fatigue, pain, and disease
Stride length	Linear distance between successive points of contact of the same foot (gait cycle); approximately 28 to 31 in. (71 to 79 cm)
Pelvic shift	Side to side (lateral) movement of pelvis necessary to align weight over stance leg
Pelvic rotation	Rotation of pelvis to lessen angle of femur with the floor to help regulate subject's walking speed and decrease center of gravity
Cadence	Number of steps per minute from heel strike to toe-off; approximately 90 to 120 per minute

Normal Gait Cycle

A normal gait cycle is made up of the swing and stance (LAREI, 2001; Perry & Burnfield, 2010). In the **swing phase**, the initial swing is the first subphase. Flexion of the hip and knee allow for initial acceleration and stabilization of the trunk in single support. The ankles will plantar flex, while the dorsiflexors help the foot clear the supporting surface. At midswing the hip continues to flex and medially rotate while the knee flexes. The body is aligned with the pelvis and trunk. Maximum knee flexion is evident as the leg moves forward, ending the acceleration phase and beginning deceleration. The terminal swing is the last phase as the leg decelerates in preparation for a heel strike. Hip flexion and rotation continue while the knee is fully extended. The trunk and pelvis maintain the support position, and the ankle is dorsiflexed and the forefoot supinated before heel strike. The hamstrings are also contracting to aid in the deceleration.

The **stance phase** begins with initial contact, or heel strike. Hip flexion is 30 degrees, with the knees slightly flexed and the ankle in a neutral position. The pelvis is level, and the heel contacts the supporting surface. In the loading response as the sole of the foot contacts the floor, the weight is transferred to the limbs. The foot is pronated to adapt to various surfaces and contacts the floor while the ankle is plantar flexed approximately 15 degrees. Hips are flexed and laterally rotate while the knee flexes approximately 15 degrees. Trunk alignment is in a neutral position with the stance leg, while the pelvis drops slightly and rotates medially on the swing leg.

The midstance phase begins when the contralateral limb leaves the ground and ends when the body is directly over the supporting limb, aligning the body over the trunk and pelvis with a neutral rotation. The hip assumes the greatest force with extension to a neutral position. The knee also flexes, and the ankle goes from plantar flexion to 10-degree dorsiflexion; the forefoot is pronated and the hindfoot inverted.

The terminal stance (heel-off) is from the midstance to point of contact with the contralateral extremity. The trunk is erect, and the hip moves from lateral to medial rotation. The knee is extended, and the ankle is in plantar flexion (with heel-off) before contact of the opposite foot. In the preswing phase, the initial contact of the contralateral extremity is before the toe-off of the reference extremity. The pelvis is level and laterally rotated, and the trunk is aligned over the lower extremities. The knee is flexed 35 degrees, and plantar flexion of the ankle is approximately 20 degrees to toe-off.

Overall the stance phase constitutes about 60 percent of the gait cycle and the swing phase about 40 percent at a normal walking speed. Two periods of double support (when both feet are in contact with the ground) overlap the stance phase for about 22 percent of the gait cycle at a normal walking speed. Any increases or decreases in walking speed will alter the percentages of time in each phase. Finally, one observes only a slight vertical displacement of the body during gait and only a slight lateral pelvic tilt or drop in the frontal plan, leading to minimal upward and sideward displacements and maximum efficiency.

Gait can also be analyzed in terms of flexion and extension phases. The flexion phase is initiated as the foot lifts off the ground and continues as the limb swings forward. This is followed by the first phase of limb extension, when the limb is extended until the foot contacts the ground. The yield phase occurs as the foot contacts the ground and supports the body. During this phase, there is a slight give as the limb absorbs ground reaction forces. Finally, the propulsive phase is enacted as the limb extends and propels the body forward.

Muscle weakness can affect the efficiency of any of these phases. For example, weakness or paralysis of the hip abductor muscles will lead to an inability to maintain a level pelvis and a hip drop during single-leg stance. With weakness or paralysis of the ankle plantar flexor muscles, the individual cannot push off during gait. This will result in a calcaneal, or heel, gait, whereby the individual lands with a stiff, dorsiflexed ankle in order to compensate for the inability to plantar flex during push-off.

Abnormal Gait

To accurately assess difficulties with gait and the accompanying movement problems, it is necessary to observe improper elements of gait to determine specific causes and dysfunctions. Table 8.3 includes several examples of gait abnormalities commonly seen in school and clinical settings (Magee, 2015; Perry & Burnfield, 2010). Although this is not a complete list of gait abnormalities, these examples should be helpful in formulating information needed to understand movement problems and develop an instructional program.

Detecting Gait Abnormalities

Gait is assessed by observing the specific joint or body segments during the gait cycle. Table 8.4, which uses information from table 8.2 (Gait Terminology) and table 8.3 (Common Gait Abnormalities), is a sample gait analysis using a screening instrument developed at the Pediatric Exercise and Motor Development Clinic at the University of Georgia. For the teacher, a simple method to screen potential problem areas is to observe the student's gait at all body segments and note any problems in each phase of the cycle.

The Rancho Los Amigos Observational Gait Analysis, a more formalized assessment, is shown in figure 8.2. This analysis helps identify significant deviations during the gait cycle that can be used to develop an intervention program. For example, after using the gait assessment in figure 8.2, a teacher can detect deviations that can be addressed to meet specific instructional needs.

Specific posture limitations and accompanying gait problems should be documented, and the relevant characteristics that contribute to the movement problem should be determined. The resulting program planning should specifically address the problem (i.e., balance or strength deficiency) and incorporate it into the program plan. Follow-up assessment and observation can then be utilized to document the effectiveness of the intervention or teaching program.

BALANCE

Balance is an essential component of movement efficiency and is included in many motor ability, development, and perceptual tests. For example, balance is measured in all the listed texts of motor development as well as the BOT-2 and MABC-2. Some form of balance is required for perceptual motor functioning.

Balance is a vital component of all sports and movement skills, especially functional tasks such as standing, walking upstairs, and lifting objects. In this context, teachers should utilize balance assessments in conjunction with other measures to determine whether the underlying component is affecting

Table 8.3   Common Gait Abnormalities

Gait abnormality	Phase	Possible cause	Characteristics	Assessment
Ataxic	Initial contact	Cerebellum; ataxia and lack of motor control; weakness of dorsiflexor; lack of lower-limb proprioception	Poor balance; broad base; exaggerated stagger to movements; foot slap; watches feet while walking; irregular, jerky gait	**Static balance**; Romberg test for standing posture; foot placement when walking line or beam
Gluteus medius (Trendelenburg gait)	Stance	Weakness of gluteus medius	Excessive lateral lean over hip to compensate for muscle weakness; bilateral weakness resulting in waddling gait	Evaluate muscle strength or pain in hip
Gluteus maximus	Stance	Weakness of gluteus maximus	Lurching or leaning trunk posteriorly; hyperextension at hip	Evaluate muscle strength and pelvic position
Hemiplegic gait	Swing	Weak hip flexors; lack of motor control	**Circumduction** or lateral movement of entire lower extremity, with adduction and internal rotation; affected upper limb may be carried across trunk for stability	Assess strength of hip flexors and extensors; range of motion in hip, knee flexion; and ankle dorsiflexion
Scissors gait	Swing	Spasticity	Lack of motor control of hip adductor causes knees to move to midline; legs are moved forward by swinging hips	Assess foot placement and control of swinging leg
Foot drop or toe drag	Swing	Weakness of dorsiflexor and toe extensor; spasticity in plantar flexors; lack of hip or knee flexion	Weak dorsiflexion of foot does not allow toes to clear the surface; loss of control of dorsiflexors causes higher knee lift to compensate for toe drops, resulting in foot slap	Assess strength and range of motion in ankle, hip, and knee
Circumduction	Swing	Weak hip flexors; spasticity	Lateral movement of affected leg to move leg forward; consists of abduction, external rotation, adduction, and internal rotation	Assess range of motion and strength of hip and knee flexors, ankle dorsiflexors

Table 8.4   Example of Observational Analysis of Gait

Body segment	Observation	Direction	Phase	Body side	Comments
Trunk	Rotation, circumduction	Lateral movement	Swing	Right	Arm adduction and flexion at elbow and wrist, forearm rotated medially
Pelvis	Rotation, circumduction	Lateral movement	Swing	Right	
Hip	Rotation, circumduction	Adduction	Swing	Right	Leg swings outward in a circle (circumduction)
Knee	Reduced flexion	Adduction	Swing	Right	
Ankle	Ankle dorsiflexion	Adduction	Swing	Right	
Feet	Toe drag	Adduction	Swing	Right	Inadequate hip flexion

Cause and remediation: neurological dysfunction; assess range of motion and strength in lower extremities.

Case Study 2
Poor Motor Function

Evan is six years old and is starting kindergarten. His gait appears unstable, and he often falls during activity. After observing him on the playground, the teacher notices his step length is very short while his step width is broad, with the feet toeing-out and arms held out at the side for balance.

By six to seven years of age, gait characteristics should be close to the mature adult pattern. Walking velocity and step length should both increase, and stability should be sufficient to support the body. Muscle structure and activation should also be appropriate for a mature gait pattern and should be assessed. If Evan has no diagnosis, an assessment of his balance and visual acuity or neurological function should be completed to see if they affect his gait.

the task performance, as illustrated in case study 3. For example, balance is multifaceted and not dependent on one factor. Several components of the sensory system affect balance, including the auditory, visual, vestibular, and somatosensory systems. The eyes, ears, vestibular apparatus of the inner ear, and muscle spindles all provide information that is transmitted via afferent nerve fibers and spinal tracts for analysis so that movement can be initiated and controlled (Shumway-Cook & Wollacott, 2001).

Vision provides information on head movement and keeps us aware of our body position and relationship to the environment. The visual system works concurrently with the vestibular system to analyze velocity and rotation and provide a reference for postural control (Shumway-Cook & Wollacott, 2001). If vision is restricted, compensations and adjustments can be made from

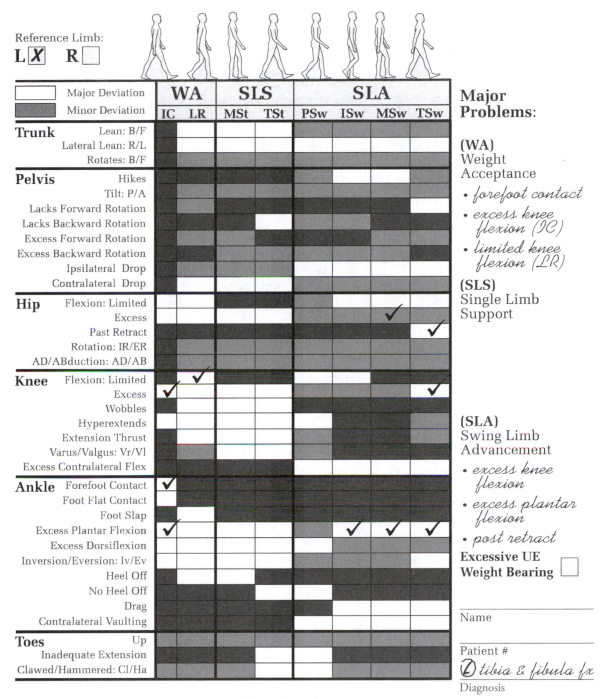

Figure 8.2 Rancho Los Amigos Observational Gait Analysis.

Adapted, by permission, from The Pathokinesiology Service and the Physical Therapy Department, *Observational gait analysis handbook,* Los Amigos Research and Education Institute, Inc., Ranchos Los Amigos National Rehabilitation Center, Downey, CA, 2001, page 56.

other sensory modalities to maintain stability. Vestibular input is used for movement and stabilization of the head during gait patterns. In conjunction with the visual system, the vestibular system stabilizes the eyes and maintains posture. Vestibular problems contribute to a loss of balance and affect the

Case Study 3
Lack of Balance and Coordination

Christa, a seven-year-old girl with Down syndrome, is experiencing difficulty walking up and down stairs and coordinating her movement. The second grader is clumsy and often trips and falls during play activities. She has difficulty maintaining her posture and often cannot recover when she exceeds her base of support. Both her vision and hearing screening are within acceptable limits, yet her movement continues to be disordered.

Christa's teacher knows that balance is multifaceted, and he wants to determine which components may be affecting her balance. For example, the teacher has already determined that Christa's lower-extremity strength is deficient in the quadriceps and plantar flexors. He's hoping a strength program targeting these muscles will help Christa, but he wants to gather some additional information on balance.

ability of the nervous system to mediate contradicting sensory information (Shumway-Cook & Wollacott, 2001).

Proprioceptive and tactile input also provide critical somatosensory feedback regarding body sway, position in space, and environmental shifts or surface changes. We use a combination of tactile and proprioceptive information to continually adjust to postural changes and maintain stability. For some students, balance or stability may be affected by a developmental disorder or loss of sensory function. Neurological or neuromuscular function may be compromised in older students. In many ways, balance disorders in students parallel the loss of function seen with aging, strokes, head injuries, and Parkinson's disease (Caciula, Horvat, Tomporowski, & Nocera, 2016). This is especially evident in a study by Biggan, Melton, Horvat, Richard, Keller, and Ray (2014), who reported that older individuals approach frailty from deficits in vision more so than chronological age.

BALANCE ASSESSMENTS

With this in mind, many of the tests discussed in this chapter have components of balance, stability, posture, and gait. Table 8.5 gives several examples of balance tests that can be used in physical education as general screening for movement difficulties, discrepancies in body symmetry, or problems with function or sport performance. Some of these tests can be included in a motor functioning test battery or used as stand-alones. Once the teacher has eliminated muscular weakness or sensory dysfunction, the functional component of balance can be addressed.

Berg Balance Scale

The Berg Balance Scale (BBS) is a widely used assessment of balance (static and dynamic) that is specific to functional movement tasks. It assesses gen-

Table 8.5 Selected Stand-Alone Balance Tests

Term	Description
Functional reach test	Student stands with feet shoulder-width apart, one arm raised to 90° of flexion. She reaches as far forward as possible without losing balance and moving the feet. The maximum the student can reach beyond her extended arm length while maintaining a fixed position is recorded.
Timed up and go	Student is assessed on the amount of time to stand up from a chair and walk to a line at 10 ft (3 m) and return to a seated position. Test scores are related to gait, speed, postural stability, and cognition (Herman, Giladi, & Hausdorff, 2011).
Romberg test	Student stands with heels and ankles together, 3 ft (1 m) from a wall, with eyes focused on a visual target. Arms are across the chest and hands touch the shoulders. Balance is recorded for 30 s with eyes open and then closed. Test is terminated if feet or hands move or if eyes open.
Sharpened Romberg	Student stands with feet in tandem (one foot in front of the other), arms across the chest and hands touching the shoulders. Balance is recorded for 30 s with eyes open and then closed. Test is terminated if feet or hands move or if eyes open.
Single-leg stance	Student stands on one leg, with arms across chest and hands touching the shoulders. Eyes are focused on visual target from a distance of 3 ft (1 m). The number of seconds is recorded with eyes open and then closed, then the test is repeated on the opposite leg. Test is stopped if legs touch, foot on floor moves, foot touches floor, arms move, or eyes open.
Standing on foam surface	Student stands on a padded surface, with hands on hips in a single-leg stance, eyes open and then closed. Balance is recorded for 30 s on each leg. Test is terminated if hands or feet move, foot touches floor, or eyes open.
Gait speed	Velocity of movement is a useful way to detect **dynamic balance** and mobility. Average time to walk 20 ft (6 m) without stopping can help determine a student's functional capabilities to cross a street or deter falls.

eral balance, transitions, foot placement, and balance with eyes open and closed. The maximum score is 56, based on a four-point scale: 0 (unable to complete task or needs assistance); 1 (minimal assistance or supervision); 2 (completes portions of the task); 3 (assuming more independence); 4 (independent function and safety). Although this scale is used primarily in the elderly population, it is especially useful to determine whether balance is affected during functional movements. The BBS assesses the following:

- Sitting to standing
- Standing unsupported
- Sitting with back unsupported but feet supported on floor or on a stool
- Standing to sitting

- Transfers
- Standing unsupported with eyes closed
- Standing unsupported with feet together
- Reaching forward with outstretched arm while standing
- Picking up object from floor from a standing position
- Turning to look behind over left and right shoulders while standing
- Turning 360 degrees
- Placing alternate foot on step or stool while standing unsupported
- Standing unsupported, one foot in front
- Standing on one leg

Performance Oriented Mobility Assessment

The Performance Oriented Mobility Assessment (POMA) is a functional battery of balance and gait. The POMA is scored on a range of 0 to 2, which proceeds from unsteady or falling to steady but supported and finally to steady and safe. The first nine items are balance oriented.

- Sitting balance (0 = leans or slides in chair; 1 = steady, safe)
- Arises (0 = unable without help; 1 = able, uses arms to help; 2 = able, without using arms)
- Attempts to arise (0 = unable without help; 1 = able to arise, requires more than one attempt; 2 = able to arise with one attempt)
- Immediate standing balance (0 = unsteady [staggers, moves feet, trunk sways]; 1 = steady, but uses walker or other support; 2 = steady without walker or other support)
- Standing balance (0 = unsteady; 1 = steady but wide stance [medial heels more than 4 inches apart] and uses cane or other support; 2 = narrow stance without support)
- Nudged (0 = begins to fall; 1 = staggers, grabs, catches self; 2 = steady)
- Eyes closed (0 = unsteady; 1= steady)
- Turning 360 degrees:
    - Steps (0 = discontinuous; 1 = continuous)
    - Steadiness (0 = unsteady [grabs, staggers]; 1 = steady)
- Sitting down (0 = unsafe [misjudged distance, falls into chair]; 1 = uses arms or not a smooth motion; 2 = safe, smooth motion)

The next seven items assess gait as the subject walks down a hallway or room at preferred pace and returns at a rapid but safe pace.

- Initiation of gait (0 = any hesitancy or multiple attempts to start; 1 = no hesitancy)
- Step length and height
    - Right foot in comparison to left foot (0 = right swing foot does not pass the left stance foot with step; 1 = right swing foot passes left stance foot)

- Right foot clearing the floor (0 = right foot does not clear floor completely with step; 1 = right foot completely clears floor)
  - Left foot in comparison to right foot (0 = left swing foot does not pass right stance foot with step; 1 = left swing foot passes right stance foot)
  - Left foot clearing the floor (0 = left foot does not clear floor completely with step; 1 = left foot completely clears floor)
- Step symmetry (0 = right and left step are not equal [estimate]; 1 = right and left step appear equal)
- Step continuity (0 = stopping or discontinuity between steps; 1 = steps appear continuous)
- Path (0 = marked deviation; 1 = mild/moderate deviation or uses walking aid; 2 = straight without walking aid)
- Trunk (0 = marked sway or uses walking aid; 1 = no sway but flexion of knees or back, or spreads arms out while walking; 2 = no sway, no flexion, no use of arms, and no use of walking aid)
- Walking stance (0 = heels apart; 1 = heels almost touching while walking)

Star Excursion Balance Test

The Star Excursion Balance Test (SEBT) is a dynamic assessment that requires the participant to maintain a single-leg stance while reaching as far as possible in eight various directions (see figure 8.3) with the other leg, tapping the foot, and returning to the initial position. The test is negated if the individual makes a heavy touch, places the foot on the floor, loses balance, or cannot return to the starting position. The average distance of three trials is recorded. A rest interval of 15 seconds is provided between each movement. Practice trials of four to six attempts are generally recommended. If this test is too difficult or there are time constraints, assessing movement in the

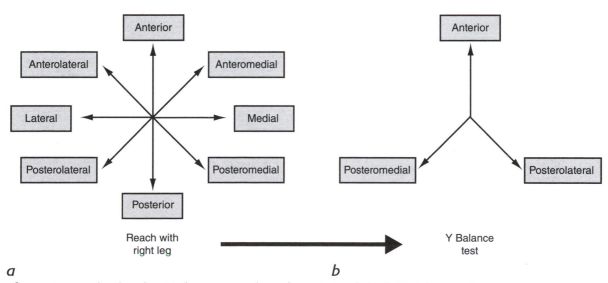

a   *b*

Figure 8.3 Directions for *(a)* the Star Excursion Balance Test and *(b)* the Y Balance Test.

Adapted, by permission, from M.P. Reiman and R.C. Manske, 2009, *Functional testing in human performance* (Champaign, IL: Human Kinetics), 109.

anterior medial, medial, and posterior medial directions (the Y Balance Test) may be more efficient.

Balance Error Scoring System

The Balance Error Scoring System (BESS) was developed by the University of North Carolina's Sports Medicine Research Laboratory and provides a portable six-item measure of static postural stability. The items are similar to the tasks included in table 8.5 and can be used to assess the effects of mild head injury on static postural stability. This helps clinicians determine safety precautions prior to a client's return to play or physical activity. The test can be performed on a floor or a foam pad. The six stance positions (figure 8.4) include a double-leg stance, a single-leg stance on the nondominant foot, and a tandem stance in which the dominant foot is placed in front of the nondominant foot. Each stance is held for 20 seconds and is scored by counting the errors, or deviations from proper form. The following are counted as errors:

- Taking the hands off the hips
- Opening the eyes
- Stepping or hopping
- Flexing or abducting the hip beyond 30 degrees
- Lifting the forefoot or heel
- Straying outside of testing position for more than five seconds

The BESS score is generated by adding an error point for each error recorded on each of the 20-second stances. Normative scores for the error scoring system are included in Khanna, Baumgartner and LaBella (2015).

CONCLUSION

Posture, gait, and balance are critical components that affect motor development and control of movement. From the foundation of sitting to standing to initiation of movement, they are indicators of achieving motor proficiency. They should be seen not as solitary components but as an interaction of abilities that allows individuals to develop a base of stability, to move, and to maintain or adjust to movement patterns in unstable environmental conditions. It is extremely important to analyze these components and establish intervention plans to restore functioning in individuals with movement limitations. Each can be analyzed to obtain information on specific needs as well as determine the effect of intervention to ensure proficient movement.

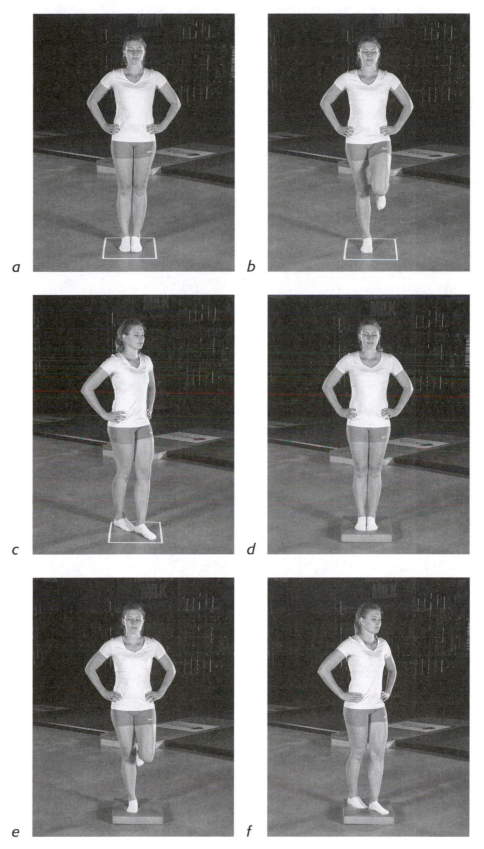

Figure 8.4 Balance Error Scoring System (BESS): *(a-c)* firm surface condition and *(d-f)* soft surface condition.

What You Need to Know

Key Terms

abduction	lordosis
adduction	postural control
body types	posture
circumduction	scoliosis
dynamic balance	spasticity
external rotation	stability
flexion	stance phase
foot drop	static balance
gait cycle	structural deviations
internal rotation	swing phase
kyphosis	

Key Concepts

1. You should be able to use assessment information regarding posture and balance to develop exercise interventions and program plans.
2. You should understand how deviations in functioning affect posture and gait.
3. You should be able to observe a gait pattern and determine possible causes of gait abnormalities.

Review Questions

1. What disabilities will affect posture?
2. Observe students of various ages and compare their posture and walking gait. What differences do you detect?
3. Discuss how muscle imbalances, symmetry, muscle spasms, or loss of sensory input affects posture.
4. Observe several people and describe their gait characteristics.
5. Describe the possible causes of gait abnormalities and the phase in which they occur. Then describe potential interventions.
6. Describe possible development effects on gait, posture, and balance.
7. What is evident in the ability to maintain postural control?
8. How does static and dynamic balance affect gait?
9. What perceptual components affect balance and postural control?
10. What components are affected when an individual suffers a head injury?
11. Why is the base of support critical to movement?

Assessing Perception and Cognition

Motor performance is based on the ability to receive and interpret sensory information prior to executing a movement. This sensory information informs the brain of the body's position in space, environmental changes, and various movement parameters that will be needed to perform a movement correctly (e.g., appropriate force, speed, and direction of the movement in question). When a student has difficulty learning or performing motor skills, teachers and therapists erroneously look merely at the student's motor execution. Rather than focusing on motor execution in isolation, professionals need to take into account all aspects of information and perceptual processing as they relate to motor performance. In this framework, when assessing a student, adapted physical education teachers and therapists must view motor performance as encompassing all aspects of sensory input, decision making, and motor output as points of emphases. This chapter is devoted to ways in which adapted physical educators and therapists can determine current levels of perception and cognition in individuals with disabilities. It defines and discusses the components of perception and information processing and describes specific tests teachers and therapists can use to assess current levels of functioning.

PERCEPTION AND COGNITION DEFINED

Perception is the process of receiving, organizing, and interpreting sensory information. Perception is multimodal and encompasses the integration and interpretation of multiple sensory inputs. For example, a student turning her head in response to olfactory, visual, and auditory cues exemplifies this type of multimodal perception. Perception is also an integral component of **cognition**. We refer to cognition broadly as encompassing high-level brain processes, such as attention, planning, motivation, and memory recall, that are essential for movement selection and execution. Perception plays a key role in an individual's experiences, while cognition is essential for planning and initiating movements based on these perceptual experiences and adjusting movements to varying environmental contexts (Horvat, Croce, Tomporowski, & Barna, 2013).

It is not surprising, therefore, that an individual's motor actions are causally related to cognitive development and functioning. It is our viewpoint that the importance of perceptual and cognitive development and functioning to movement execution has been critically understated, and that cognition and perception can vary greatly by degree of impairment in individuals with disabilities. It is important that adapted physical educators and therapists understand how both directly affect functional movement and also become familiar with the instruments used to assess levels of perceptual and cognitive functioning.

COMPONENTS OF COGNITION

The following components of cognition need to be considered by adapted physical educators and therapists. This list is not exhaustive, but it does provide an overall picture of what abilities constitute cognition. Everyone on the MPT must understand the constituents of a cognitive assessment and how this information can ultimately be used for program planning.

Attention and concentration. The ability to attend to, and concentrate on, stimuli in the environment forms the basis for nearly all cognitive functions. **Attention** is the ability to focus on internal or external stimuli and defines the length of an individual's focus, or attention span. Closely related to attention is concentration. **Concentration** entails the ability to focus one's attention on the task at hand and not be affected by internal or external distractions. Both attention and concentration require integration of several nervous system structures that work together to process information such as alertness (arousal), the ability to select specific environmental stimuli, the ability to shift focus (i.e., to cease attention on one task and give attention to another) and to sustain it over time, and the ability to process information. Essentially, a concussion or any lesion in the brain (e.g., vascular events, traumatic injury, tumors) can affect any one of these processes and impair a student's ability to learn or to engage in daily activities. Observable behaviors often seen with attentional problems include distractibility, perseveration (inability to shift attention to other tasks), decreased concentration, retarded information processing, confusion, and impersistence. Most cognitive assessments use a scale to measure attention. Many tests present a series of letters or patterns and ask the individual to replicate the pattern when it is no longer visible.

Orientation. Hand in hand with attention and concentration is **orientation**, which is often affected when there is diffuse brain impairment. Orientation generally encompasses awareness of person (awareness of self and knowing who you are), place (knowledge of where you are and how you can move about in the environment), and time (awareness of time of day, seasons, months, and passage of time).

Memory. Memory is the ability to take in, store, and retrieve information, or simply the ability to learn and retrieve information. **Short-term memory (STM)** is capacity-limited in that a person can absorb and work with only a small amount of information at a time. **Long-term memory (LTM)** is the ability to remember for longer periods and involves the ability to transfer information from short-term memory to long-term storage and retrieval. Many academics break down memory into several types: episodic (memory of autobiographical events), semantic (memory of meanings, rules, and concepts), and procedural (memory of how to do skills). Short-term memory in a cognitive assessment is the ability to recall information that was learned minutes to months previously. Thus, it differs from immediate recall, which is the ability to repeat information (often measured by having the individual repeat a string of digits).

Executive functions. Much of a person's cognitive function falls under the umbrella term **executive functions**. Executive functioning includes a person's ability to self-regulate, ignore or act upon inhibitions, or perform multiple tasks simultaneously. Some of the most recognizable executive skills include the ability to make decisions, plan, problem-solve, reason, and anticipate consequences of one's behavior. Metacognition is an executive function pertaining to a person's ability to predict performance on a given task. A cognitive assessment will usually measure the person's initial ability to make decisions.

Information processing speed. **Information processing speed** is how rapidly an individual can input, integrate, store, and output information, which are fundamental aspects of almost all learning and performance activities. Input is related to how information from the senses enters the brain. Integration is the process of interpreting and processing the information. Storage involves storing information for later retrieval. Output is the process of expressing information via language or motor (muscle) activity. Speed of processing is affected by working memory deficits and information processing deficits and the use of strategies. Sometimes this concept is referred to as reaction, psychomotor, or processing speed.

Motor skills. The use of motor skills tests in a cognitive assessment is probably the largest difference between it and an IQ test. Many educators and clinicians fail to realize that motor function involves cognitive functioning. Many times, difficulty with fine motor skills can be indicative of cognitive impairment.

Perception. Perceptive components of a cognitive assessment measure a person's ability to identify or recognize external stimuli using their senses (sight, hearing, touch, and sometimes smell). Common tests include the use of optical illusions, such as a visual object that looks like a vase from one perceptive angle, while the negative space reveals two faces looking at one another.

Task sequencing. Tasks with multiple movement components performed in a specific order or sequence require complex information and cognitive processing by the brain. For some individuals, even simple tasks can present complex challenges. Understanding all the steps involved for a particular task can assist professionals in identifying any steps that may need extra instruction and will help in teaching the task in a logical progression to help with **task sequencing**.

Visual search and scanning. **Visual search and scanning** are types of perceptual tasks requiring attention that typically involve an active scan of the visual environment for a particular object or feature (the target) among other objects or features (the distracters).

Visual and auditory processing. **Visual processing** refers to the ability to make sense of information taken in through the visual system, whereas **auditory processing** refers to the ability to make sense of information taken in through the auditory system. Difficulties with visual and auditory processing affect how these types of sensory information are interpreted, or processed, by the brain.

Fluid cognition (ability). **Fluid cognition** (or ability) is the ability to solve new problems, to use logic in new situations, and to identify patterns. Fluid cognition is one's on-the-spot reasoning capability and pertains to the capacity to think and reason out. It also governs memory capacity, attention, and information analysis.

COGNITIVE ASSESSMENTS

Cognitive assessments may include a variety of formal and informal assessments of a person's perceptual and cognitive abilities and skills. Testing may cover a wide range of areas that might measure, for example, an individual's level of intelligence, perceptual abilities, verbal and nonverbal skills, attention, and processing or memory abilities. Unlike cognitive and perceptual tests administered by qualified clinical psychologists or diagnosticians, cognitive tests administered by adapted physical educators and therapists are geared more toward analyzing an individual's perceptual and cognitive abilities as they relate to movement. In addition, it is critical to appreciate that most standard cognitive assessment instruments are geared for adults—in particular adults recovering from brain injury or stroke or who have Alzheimer's disease. Consequently, there are few cognitive assessment instruments that can be applied to individuals with disabilities in the school setting. Of those instruments available, the Trail Making Test (TMT) is one of the most reliable for use by adapted physical educators and therapists in schools, and it has been used extensively since its development as part of the Army Individual Test Battery (1944).

Briefly, the TMT requires subjects to connect a sequence of consecutive targets on a sheet of paper or computer screen, in a similar manner to what a child would do in a connect-the-dots puzzle. There are two parts to the test. In the first part, the targets are 25 numbers randomly distributed in space (1, 2, 3, and so on), and the test takers need to connect them in sequential order. The subjects start at the circle marked Begin and continue linking numbers until they reach the endpoint, a circle marked End. Part B is similar to A; however, instead of linking only numbers, the subjects must alternately switch between a set of numbers (1 to 13) and a set of letters (A to L), again linking them in ascending order (1-A, 2-B, 3-C, 4-D, and so on). At the same time, the subjects connect the array of circles as fast as possible without lifting the pencil.

A commonly reported performance index in the TMT is time to completion. A difference score (B – A) is often reported, meant to remove the speed element from the test evaluation. The first part of the test reflects speed of processing, while the second part reflects executive functioning or fluid cognitive ability. Extensive research indicates that the TMT assesses a variety of cognitive functions including attention, visual scanning, switching speed, mental flexibility, and the ability to initiate and modify an action plan (Bowie & Harvey, 2006; Salthouse, 2011; Strauss, Sherman, & Spreen, 2006; Zakzanis, Mraz, & Graham, 2005).

Recently, Horvat and colleagues (Horvat, Fallaize, Croce, & Roswal, in preparation) focused on modifying the TMT to develop a more cognitive-motor-based assessment better suited for use by adapted physical educators and therapists. In this variation, the TMT compares speed of processing and fluid cognitive ability with a running task (subsequently termed a cognitive dash by the authors). Individuals complete a computerized version of the TMT, which is then compared with the time it takes to complete running on a basketball court from baseline to midcourt (42 ft, or 13 m). In condition A, participants pick up a poly spot placed around the center court circle in the appropriate number sequence (1-2-3, and so on), place the poly spot in a bucket, and return to the starting point. Condition B requires the participants to alternatively pick up a number, then a letter (1-A, 2-B, 3-C, 4-D, and so on), place them both into a bucket, and run back to the starting line. Similar to the TMT, condition A requires connecting a series of numbers, reflecting speed of processing. Condition B, which includes a number and letter in unison, is used to detect executive function and **verbal fluency**. Here, verbal fluency refers to a cognitive function that facilitates information retrieval from memory, requiring executive control over several cognitive processes such as selective attention, selective inhibition, and response generation. The correlation between the TMT and actual movement times from the cognitive dash gives teachers additional information to assess processing speed and planning a movement sequence.

Table 9.1 provides a brief list of cognitive assessments that adapted physical educators and therapists can use in the school setting. Many of these tests are specific to a singular component of cognition (e.g., memory, reaction time, visual processing, executive function). There is no one perceptual or cognitive assessment instrument that can test them all.

Table 9.1 Cognitive Assessments

Test name	Test description	Cognitive abilities used
Speed-based tests		
Simple reaction time (SRT)	To react ASAP to a fixed visual stimulus. The participant rests the index finger of the dominant hand on the space bar and taps it as soon as a white circle appears in the middle of the black screen at random time intervals. Practice trials are followed by 12 test trials.	Reaction and decision speed
Complex reaction time (CRT)	Similar to SRT but includes 16 distracters appearing randomly in the middle of the screen among the 12 targets. The only action required is to tap when a circle appears.	Reaction and decision speed, selective attention
Simple visual search (SVS)	To react ASAP to a random visual stimulus. In this touch-screen-based subtest, the participant sits in front of the screen and taps 12 times as fast as possible with the preferred hand in the middle of the circle when it appears on the screen at randomized time intervals and randomly chosen spots.	Processing speed
Complex visual search (CVS)	Similar to SVS but with a distracting background. The appearing circle gradually becomes more intense and visible.	Processing speed, visual processing
Short-term memory test		
Corsi Block-Tapping Task (CBTT)	To memorize increasing sequences of squares. The participant reproduces randomly generated block-tapping sequences, with the provision that no block is repeated in any sequence. All squares turn blue when the sequence is finished, cueing the participant to start tapping blocks in the same order they lit up. The sequence length starts with two blocks and increases by one after correct recalls and decreases by one if an error is made. The computer automatically stores the length of each sequence. The final score is the best average score of five subsequent trials.	Short-term memory, spatial memory span
Executive function test		
Tower of London (TOL)	To replicate configurations in the least number of moves. This test ends after 14 items with a six-move problem. For participants scoring more than 90%, four additional test items are presented. The emphasis is accuracy rather than speed, but for practical purposes an upper time limit (120 s) is set for solving each item, with two trials for each. To limit potential distress because of repeated failure, a cessation trial is applied when the participants indicate the task is too difficult. The test score is based on the number of correctly solved items (in the least number of moves).	Executive functioning

Test name	Test description	Cognitive abilities used
Fluid reasoning and visual processing tests		
WASI Block Design test (WBD)	To replicate 2D block patterns with nine 3D cubes. Absolute test scores are used for data analysis, with a maximal obtainable test result of 72 points.	Fluid cognitive ability and reasoning, visual processing
WASI Matrix Reasoning test (WMR)	To complete gridded patterns (multiple choice). Absolute test scores are used for data analysis, with a maximal obtainable test result of 35 points.	Fluid cognitive ability and reasoning, including induction, general sequential reasoning, and speed of reasoning pattern recognition
Match to Sample Visual Search (MTS)	A matching test, with a speed/accuracy trade-off. It is a simultaneous visual search task with response latency dissociated from movement time. Efficient performance on this task requires the ability to search among the targets and ignore the distracter patterns.	Fluid visual processing, visual search
Additional tests		
Trail Making Test Part A and B (TMT)	Computerized or paper matching test. Part A consists of connecting numbers in numerical order, while Part B consists of connecting numbers and letters in alternating order (1-A, 2-B, 3-C, and so on).	Visual scanning, attention, information processing, psychomotor speed
Symbol Digit Modalities Test (SDMT)	Student substitutes a number for randomized geometric figures. Responses can be given verbally or written.	Psychomotor speed, attention, concentration
Stroop Color and Word Test (SCWT)	Consists of cards with color words printed in black, color words printed in the color the word represents, and color words printed in a color other than what the word represents. Student must correctly identify the color word each time.	Attention, information processing speed

Based on Van Biesen, Mactavish, McCulloch, Lenaerts, & Vanlandewijck 2016.

CONCUSSION ASSESSMENTS

Given the current interest in concussions and concussion-related screening, a brief discussion of this information is warranted. The word *concussion* comes from the Latin *concussus*, which means to shake violently. Quite often **concussion** is viewed as a subset of mild traumatic brain injury (mTBI). In the past, a concussion was thought to involve only transient disturbances of brain functioning without any significant gross structural changes. Today, however, it is recognized that many concussions involve structural damage to the brain. Recreational- and sport-related concussion is defined as a complex pathophysiological process affecting the brain, induced by traumatic mechanical forces. These forces can both bruise and stretch the brain tissue, resulting in a typical set of neurological symptoms. Several common features and symptoms of a concussive event include, but are not limited to, the following (McCrory, Meeuwisse, Aubry, et al., 2013):

Case Study 1
Overcoming Memory Problems

Ashley is a 10th grader diagnosed with memory and learning problems. Her initial individualized education plan requested adapted physical education, with a particular focus on learning and retention of simple motor tasks. Ashley's visual-spatial short-term working memory was assessed with the Corsi Block-Tapping Task. In the CBTT, the subject observes a sequence of blocks "tapped" (or lit up in the computer version) and repeats the sequence in order. The task starts with a small number of blocks and gradually increases in length up to nine blocks; it measures both the number of correct sequences and the longest sequence remembered. The longest sequence Ashley remembered was two blocks (this number is known as the Corsi Span and averages about five in most individuals).

With the results of this test in mind, the motor performance team designs a program for Ashley that involves sequentially learning motor tasks from simple to more complex, using continuous repetition and a criterion of 90 percent correct responses before moving on to more complex performances. The key to this motor program is to repeat exercises, with intervals, on a daily basis, as motor memories are not created without repeated exercise.

1. Concussion may be the result of a direct blow to the head, face, or neck regions, or even a blow elsewhere on the body whereby the force is transmitted to the head.

2. Concussion typically results in a rapid onset of short-lived impairment of neurological functioning that will resolve spontaneously.

3. Concussion may result in neuropathological changes.

4. Concussion results in a graded set of clinical disturbances that may or may not involve loss of consciousness.

5. The majority of concussions resolve in a relatively short time (usually between 1 and 2 weeks), although in children this time frame may be longer. These types of concussion are often referred to as "simple" concussions. Complex concussions are those whereby the event leads to a prolonged loss of consciousness (more than 1 minute) and the symptoms persist beyond 10 days or the individual has prolonged cognitive impairment. Persistent symptoms such as headaches, dizziness, loss of balance, sleep disturbances, and poor concentration and memory problems are often referred to as postconcussion syndrome.

6. The most common symptoms encountered with concussions are severe or persistent headaches; decreased cognitive functioning, including memory loss and trouble attending to tasks; dizziness and loss of coordination; poor balance; nausea; blurred vision or sensitivity to light; emotional outbursts; slurred speech; disturbed sleep; and in more severe cases even amnesia.

Case Study 2
Problems Executing Multistep Motor Tasks

Martin is a 15-year-old student who demonstrates increasing problems with remembering and executing multistep motor tasks. When he responds to stimuli his movements are slow, and over the past several years, he's been taking increasingly longer to complete tasks. The primary information processing problem noted during his evaluation (Tower of London test) was task execution. Martin perceives sensory stimuli well but has trouble with attention and response selection. When tasks increase in movement complexity (i.e., more steps are required to complete the movement), he essentially stops attempting the task. After further evaluation, the motor performance team broke Martin's problems into deficits in executive functioning and in preprogrammed motor tasks that are not under feedback control.

To help remediate the problem, the team has Martin performing a variety of quick movements whereby he reacts to stimuli in the environment. Items emphasized include detecting relevant cues; decision making (working on set pieces and game situations); and changing attention focus (being able to switch quickly from one stimulus to another) to concentrating on the field of play in invasion games. A key activity is improving reaction time to a stimulus. Drills include controlling an object (e.g., football or hockey puck). The cue for the reaction to take place can be visual (movement of an object), a specific command (voice), or a sound (buzzer).

The most recent concussion consensus statements recommend neuropsychological (NP) testing in making return-to-play decisions. Moreover, to obtain the most reliable results from such testing, baseline NP screening of athletes in sports with a high risk of concussive events (e.g., football, hockey, lacrosse, soccer) is highly recommended. The importance of this preseason baseline screening cannot be overemphasized. A baseline neurocognitive exam measures cognitive functioning a priori, generating a score that then serves as a reference point against which medical and clinical professionals can compare scores on tests performed after the concussive event. Baseline results are also helpful in identifying preexisting conditions that have nothing to do with the concussive event and postconcussion test scores.

In nearly all professional and collegiate sports, baseline preinjury and post-injury NP testing is now commonplace, and more recently, baseline screening has become common in high school and youth sports as well. In the absence of reliable and valid NP testing, the Zurich consensus statement on concussion (McCrory, Meeuwisse, Aubry, et al., 2013) recommends a conservative approach to return to play, especially for children and youth.

The basic assertion is that all concussed individuals should be asymptomatic at rest before returning to any type of training, game involvement, or physical exertion. And if symptoms return during or after physical exertion, participation should be terminated immediately. A typical return-to-play protocol involves six steps:

1. No activity with complete rest
2. Light exercise away from the game field (walking, stationary bike)
3. Sport-specific activity with no body contact
4. On-field practice without body contact
5. Once cleared by a physician, on-field activity with body contact
6. Return to competitive participation

Although most concussions lead to subtle changes, making clinical evaluation challenging, numerous assessment tools are available to aid in diagnosis and management. Moreover, using just one test exclusively is not as effective as combining tests to increase sensitivity and specificity. As mentioned previously, assessment tools are most beneficial when baseline measurements are available for comparison.

Postconcussion assessment tools are often listed by type and fall into three main categories:

1. Symptom checklists, such as the Postconcussion Symptom Scale (the most commonly used of this type), the Concussion Symptom Inventory (a quick, easy, and cost-effective assessment tool, allowing participants to self-report symptoms), and the Graded Symptom Checklist
2. Postural stability tests, such as the Sensory Organization Test (SOT), which identifies abnormalities in the participant's somatosensory, visual, and vestibular systems
3. NP tests, both pencil and paper (e.g., Trail Making Test, Stroop Color and Word Test) and computer based (e.g., Immediate Post-Concussion Assessment and Cognitive Testing [ImPact] and Sport Concussion Assessment Tool, 3rd Edition [SCAT-3])

Because the SCAT-3 has become one of the more commonly used NP tests clinically, it is discussed briefly here. Generally speaking, computer-based NP tests have several advantages over more traditional paper and pencil NP tests in that

- they take less time and can be scored rapidly;
- they do not need to be administered by a neuropsychologist, so there is ease of administration;
- many allow for a countless variety of test questions, mitigating practice learning effects; and
- they are more widely accessible to a wider range of clinicians.

The SCAT-3 is a comprehensive tool developed by a group of international experts at the Fourth International Conference on Concussion in Sport held in Zurich, Switzerland, in November 2012. This standardized assessment instrument can be used for athletes 13 years and older and is the most recent version of the original SCAT-1 (2005) and SCAT-2 (2009), respectively (Chin, Nelson, Barr, McCrory, & McCrea, 2016). For younger persons, aged 12 and under, clinicians are instructed to use the Student SCAT-3. Both tests are designed for use by medical professionals. Unsurprisingly, preseason baseline testing with the SCAT-3 is most helpful for interpreting postinjury test results. The test preface strongly states that diagnosis of a concussion is a clinical judgment made ideally by medical professionals, and therefore the test should not be used solely to make or exclude a diagnosis of concussion in absence of clinical judgment, as an athlete may have a concussion even with a "normal" SCAT-3 test result. Although adapted physical educators and other clinicians would not directly perform this assessment, knowledge of the test and its interpretations is, nonetheless, important for understanding results obtained with its use.

The SCAT-3 includes multiple subtests, some of which are scored on a Likert scale: (0) indicating none and (6) indicating severe. Test administration, as well as what the tester should look for, are provided in the manual. Tested areas include the following:

- Two immediate sideline assessments with indications for emergency management (Glasgow Coma Scale and a Maddocks score)
- Symptom evaluation
- Cognitive evaluation, assessing orientation, immediate memory, and concentration
- Neck evaluation
- Balance examination (using a modified version of the BESS)
- Upper-limb coordination examination, involving a finger to nose task
- A delayed recall score

From these subtests, a scoring summary is developed with recommendations. The SCAT-3 uses an abbreviated version of the Standardized Assessment of Concussion (SAC). The full SAC is a paper and pencil assessment that can be utilized on the sidelines. The SAC itself measures

- orientation (month, date, day of week, year, time);
- immediate memory (recall of five words in three separate trials);
- neurological screening such as loss of consciousness (occurrence, duration), amnesia (either retrograde or anterograde by recollection of events pre- and postinjury), sensation, coordination, strength, and concentration;
- exertional maneuvers (jumping jacks, sit-ups); and
- delayed recall (five words).

Case study 3 highlights how even when high school students know the risks, they are willing to overlook them and continue playing.

PERCEPTUAL-MOTOR TESTS

Similar to cognitive abilities, perceptual-motor abilities are traits—in this case, specifically sensory and perceptual traits—underlying the ability to perform various motor skills. Being able to accurately receive information (sensation) and then accurately interpret this information (perception) is critical for virtually all movements. There are six different perceptual modalities: visual (sight), auditory (hearing), kinesthetic (body awareness), tactual (touch), olfactory (smell), and gustatory (taste). Of these, visual and

Case Study 3
Symptoms of Concussion

Robert is a star football player for his high school team who recently sustained a concussion in a game. The 16-year-old continued to participate in his sport even though he knew the risks of playing while showing concussion symptoms. He did not report them and continued playing until the season ended. In physical education class, the teacher realized that Robert was displaying some of the more common long-term symptoms of a concussion: persistent headaches, problems sleeping and attending to tasks, and blurred vision. The motor performance team recommended that Robert be screened for a concussion. The SCAT-3 used to evaluate Robert showed he had postconcussion symptoms. Thanks to the physical education teacher's knowledge of concussion symptoms and recommendation for a concussion screening, more severe problems were prevented. Recent research indicates that mild aerobic exercise aids in postconcussion recovery, so the MPT prescribed a program of mild-intensity stationary cycling.

kinesthetic perception are most critical to physical educators and therapists because these two areas are most directly related to successful motor skill performance (Gabbard, 2018).

Visual perception has several subareas, including perceptual constancy, spatial orientation, figure-and-ground perception, depth perception, field of vision, perception of movement, and visual-motor coordination. Kinesthetic perception refers to the ability to sense, or to be aware of, movement and body position. Unlike the visual system, which receives information from the environment, the kinesthetic system receives information from within the body through sensory receptors predominately in the muscles, tendons, and joints as well as through the vestibular system (balance system) located in the inner ear. **Perceptual-motor tests** evaluate normal development of visual and kinesthetic perceptual systems and determine whether a student has a significant deficit in one or more subareas within these systems (Horvat, Kalakian, Croce, & Dahlstrom, 2011).

The premise of these tests is that students who have difficulty receiving information, making sense of information they receive, or forming a movement to match the information from the environment ultimately will demonstrate movement problems. The Purdue Perceptual-Motor Survey (PPMS) was one of the first and most popular perceptual-motor tests. It was developed at a time when perceptual-motor development was linked to academic performance and was constructed to determine whether a student who had academic problems might have related perceptual-motor deficits. The PPMS was validated in the early 1960s on a sample of 200 children. Although test–retest reliability results were high (95%), the limited number of subjects in the sample and the limited standardization procedures make the true reliability of this test a bit suspect. Its use by physical educators and therapists is currently limited.

Case Study 4
Student With Visual Perception Problems

Michael is a 10-year-old student who appears to have sensory-integrative and perceptual problems relating to vision. Fortunately, Michael does not demonstrate problems with attention, cognition, flexibility and range of motion, or muscular strength and endurance. His physical education teacher must determine to what extent his visual perception is compromised so as to develop the most appropriate intervention and education program. To accomplish this goal, the teacher administers a test that assesses Michael's ability to process information. Results from the test indicate he has moderate problems discerning objects in the environment and reacting quickly to them.

Now aware of Michael's visual acuity strengths and weaknesses, the motor performance team initiates a physical education program centering around visual-motor activities that include discerning targets in a visual surround. Activities prescribed include visual-motor integration tasks (controlling movement guided by vision) such as (1) ball play with medium and small balls to catch and throw; (2) beanbag toss games where Michael tosses beanbags at a target such as a container; and (3) balloon volleyball or hitting a balloon with a tennis racket or paddle.

Another major test is the Developmental Test of Visual Perception, now in its third edition (DTVP-3, 2014). Of all the tests of visual perception and visual-motor integration, the DTVP-3 is somewhat unique in that its scores are reliable at the 0.80 level or above for all subtests and 0.90 or above for the composites for all age groups; its scores are validated by many studies, and its most recent norms are based on a representative sample of 1,035 individuals; it yields scores for both visual perception (no motor response) and visual-motor integration ability; and it is shown to be unbiased relative to race, gender, and handedness. The new normative data were collected in 2010 and 2011, and norms were extended upward to age 12 years, 11 months. The DTVP-3 has five subsets: eye–hand coordination, copying, figure-and-ground perception, visual closure, and form constancy. The results of these subsets are combined to form three composites: motor-reduced visual perception, visual-motor integration, and general visual perception. As one can see, this test concentrates primarily on visual-perceptual abilities and does not assess other perceptual components.

There are drawbacks to pure perceptual tests. Many of these tests are used in laboratory and clinical settings and are often extremely difficult to generalize to a school setting for developing program plans. In addition, other than the DTVP-3, most of these tests have not been updated, revised, or reevaluated for decades. Finally, current theories on motor skill acquisition and performance indicate that separating perceptual and motor aspects of a student's motor ability and performance is difficult as both the receiving and responding elements in motor performance are inextricably intertwined.

Consequently, the use of these tests has become somewhat limited, and they have been supplanted by more general motor development and motor ability assessments such as the Bruininks-Oseretsky Test of Motor Proficiency 2 (BOT-2) and the Movement Assessment Battery for Children, Second Edition (MABC-2). These and other motor assessment instruments are described in detail in chapter 6.

CONCLUSION

Perception is the organization, identification, and interpretation of sensory information in order to represent and understand the environment. Cognition, or cognitive processes, can be conceived as procedures we use to incorporate perceptual information and new knowledge and to make decisions based on existing knowledge. Different cognitive functions play a role in these processes, and all these cognitive functions work together to integrate new knowledge and allow us to interpret the world as we see it. Components of cognition include attention, memory, language, and learning, just to name a few. Perception and cognition are inextricably intertwined with motor performance and thus should be assessed by adapted physical educators and therapists alike. A key point in the assessment and screening debate is the suitability of available instruments: Few instruments have been validated in the populations for which they are intended to be used, many have low validity for mild levels of cognitive impairment, and there are often biases in scoring. Although no single instrument for cognitive screening is suitable for global use, the chapter discusses several of the more popular assessment instruments.

What You Need to Know

Key Terms

attention
auditory processing
cognition
concentration
concussion
executive functions
fluid cognition
information processing speed
long-term memory (LTM)

orientation
perception
perceptual-motor tests
short-term memory (STM)
task sequencing
verbal fluency
visual processing
visual search and scanning

Key Concepts

1. You should understand the importance of perception and cognition to motor performance.
2. You should understand the various components of cognition that make up a typical cognitive assessment.
3. You should understand the various components of perception and those components that are most directly related to motor performance and assessment.

4. You should understand what signs and symptoms constitute a concussion and the types of concussion-related screening tests available.
5. You should be able to use cognitive and concussion assessments to develop intervention programs.

Review Questions

1. What factors make up cognition?
2. Observe students of various ages and compare their abilities to perceive and respond to various stimuli. What differences do you detect?
3. Discuss how various cognitive limitations affect social interactions and motor functioning.
4. Explain the purpose of cognitive assessment and what assessment tools might be used to develop appropriate intervention programs.

Chapter 10

Assessing Behavior and Social Competence

Behaviors, social skills, and how well a student plays with equipment are important yet often undermeasured concepts in general and adapted physical education. Yet many referrals for adapted physical education are for behavior or social interaction problems students display in general physical education rather than physical or motor problems. It is often said that physical education can improve self-concept, but how a student feels about himself or herself in relation to physical education is rarely measured. Finally, many teachers talk about the importance of helping students without disabilities gain a positive, empathetic, caring attitude toward peers with disabilities. This chapter reviews common assessment tools and practices used to measure students' behaviors, social skills, self-concept, play, and attitudes. Each section begins with a short case study relating a real-life situation of a student with a disability.

Students who present difficult behaviors are often the most challenging for both general and adapted physical educators. Difficult behaviors can include passive aggression (refusing to participate), verbal outbursts,

Case Study 1
Rachel: Child with Aggressive Behaviors

Rachel, a nine-year-old fourth grader with Down syndrome at Woodfield Elementary School, is known to her teachers and her peers as a "mean little girl." No one knows why Rachel is so mean to her classmates, but everyone knows to avoid Rachel whenever possible (even though her peers have been encouraged to interact and play with her). Rachel's meanness is displayed through physical aggression. She has been known to bite, hit, scratch, pinch, kick, and push other students for no apparent reason. This has been going on ever since Rachel was moved from a self-contained special education class to a general education fourth-grade class. Rachel's teacher (and Rachel's classmates) want to know exactly how often Rachel displays these aggressive behaviors, why she is displaying them, and what to do to help her develop more appropriate behaviors.

running away, destroying equipment, and even physical violence toward peers and staff. Before the IEP team can determine an appropriate program for a student with challenging behaviors, the team needs to determine the types of behaviors being displayed, the intensity of the behaviors, and possible causes of the behaviors.

The ability to effectively meet social and community expectations for personal independence, physical needs, and interpersonal relationships expected for one's age and cultural group is termed **adaptive behavior** (Brown, McDonnell, & Snell, 2016). Behavior that interferes with everyday activities is called **maladaptive behavior**, or more often, problem behavior. Maladaptive behavior is undesirable, is socially unacceptable, or interferes with the acquisition of desired skills or knowledge (Bruininks, Woodcock, Weatherman, & Hill, 1996). Problems in acquiring adaptive skills may occur at any age—in developing and mastering basic maturational skills for young children (e.g., the ability to walk or perform self-help skills), in learning academic skills and concepts for school-age children (e.g., basic reading, writing, and math), or in making social and vocational adjustments for older individuals (e.g., getting along with others and developing basic job skills).

Maladaptive behavior ultimately limits independence, the ability to do things on one's own without getting into trouble. Independence is critical for success at school, at home, and in the community. It means not only being able to perform a task but also knowing *when* to do it and having the willingness to do so. When students exhibit behavior problems that affect independence, it leads to restrictions, extra supervision, additional assistance with behaving more appropriately, and possibly a more segregated placement (Bruininks, Woodcock, Weatherman, & Hill, 1996).

With regard to physical education, adaptive behavior includes following directions, getting along with peers, using equipment appropriately, putting forth an appropriate amount of effort, and generally behaving appropriately for the setting (e.g., not running away or getting into fights). Good adaptive behavior and a lack of behavior problems in physical education allow the student to be more independent (does not need a teacher assistant), be more successful, and be accepted more readily by the general physical education teacher and by peers.

In behavioral assessments, the first step is defining the targeted behavior to determine the extent of its occurrence before treatment. The assessment of behavior depends on accurate observation and precise measurement. Therefore, it is important that the examiner clearly and objectively define the behaviors to be assessed and then accurately observe and record these defined behaviors (Bambara, Janney, & Snell, 2015). For example, saying a student is "always getting in trouble" is vague and not measurable. Even a statement such as "Emily is aggressive toward her peers" is too vague to target for intervention. *Aggressive* could mean that she hits, bites, yells, or displays other forms of aggression. A better definition might be that "Emily touches and pushes other children two or three times while waiting in line to drink water and four or five times when sitting in a group waiting for instructions."

It is also important to examine **antecedents** (things that happen just before a behavior occurs that may cause the behavior) as well as **consequences** (things that happen immediately after a behavior occurs that may reinforce the behavior). For example, being paired with a particular peer may upset a student and cause an inappropriate behavior (screaming when the student sees that peer coming toward him), while chasing after a student who runs away may reinforce that behavior (running away becomes a game) (see the section on functional behavioral analysis in this chapter for more details on measuring antecedents and consequences).

Traditional behavioral assessments usually focus on two areas: adaptive behaviors and behavior problems. Assessing adaptive behaviors involves information such as a student's ability to perform certain adaptive behaviors (e.g., dressing, getting from one place to another, staying on task), how often he performs an adaptive behavior, and how well he performs an adaptive behavior. Assessing behavior problems includes types of maladaptive behaviors, frequency of such behaviors, and intensity of such behaviors. For example, a question on the Scales of Independent Behavior–Revised (SIB-R) (Bruininks, Woodcock, Weatherman, & Hill, 1996) asks whether or not the student is hurtful to others (e.g., biting, kicking, pinching, pulling hair, scratching, or striking). The scale includes a place for the examiner to note the frequency (*never* to *one or more times per hour*) as well as the perceived severity of the problem (*not serious, not a problem* to *extremely serious, a critical problem*). Thus, the examiner is able to obtain an idea of the student's present abilities, strengths, and deficits with regard to adaptive behaviors and problem behaviors. This information can then be translated into behavioral goals such as "demonstrates the ability to wait turn when playing small-group game in physical education" or "maintains appropriate personal space when playing games and interacting with peers in physical education."

Information from this type of assessment can also help the general physical education teacher determine whether a behavior is significant enough (i.e., occurs fairly frequently and at a serious level) to warrant additional support—such as a teacher assistant or adapted physical educator—or perhaps removal from general physical education into a self-contained setting. Other areas that are measured in behavioral tests include the following (Kazdin, 2000):

- *Frequency:* number of behaviors during a designated time period
- *Response rate:* number of responses divided by the time interval
- *Intervals:* behaviors during a specified time rather than by discrete responses that have a beginning and end point
- *Time sampling:* observations conducted for brief periods at different times rather than during a single block of time
- *Duration:* amount of time the response is observed (effective for measuring continuous rather than discrete behaviors)
- *Latency:* duration measure that observes the time lapse between the cue and the response
- *Categorization:* classifying responses according to their occurrence (correct or incorrect, appropriate or inappropriate)
- *Group:* number of individuals who perform a specific behavior or response as opposed to individual responses

BEHAVIORAL TESTS

This section reviews four different adaptive behavior assessment scales. The first is a teacher-developed checklist specifically designed for physical education: the University of Virginia Adapted Physical Education Program (UVA-APE) Initial Observation and Referral Form. This is followed by a review of three well-known adaptive behavior scales: Adaptive Behavior Assessment System, Third Edition (ABAS-3); the Vineland Adaptive Behavior Scales, Third Edition (VABS-3); and the AAMR Adaptive Behavior Scale–School (ABS-S:2). Each test measures everyday living skills—skills that are related to, but distinct from, academic ability and intelligence. These commercially available tests provide results that can be described qualitatively or as age equivalents, percentile ranks, or standard scores.

Note that adaptive behavior measures have been criticized over the years. First, adaptive behavior can be difficult to evaluate because the concept of this type of behavior is vague. For example, although self-help skills are relatively easy to measure, demonstration of age-appropriate social and emotional behaviors can be difficult to quantitatively assess. Second, adaptive behavior scales do not usually focus on the student's ability to adapt to changes in the environment and to problem-solve when something unexpected arises. Finally, adaptive behavior measures focus on what the student can and cannot do rather than on what might be causing the particular behaviors (Brown, McDonnell, & Snell, 2016). Despite these concerns, adaptive behavior measures are still popular with special education teachers and behavioral specialists, and it is helpful for physical educators and physical therapists to have a basic understanding of them.

An alternative way to assess behaviors of students with disabilities is to conduct a **functional behavior analysis**. In this process, the IEP team attempts to determine why a student displays a particular behavior in hopes of planning a program that can prevent it. This tactic is part of the **positive behav-**

ioral support approach to working with students with behavioral problems (Bambara, Janney, & Snell, 2015). This approach finds positive ways to help students develop more appropriate adaptive behavior and become more independent. The advantage of a positive behavioral support approach compared with simply noting the student's adaptive behaviors and behavior problems is it gives an idea of why the student is displaying the inappropriate behaviors. If the physical education teacher can determine why a student behaves the way she does, then the teacher will have a better chance of finding a strategy to prevent the student from exhibiting the behavior while at the same time teaching the student more appropriate behaviors. Since there are no specific functional behavioral assessment tools, key questions used in the functional assessment process are presented.

UVA-APE Initial Observation and Referral Form

As noted earlier, many students with disabilities are referred to adapted physical education because of problems in general physical education. It is important that both adapted and general physical educators have a quick way of determining if a student's behaviors are significant enough to warrant further testing, extra support, or perhaps adapted physical education services. The UVA-APE Initial Observation and Referral Form (figure 10.1) is a quick, simple-to-use screening tool that helps general and adapted physical educators determine the significance of a student's behavioral problems in physical education. The form is divided into five main categories:

1. Transition to and from physical education
2. Responding to the teacher
3. Relating to peers and equipment
4. Effort and self-acceptance
5. Cognitive abilities

Each category has four to six different behaviors that are important for success in general physical education. Each behavior is observed and then scored on a three-point scale: adequate, needs improvement, and significantly inadequate. There is also a place to note when a behavior was not observed. The general or adapted physical educator should observe the targeted student in general physical education on at least two different occasions. The teacher fills out the form by putting a mark by the behavior in one of the three scoring boxes or in the "not observed" box. Observations on the second day as well as any subsequent observations are used to fill in behaviors not observed on the first day and to confirm behaviors seen on the first day.

Analysis of the scale involves simply scanning the results of the form. If most of the items are scored at the "needs improvement" level, then the recommendation to the IEP team might be peer tutor or teacher assistant support as well as training the general physical educator on ways to modify instruction, motivate the student, and deal with behavior problems. If most of the items are scored at the "significantly inadequate" level, then the recommendation might be a teacher assistant part of the time and adapted physical education part of the time within general physical education, or perhaps pull-out adapted physical education. For example, Jorge has general physical

UNIVERSITY OF VIRGINIA ADAPTED PHYSICAL EDUCATION INITIAL OBSERVATION AND REFERRAL FORM

Part II–Behaviors, Cognitive Abilities, and Social Skills in Physical Education

Child's name: _____   Evaluator: _____

School: _____   Date: _____

Use this form when first observing a child with a disability who has been referred for adapted physical education. Rate each item based on how the child compares with other children in his or her physical education class.

	Adequate 3	Needs improvement 2	Significantly inadequate 1	Not observed 0
Transition to and from physical education				
Enters without interruption	☐	☐	☐	☐
Sits in assigned area	☐	☐	☐	☐
Stops playing with equipment when asked	☐	☐	☐	☐
Lines up to leave when asked	☐	☐	☐	☐
Responding to teacher				
Remains quiet when teacher is talking	☐	☐	☐	☐
Follows directions in a timely manner: warm-up	☐	☐	☐	☐
Follows directions in a timely manner: skill focus	☐	☐	☐	☐
Follows directions in a timely manner: games	☐	☐	☐	☐
Accepts feedback from teacher	☐	☐	☐	☐
Uses positive or appropriate language	☐	☐	☐	☐
Relating to peers and equipment				
Works cooperatively with a partner when asked (e.g., shares, takes turns)	☐	☐	☐	☐
Works cooperatively as a member of a group when asked	☐	☐	☐	☐
Uses positive or appropriate comments with peers	☐	☐	☐	☐
Seeks social interactions with peers	☐	☐	☐	☐
Displays sportsmanship by avoiding conflict with others	☐	☐	☐	☐
Uses equipment appropriately	☐	☐	☐	☐
Effort and self-acceptance				
Quickly begins the activity once instructed	☐	☐	☐	☐
Continues to participate independently throughout activity	☐	☐	☐	☐
Adapts to new tasks and changes	☐	☐	☐	☐
Strives to succeed and is motivated to learn	☐	☐	☐	☐
Accepts his or her own skill whether successful or improving	☐	☐	☐	☐
Cognitive abilities				
Understands nonverbal directions	☐	☐	☐	☐
Understands verbal directions	☐	☐	☐	☐
Processes multistep cues	☐	☐	☐	☐
Attends to instructions	☐	☐	☐	☐

Comments regarding behaviors, social abilities, or cognitive abilities: _____

Figure 10.1   UVA-APE Initial Observation and Referral Form, Part II–Behaviors, Cognitive Abilities, and Social Skills in Physical Education.

From Horvat, M., Kelly, L.E., Block, M.E., and Croce, R., *Developmental and adapted physical activity assessment*, 2nd ed. (Champaign, IL: Human Kinetics, 2019). From the University of Virginia, *Adapted physical education initial observation and referral form,* courtesy of M.E. Block.

education two times per week. If he scored "significantly inadequate," then he could be accompanied by the teacher assistant to general physical education once a week and also see the adapted physical education specialist once a week. His program would continue to focus on motor and fitness goals but also include additional goals that focus on behaviors. The adapted physical educator would be in charge of training the teacher assistant and the general physical educator as well as peers without disabilities.

There have been no reports of validity or reliability on this observation and referral form. It is a quick screening tool, and results can be used to develop a basic behavioral intervention plan in physical education as well as to recommend more formal behavioral assessment. For example, this tool has been used to find out if a student can follow simple directions, stay on task, and generally display appropriate behaviors, either without support or with a peer tutor, and to determine whether the student needs a teacher assistant to be successful in general physical education.

Adaptive Behavior Assessment System, Third Edition (ABAS-3)

The Adaptive Behavior Assessment System, Third Edition (ABAS-3) is a norm-referenced assessment used with individuals from birth to age 89 to assess three general areas of adaptive behavior outlined by the American Association on Intellectual and Developmental Disabilities (AAIDD): conceptual, social, and practical skills. Scores for each area can be used to determine level of functioning, strengths and weaknesses, and training goals. Specifically, the ABAS-3 can be used to determine how well an individual responds to daily demands from the environment as well as whether adults can live independently (Harrison & Oakland, 2015). Although not as popular as the Vineland Adaptive Behavior Scales, the ABAS-3 has been used by both clinicians and researchers (e.g., Ogg, Montesino, Kozdras, Ornduff, Lam, & Takagishi, 2015).

Items on the ABAS-3 focus on everyday activities within the following areas: communication, community use, functional academics, health and safety, home or school living, leisure, self-care, self-direction, social, work, and motor. Scores are rated on a four-point response scale; raters indicate whether, and how frequently, the individual performs each activity. There are five rating forms, each for a specific age range and respondent. These forms can be completed by parents, family members, teachers, daycare staff, supervisors, counselors, or others who are familiar with the daily activities of the individual being evaluated. The adult form can function as self-rating. Software can be used for scoring, and the Intervention Planner and the Scoring Assistant identify appropriate interventions and monitor progress (Harrison & Oakland, 2015). ABAS-3 is best used by a trained behavior interventionist or school psychologist, but the information could be useful for physical educators and physical therapists in understanding a student's behavior and possible behavior planning.

Vineland Adaptive Behavior Scales, Third Edition (VABS-3)

The Vineland Adaptive Behavior Scales, Third Edition (VABS-3) (Sparrow, Cicchetti, & Saulnier, 2016) is a semi-structured parent interview used to obtain parent ratings of children's level of adaptive behavior functioning in individuals from birth to 21 years of age. The assessment also can be completed by clinicians and physicians who are familiar with the child. The assessment contains questions about behaviors and skills designed to aid in diagnosing and classifying intellectual and developmental disabilities. The scales are organized using three domains: communication (receptive, expressive, written), daily living skills (personal, domestic, community), and socialization (interpersonal relationships, play and leisure, coping skills). These domains correspond to the three broad domains of adaptive functioning specified by the American Association on Intellectual and Developmental Disabilities (AAIDD) and by the *Diagnostic and Statistical Manual of Mental Disorders, Fifth Edition* (DSM-5). In addition, VABS-3 offers optional domains for motor skills (fine motor, gross motor) and maladaptive behavior (internalizing, externalizing) for situations in which these areas are of concern.

Similar to IQ tests, the global VABS-3 score (scores from three major domains taken together) has a mean of 100 ± 15, with lower scores indicating greater impairment. Domain-level scoring is also available. VABS and VABS-2 have been the most widely used instruments to determine whether a student qualifies as having an intellectual disability, and VABS-3 should continue to be the gold standard in measuring adaptive behaviors. In addition, VABS and VABS-2 have often been used in research to measure present level of adaptive behavior as well as the effects of treatment on adaptive behavior (e.g., Ashwood, Tye, Azadi, Cartwright, Asherson, & Bolton, 2015; Doobay, Foley-Nicpon, Ali, & Assouline, 2014; Paynter, Riley, Beamish, Scott, & Heussler, 2015; Ventola, Friedman, Anderson, Wolf, Oosting, Foss-Feig, & Pelphrey, 2014). Changes in the VABS-3 from previous editions include updated item content and norms, choice of digital or paper-based administration, separation of interview and parent/caregiver forms, and clarification of basal and ceiling rules to shorten administration.

The adapted physical education specialist might find that the special education teacher uses this test to get an accurate measurement of a student's present adaptive behaviors in various settings, including physical education, and the special education teacher may ask the APE specialist to complete part of the form with reference to the student's behaviors in physical education. Similar to the ABAS-3, the VABS-3 is best used by a trained behavior interventionist or school psychologist, but the information could be useful for physical educators and physical therapists in understanding a student's behavior and possible behavior planning.

AAMR Adaptive Behavior Scale–School (ABS-S:2)

An older but still popular test is the AAMR Adaptive Behavior Scale–School (ABS-S:2), which was revised in 1993 from an earlier version. It is a popular norm- and criterion-referenced test that measures both adaptive and maladaptive behaviors. Divided into two parts, the test's first part measures adaptive behaviors in nine behavioral domains: independent functioning, physical development, economic activity, language development, numbers and time, prevocational and vocational activity, self-direction, responsibility, and socialization. The second part measures social maladjustment and is divided into seven behavioral domains (related to personality and behavior disorders): social behavior, conformity, trustworthiness, stereotyped and hyperactive behavior, self-abusive behavior, social engagement, and disturbing interpersonal behavior.

The age range for the ABS-S:2 is 3 to 18 years, and testing time is estimated at 15 to 30 minutes. Information is obtained via a standardized interview format conducted by a trained examiner (usually a school psychologist who has been trained on this test). Some items are measured on a Likert scale, ranging from 0 (behavior not present) to 3 (behavior present in highest form). An example is how well a person functions when visiting a fast-food restaurant. Other items require a yes or no (1 or 0) response. Examples of these items include taking food off others' plates, eating too fast or too slow, and swallowing food without chewing.

The ABS-S:2 was standardized on more than 2,000 children with disabilities and 1,000 children without disabilities from 31 states. Percentiles, age equivalents, and standard scores can be produced from the data. As was the case with the VABS, adaptive behavior quotients can be derived that have a mean of 100 and a standard deviation of 15 to match typical IQ tests. Data can also be easily translated for use with an IEP. For example, a teacher can identify a student's deficits in adaptive behavior as well as the presence of maladaptive behavior. She can then create objectives that focus on areas needing attention and instruction (Lambert, Nihira, & Leland, 1993). The test is reported to have high reliability and validity.

Also similar to the Vineland, the APE specialist might find that special education teachers in the district use this test to get an accurate measurement of a student's present adaptive behaviors and behavior problems in various settings, including physical education, and the special education teacher may ask the APE specialist to complete part of the form with reference to the student's behaviors in physical education. Similar to the ABAS-3 and the VABS-3, the ABS-S:2 is best used by a trained behavior interventionist or school psychologist, but the information could be useful for physical educators and physical therapists in understanding a student's behavior and possible behavior planning.

FUNCTIONAL BEHAVIORAL ANALYSIS

As noted earlier, functional behavioral analysis is a process in which the IEP team attempts to determine why a student displays a particular behavior. The purpose of the assessment is to understand the underlying cause of the behavior in hopes of planning a program that can prevent it. The focus of a functional behavioral assessment (and the subsequent positive behavioral support program) is on creating positive ways to help the student develop more appropriate adaptive behavior and become more independent.

There is no array of functional behavior assessment tools on the market. Rather, there are specific questions that any functional behavioral assessment tool should include. The questions listed in figure 10.2 are modified from worksheets created by Bambara, Janney, and Snell (2015). The functional behavioral assessment begins with a clear description of the student's targeted behavior written in an objective way, including the type of behavior (destructive, disruptive, or distracting) as well as the frequency, intensity, and duration of the behavior. For example, a student who is aggressive toward peers in physical education (further defined as hitting, pushing, and scratching) is demonstrating destructive behavior. The IEP team would note how often the student (Joey) is disruptive and the intensity of this disruptive behavior. The team might observe that Joey is aggressive on average three times per 30-minute physical education class, and the aggressiveness is at a moderate level (pushing and grabbing at peers, but not to the point where the peers get hurt).

The second step in the assessment process is a functional analysis of the cause of the behavior. In other words, what triggers the behavior? This is also known as examining the antecedents, or what happened just before the behavior occurred. The analysis includes questions and observations of who is present when the behavior occurs, what is going on when the behavior occurs, and finally where the behavior occurs. The focus at this point in the assessment is determining if something in the student's setting (person, place, activity, or time) is causing the behavior. Continuing with the previous example, the team observes Joey in physical education and notes that aggressive behaviors seem to focus on two specific peers (who). Joey shows these aggressive behaviors only when the general physical educator has the students grouped together to give instructions (when the behavior occurs, what is happening, and where it happens). Further observation reveals that aggressiveness can be expected nearly 100 percent of the time when the teacher asks the students to sit and wait while she sets up equipment or when instructions take several minutes.

The next step involves observing what happens to the student after he engages in the problem behavior (consequences). The team is watching for anything that occurs immediately after the student displays the behavior that might be reinforcing or maintaining the behavior. For example, Joey might get a lot of attention from his peers as well as from the general physical education teacher when he starts to push other students. He can be seen smiling and continuing the behavior while peers try to stop the behavior. He does not stop the behavior until the teacher comes over and places him in time-out.

The fourth step in the functional assessment process is determining the reason for the behavior, or what the student gets or avoids when he or she displays the behavior. In other words, what is the purpose of the behavior? Functional purposes of problem behaviors include getting attention, escape, getting something tangible, self-regulation, and play or entertainment (Bambara, Janney, and Snell, 2015). In our example, Joey might be displaying aggressive behavior to escape the activity (he seems to keep up the behavior until the teacher comes and puts him in time-out). Or he might be displaying the behavior to get attention (he seems to enjoy having peers try to stop him). Getting attention might make sense because the behavior occurs during "downtime" when no one is attending to Joey and he is bored.

FUNCTIONAL BEHAVIOR ASSESSMENT

Student: _____   Date: _____

School: _____   DOB: _____

1. **Define the student's problem behaviors:**
   Is the behavior destructive? ☐   disruptive? ☐   distracting? ☐

2. **Describe the behavior** in detail (frequency, intensity, duration).

3. What seems to **trigger** the behavior?
   - Who is present when the problem behavior occurs?
   - What is going on when the problem behavior occurs?
   - When does the problem behavior happen?
   - Where does the problem behavior occur?

4. **What happens to the student** immediately after he or she engages in the problem behavior (consequences)?

5. **What does the student get or avoid** by behaving this way (tangible items, escape or avoid, attention, self-entertainment)?

6. **Hypothesis statement:** "When (antecedent) happens in (specific setting), he or she does (problem behavior) in order to (perceived function)."

7. What are some **strengths and likes** of the student?

8. What are some ways to **prevent** the problem behavior?

9. What **alternative behaviors** can be **taught** and used in place of the problem behavior?

10. Describe ways to **respond** to the problem behavior when it occurs.

Figure 10.2   Functional behavior assessment.

From Horvat, M., Kelly, L.E., Block, M.E., and Croce, R., *Developmental and adapted physical activity assessment*, 2nd ed. (Champaign, IL: Human Kinetics, 2019). Modified from the *Albemarle County Schools functional behavior assessment form*, Form 80.01. Reprinted with permission of M.E. Block.

This leads to the next step, creating a hypothesis statement that includes when (antecedent), where (specific setting), what (problem behavior), and why (perceived function). For Joey, the hypothesis statement might read: When the physical education class is sitting and waiting for the teacher to set up equipment, or when the teacher is giving a great deal of instruction and the students have to sit and wait, Joey is aggressive toward peers (hits, pushes, scratches) in order to gain their attention. With a strong hypothesis statement, the team can then continue with the assessment process to determine Joey's strengths and likes (to see if there is a powerful reinforcer the student might like to work for), ways to prevent the behavior (e.g., allow this student to start at a station or do an activity with a peer when a lot of wait time is anticipated), alternative behaviors to be taught in place of the maladaptive behavior (e.g., holding hands with a peer while the teacher gives instruction), and how the team might respond to the behavior in a positive way if the behavior does occur. (See Bambara, Janney, and Snell, 2015, for more details on the positive behavioral support process.)

SOCIAL COMPETENCE

Displaying appropriate **social competence** is important for a student with disabilities to be successful in general physical education (or for that matter, in school, at work, or in the community). Students who cannot get along with peers, who cannot deal with basic interactions, who do not understand

Case Study 2
Documenting Problem Behaviors

Malcolm is a wonderfully energetic and physically skilled seven-year-old second grader in Mr. Johnson's fifth-period physical education class. In fact, Malcolm's motor skills and fitness put him at the top of the class compared with his peers. Unfortunately, his behaviors often get him into trouble in physical education. Malcolm's problems often begin as soon as he enters the gym. Mr. Johnson expects Malcolm and his classmates to enter the gymnasium quietly and sit in a "good" space away from peers and equipment. Malcolm often enters the gymnasium and runs to whatever equipment has been set out, whether it is a ball or jump rope or even cones marking boundaries. Then he begins to play with the equipment until Mr. Johnson reminds him that he is supposed to sit and wait for instructions. But this is only the beginning of Malcolm's problems. He will sit too close to his peers and begin conversations with them when all the students are supposed to be listening to the teacher. When Mr. Johnson asks questions to the class, Malcolm often blurts out answers without raising his hand. When the class is engaged in a fitness activity, skill activity, or game, he is often loud and physically aggressive with his peers, bumping and pushing them or running by them very fast to scare them. Mr. Johnson knows Malcolm has a behavior problem, and he would like to clearly document his concerns so both he and Malcolm can get the help they need. What types of assessment tools measure and detect students who display behavior problems in physical education?

basic safety as well as rules of games, and who cannot cope with criticism or situations such as losing will have a problem in most general physical education settings.

Social competence includes many subareas such as basic classroom skills (e.g., listening to the teacher, doing your best), basic interaction skills (e.g., making eye contact, using the right voice, turn-taking when talking), getting-along skills (e.g., using polite words, sharing, following rules), making-friends skills (e.g., good grooming, smiling), and coping skills (responding appropriately when someone says "no," responding appropriately when expressing anger) (Snell & Janney, 2006). Social skills and expectations differ for preschool students compared with elementary students compared with middle and high school students. Sharing toys may be important in preschool, while participating appropriately in a conversation is more important in high school. Nevertheless, all social skills are interrelated and reveal the ability of a student with disabilities to get along with peers and demonstrate socially acceptable behaviors.

A student who lacks basic social skills has problems with social acceptance. He may be known as the "weird kid" or be the student the general physical educator will notice. But without assessing the array of behaviors that fall under the umbrella term *social competence*, it is difficult for the general physical educator to determine exactly what social competencies the student is lacking. Also, assessing social skills allows the teacher to determine the student's present strengths and weaknesses with regard to social competence, identify goals for social competence, and determine whether the student is making progress toward these social goals. Four social skills tests are reviewed in this section. The first two tools are designed specifically to evaluate social skills in children with autism. This is followed by the Walker-McConnell Scale, which can be used with a variety of children. Finally, a more informal tool specific to physical education is reviewed—the University of Virginia Adapted Physical Education Program (UVA-APE) Social Skills Inventory.

Autism Diagnostic Observation Schedule (ADOS)

The Autism Diagnostic Observation Schedule, or ADOS, is considered by most to be the gold standard for diagnosing autism spectrum disorder (ASD). The ADOS directly assesses an individual for the common characteristics of ASD instead of using parental report as a proxy for diagnosing the behaviors associated with ASD (Akshoomoff, Corsello, & Schmidt, 2006; Lord, Rutter, DiLavore, & Risi, 2001). The second edition of the Autism Diagnostic Observation Schedule (ADOS-2) includes four modules (1-4) and one toddler module (Lord, Rutter, Dilavore, Risi, Gotham, & Bishop, 2012; Lord, Luyster, Gotham, & Guthrie, 2012). Each module consists of 10 to 15 tasks that are administered by a clinician or researcher, taking about 30 to 40 minutes to complete. Each task is designed to elicit social behaviors and communicative responses that are coded by the administering clinician or researcher as typical or nontypical, such as shared enjoyment, eye contact, repetitive behaviors, and self-stimulatory behaviors. The reliability and validity of the ADOS-2 are centered on the rigid training protocols that need to be completed prior to use in a clinic or in research.

Typically, the ADOS-2 is used with the Autism Diagnostic Interview–Revised (ADI-R) for diagnostic purposes to ensure that each participant has ASD (Jansiewicz, Goldberg, Newschaffer, Denckla, Landa, & Mostofsky, 2006; Lloyd, MacDonald, & Lord, 2013; Ming, Brimacombe, & Wagner, 2007). In one analysis (MacDonald, Lord, & Ulrich, 2014), the ADOS-2 was used as a calibrated autism severity score to understand the relationship between the severity of ASD (i.e., the amount of stereotypic behavior present) and gross motor skills. Results from this analysis suggest that as severity of ASD increases, there is a related severity in gross motor deficits. Extensive training is required to be certified to administer the ADOS, so practicing physical educators and therapists will not be the one administering the test but will be interested in the results.

Social Responsiveness Scale, Second Edition (SRS-2)

The SRS-2 is a 65-item parent report scale for use with children and adults with autism to quantitatively measure the ability to participate in reciprocal social behavior in typical social settings. Constantino (2012) notes that although some autism tests require trained professionals to code behaviors observed in clinical settings, the SRS-2 asks teachers, parents, and others to rate symptoms they've noticed over time at home, in the classroom, or elsewhere. Raters evaluate characteristics using a quantitative scale representing a range of severity. Each item examines an observed aspect of reciprocal social behavior that is rated on a scale from 0 (never true) to 3 (almost always true). Behaviors are assessed across five domains: social awareness, social cognition, social communication, social motivation, and autistic mannerisms. He further notes that the quantitative nature of the SRS-2 and wide age range make it ideal for measuring response to intervention over time, which in turn makes it easy to use in clinical, research, and educational settings. The total score provides an index of severity of social deficits. Subdomain severity can also be scored, which can then be translated to intervention needs and protocols (Constantino, 2012).

The SRS-2 offers four forms, each with 65 items and each for a specific age group:

- *Preschool form:* for ages 2-1/2 to 4-1/2, completed by parent or teacher
- *School-age form:* for ages 4 through 18, completed by parent or teacher (composed of the same items that appeared on the original SRS)
- *Adult form:* for ages 19 and up, completed by relative or friend
- *Adult self-report form:* self-report option for ages 19 and up

SRS-2 has been used in studies focusing on children with autism (e.g., Ventola, Friedman, Anderson, Wolf, Oosting, Foss-Feig, & Pelphrey, 2014). The assessment was standardized on a sample that included 4,891 children with autism and 3,030 siblings without autism. Alpha internal consistency for the ASD sample was .95 and .97 for the sibling sample. Test–retest reliability ranged from r = .88 to .97. The SRS-2 also has strong convergent validity (Constantino, 2012). Physical educators and therapists will not use this tool, but they will be interested in the results and how this information can inform understanding of the student with autism and related behaviors.

Walker-McConnell Scale (WMS)

The Walker-McConnell Scale of Social Competence and School Adjustment (WMS) rates students' social behaviors. It focuses on behaviors that are relatively easily observed during the school day, many of which occur in a physical education setting (e.g., accepts constructive feedback, sensitive to needs of others, uses free time appropriately). There are two versions of the WMS: one for elementary-aged children (K-6) and one for adolescents (grades 7 to 12). The elementary version consists of three subscales (teacher-preferred social behavior, peer-preferred social behavior, and school adjustment) totaling 43 items. The scale relies on teacher ratings of how frequently (never, sometimes, frequently) a student exhibits a particular social behavior. The 43 items of the elementary scale typically require no more than 10 minutes to complete for each student. The adolescent version contains four subscales (self-control, peer relations, school adjustment, and empathy) totaling 53 items. The adolescent scale also relies on teacher ratings of how frequently (never, sometimes, frequently) a student exhibits a particular social behavior, and the entire scale typically takes no more than 10 minutes to complete per student (Walker & McConnell, 1995). The scale can be used as a pretest to determine present level of social competence and ongoing progress toward development of specific social skills. Both the elementary and adolescent versions of the WMS have excellent validity and reliability, and the scales are widely used in schools across the United States.

The adapted physical education specialist might find that special education teachers in a district use the WMS to measure social competence, and they may ask the APE specialist to participate in the administration of this test in the physical education setting. Information from this test will also cue the APE specialist as to the specific social competencies and problems a particular student may have in various settings during the school day, including physical education. This information could then be used to create an intervention program to help the student improve his or her social skills and competencies.

UVA-APE Social Skills Inventory

The University of Virginia Adapted Physical Education Program (UVA-APE) Social Skills Inventory is a simple criterion-referenced tool that measures the social competence of students with disabilities. The inventory is divided into 10 subcategories, with descriptions of appropriate social behaviors listed under each category (figure 10.3). Categories include such social competence areas as accepting authority (e.g., complying with requests of adults, knowing and following classroom rules, following rules in the absence of a teacher), gaining attention (e.g., raising hand, waiting quietly for recognition, asking peer for help), making conversation (e.g., paying attention in a conversation, talking to others in appropriate tone of voice, waiting for pause in conversation before speaking), and care of property (e.g., taking care of personal property, asking permission to use another's property, sharing personal property).

UNIVERSITY OF VIRGINIA ADAPTED PHYSICAL EDUCATION PROGRAM SOCIAL SKILLS INVENTORY

Child's name: _____   Evaluator: _____

School: _____   Date: _____

Use this form when first observing a child with a disability who has been referred for adapted physical education. Rate each item based on how the child compares with other children in his or her physical education class.

Interpersonal Relations

	Adequate 3	Needs improvement 2	Significantly inadequate 1	Not observed 0
Accepting authority				
Complies with request of adult in position of authority	☐	☐	☐	☐
Complies with request of peer in position of authority	☐	☐	☐	☐
Knows and follows classroom rules	☐	☐	☐	☐
Follows classroom rules in the absence of the teacher	☐	☐	☐	☐
Questions rules that may be unjust	☐	☐	☐	☐
Coping with conflict				
Responds to teasing or name calling by ignoring, changing the subject, or some other constructive means	☐	☐	☐	☐
Responds to physical assault by leaving the situation, calling for help, or some other constructive means	☐	☐	☐	☐
Walks away from peer when angry to avoid hitting	☐	☐	☐	☐
Expresses anger with nonaggressive words rather than physical actions or aggressive words	☐	☐	☐	☐
Constructively handles criticism or punishment perceived as undeserved	☐	☐	☐	☐
Gaining attention				
Gains teacher's attention in class by raising hand	☐	☐	☐	☐
Waits quietly for recognition before speaking out in class	☐	☐	☐	☐
Uses "please" and "thank you" when making requests of others	☐	☐	☐	☐
Approaches teacher and asks appropriately for help, explanations, instructions, and so on	☐	☐	☐	☐
Asks a peer for help	☐	☐	☐	☐
Greeting others				
Looks others in the eye when greeting them	☐	☐	☐	☐
States name when asked	☐	☐	☐	☐
Smiles when encountering a friend or acquaintance	☐	☐	☐	☐
Greets adults and peers by name	☐	☐	☐	☐
Responds to an introduction by shaking hands and saying, "How do you do?"	☐	☐	☐	☐
Introduces self to another person	☐	☐	☐	☐
Introduces two people to each other	☐	☐	☐	☐
Helping others				
Helps teacher when asked	☐	☐	☐	☐
Helps peer when asked	☐	☐	☐	☐

Figure 10.3   University of Virginia Adapted Physical Education Program Social Skills Inventory.

(continued)

	Adequate 3	Needs improvement 2	Significantly inadequate 1	Not observed 0
Helping others				
Gives simple directions to a peer	☐	☐	☐	☐
Offers help to teacher	☐	☐	☐	☐
Offers help to a classmate	☐	☐	☐	☐
Comes to defense of peer in trouble	☐	☐	☐	☐
Expresses sympathy to peer about problems or difficulties	☐	☐	☐	☐
Making conversation				
Pays attention in a conversation to the person speaking	☐	☐	☐	☐
Talks to others in a tone of voice appropriate to the situation	☐	☐	☐	☐
Waits for pauses in a conversation before speaking	☐	☐	☐	☐
Makes relevant remarks in a conversation with peers	☐	☐	☐	☐
Makes relevant remarks in a conversation with adults	☐	☐	☐	☐
Ignores interruptions of others in a conversation	☐	☐	☐	☐
Initiates conversation with peers in an informal situation	☐	☐	☐	☐
Initiates conversation with adults in an informal situation	☐	☐	☐	☐
Organized play				
Follows rules when playing a game	☐	☐	☐	☐
Takes turns when playing a game	☐	☐	☐	☐
Displays effort in a competitive game	☐	☐	☐	☐
Accepts defeat and congratulates the winner in a competitive game	☐	☐	☐	☐
Positive attitude toward others				
Makes positive statements about qualities and accomplishments of others	☐	☐	☐	☐
Compliments another person	☐	☐	☐	☐
Displays tolerance for persons with characteristics different from his or her own	☐	☐	☐	☐
Informal play				
Asks another student to play on the playground	☐	☐	☐	☐
Asks to be included in a playground activity in progress	☐	☐	☐	☐
Shares toys and equipment in a play situation	☐	☐	☐	☐
Gives in to reasonable wishes of the group in a play situation	☐	☐	☐	☐
Suggests an activity for the group on the playground	☐	☐	☐	☐
Care of property				
Distinguishes own property from the property of others	☐	☐	☐	☐
Lends possessions to others when asked	☐	☐	☐	☐
Uses and returns others' property without damaging it	☐	☐	☐	☐
Asks permission to use another's property	☐	☐	☐	☐

Comments: _____

_____

Figure 10.3 *(continued)*

From Horvat, M., Kelly, L.E., Block, M.E., and Croce, R., *Developmental and adapted physical activity assessment*, 2nd ed. (Champaign, IL: Human Kinetics, 2019). Created by Martin Block. Based on Stephens, Hartman and Lucas 1982.

These categories were determined by practicing APE specialists in Albemarle County, Virginia, to be the most important social categories for success in general physical education. The inventory has not been tested for validity or reliability, but practicing general and adapted physical educators find it useful for determining the basic social competencies of students with disabilities in physical education.

To administer the inventory, the teacher observes the student in a general physical education setting in situations that require the demonstration of social competence. This may take several observations and some staging of social situations to view all the various social competencies on the inventory. For each behavior observed, the student is scored on a three-point Likert scale (adequate, needs improvement, and significantly inadequate). Students who receive a "significantly inadequate" rating on 50 percent or more of the behaviors on the overall checklist, or students who receive a "significantly inadequate" rating on all the items in two or more subcategories, clearly have social competency inadequacies that require intervention (even significantly inadequate ratings on a handful of social behaviors may be worth noting and planning intervention for). Social behaviors that are inadequate can be targeted for instruction, and follow-up assessments can be administered to chart improvement.

SELF-CONCEPT

Positive **self-concept** is critical in order for students with disabilities to stay motivated to try their best in school, including physical education. If a student is not successful in physical education, there is a good chance she will not feel good about herself. There are many specific terms associated with self-concept. **Self-esteem** is defined as a general positive self-regard, self-worth, or overall good feeling about oneself. Self-esteem is most directly related to self-concept. Students who have a strong self-esteem feel good about themselves and are not troubled by sadness, loneliness, or depression. Self-esteem is believed to be a global concept that is different from perceived competence and self-perception. **Perceived competence** and **self-perception** refer to how competent one feels in particular activities or pursuits (Harter, 1988). Typical domains associated with perceived competence include school, sports, work, close friendships, social acceptance, romantic appeal, physical appearance, and behavioral conduct.

For adapted physical education, it might be important to determine how some students feel about themselves globally (self-worth or self-esteem) as well as how they feel specifically about certain characteristics (e.g., appearance, athletic ability, social acceptance). This is particularly true for adolescents with physical or sensory disabilities who may begin to think they are not as capable or as worthy as their nondisabled peers. For this reason, adapted physical educators may want to seek out instruments that measure self-esteem and perceived competence. Two scales in particular seem to be most appropriate for adapted physical education: Harter's Self-Perception Profile for Adolescents (SPPA) and Ulrich's Pictorial Scale of Perceived Physical Competence (PSPPC).

Case Study 3
Sarah: Low Physical Self-Perception

Sarah is a 13-year-old eighth grader at Eastern Middle School. She was born with a severe hearing impairment that cannot be corrected with hearing aids or surgery. She is fluent in sign language and has an interpreter for all her classes. She can read lips a little when she is one on one with someone, and she can speak, but her speech is difficult to understand. Sarah has always gone to general education classes, including general physical education. She does receive special speech services, and she goes to a resource room for about an hour a day for academic help, but she is basically on age level academically. Physical education has never been a problem for Sarah because she has relatively typical motor skills and physical fitness, so she has never received any special physical education services.

Sarah has had the same physical education teacher, Ms. Avery, for all three years she has been at Eastern Middle School. Ms. Avery has never considered Sarah a behavior problem or someone she has any concerns about. However, she has noticed that Sarah has gradually become less enthusiastic and less involved in physical education activities. Sarah dresses and participates, but Ms. Avery considers Sarah's effort less than what she sees from the other eighth graders. The teacher has also begun to notice that Sarah stays on the periphery in games rather than trying to get involved. Finally, this year Ms. Avery has noticed that Sarah often chooses her interpreter as her partner rather than seeking out a peer. Sarah's physical educator would like to see her become more socially included in the class. What are some simple ways Ms. Avery can get Sarah's peers to embrace her?

Harter's Self-Perception Profile for Adolescents (SPPA)

Susan Harter from the University of Denver has created several scales to measure self-perception in children and adults. The scales most appropriate for adapted physical education are her Self-Perception Profile for Children and her Self-Perception Profile for Adolescents. Both scales assess self-perceptions in several different domains. The childhood scale measures self-perceptions in global self-worth as well as in five domains: scholastic competence, social acceptance, athletic competence, physical appearance, and behavioral conduct. The adolescent scale covers these six areas plus friendship, romantic appeal, and job competence (Harter, 2012).

The SPPA utilizes a structured alternative-response format. Subjects are given two descriptions and asked to choose which description they are most like. Then within the description they choose, they select "really true for me" or "sort of true for me". Harter suggests that this type of format increases the likelihood that subjects will respond based on how they truly feel rather than in a way they think is desirable or expected. The profile also includes an importance scale, which asks subjects to rate whether or not something is important to them. The format for the importance scale is the same as for the Self-Perception Profile (i.e., structured alternative-response format). Harter's Self-Perception Profile for Children and Self-Perception Profile for Adolescents have both been widely used in sport psychology research (see figure 10.4). Both instruments have very good reliability (both internal consistency and test–retest reliability) as well as validity supported through factor analysis (Harter, 2012).

Of interest to physical educators is the athletic competence subscale (see figure 10.4). Results from the five items in this subscale provide a sense of how students feel about their athletic abilities and to a lesser degree their abilities in physical education. This information could be used for students with physical or sensory disabilities or mild cognitive disabilities to get a general sense of how they feel about their physical athletic competence. The adapted physical educator could also create other items more directly related to physical education. The following are examples of statements using Harter's structured alternative-response format that adapted physical educators can use for students with disabilities to get a more accurate idea of their self-perception and self-confidence in physical education:

- Some students enjoy physical education, but other students do not enjoy physical education.
- Some students do well in most physical education activities, but other students do not do well in most physical education activities.
- Some students enjoy physical fitness activities, but other students do not enjoy physical fitness activities.
- Some students enjoy working with a partner in physical education, but other students do not enjoy working with a partner.
- Some students enjoy playing group games in physical education, but other students do not enjoy playing group games.
- Some students wish games could be modified more so that everyone could be successful, but other students like playing the games following the regulation rules.
- Some students get a little embarrassed when they cannot do a skill in physical education, but other students don't really care if they have trouble doing a skill.

Ulrich's Pictorial Scale of Perceived Physical Competence (PSPPC)

Ulrich and Collier (1990) adapted Harter's Pictorial Scale of Perceived Competence and Social Acceptance for use with children with mild intellectual disabilities. The adapted scale became known as Ulrich's Pictorial Scale of Perceived Physical Competence (PSPPC). The PSPPC assesses the self-perceptions of motor skills competence among elementary-aged students and students with an intellectual disability. Since this is a pictorial scale, it is ideal for students who cannot read, such as young elementary students and students with mild intellectual disabilities and learning disabilities (Ulrich & Collier, 1990). Subjects are

WHAT I AM LIKE

Really true for me	Sort of true for me				Sort of true for me	Really true for me
		Sample Sentence				
_____	_____	Some teenagers like to go to movies in their spare time	BUT	Other teenagers would rather go to sports events	_____	_____
		Items from the Athletic Competence Subscale				
_____	_____	Some teenagers do very well at all kinds of sports	BUT	Other teenagers don't feel that they are very good when it comes to sports	_____	_____
_____	_____	Some teenagers think they could do well at just about any new athletic activity	BUT	Other teenagers are afraid they might not do well at a new athletic activity	_____	_____
_____	_____	Some teenagers feel that they are better than others their age at sports	BUT	Other teenagers don't feel they can play as well	_____	_____
_____	_____	Some teenagers don't do well at new outdoor games	BUT	Other teenagers are good at new outdoor games right away	_____	_____
_____	_____	Some teenagers do not feel that they are very athletic	BUT	Other teenagers feel that they are very athletic	_____	_____

Figure 10.4   Select items from Harter's Self-Perception Profile for Adolescents.

From Horvat, M., Kelly, L.E., Block, M.E., and Croce, R., *Developmental and adapted physical activity assessment*, 2nd ed. (Champaign, IL: Human Kinetics, 2019).

shown a series of two contrasting pictures of children performing gross motor skills such as throwing or jumping (see list that follows). One picture shows a child who is "pretty good" at the skill, and the other picture shows a child who is "not very good" at the skill. Subjects are then asked to point to the picture of the child they feel most like and to indicate if they feel "a lot" like the child they chose or "a little" like the child they chose. Thus, the scale is a four-point scale, with a 1 indicating a subject selected the picture of the child who is not very good at a skill and then stated he feels "a lot" like that child. A score of 4 indicates a subject selected the picture of the child who is very good at a skill and then stated he feels "a lot" like that child (figure 10.5).

As noted already, the PSPPC was modified from Harter's original pictorial scale. Modifications focused on adding fundamental gross motor skills commonly seen in elementary physical education programs as well as items recommended by adapted physical educators (hopping was eliminated, and

This boy is pretty good at jumping.

Are you:

Pretty good   or   Really good at jumping

This boy is not very good at jumping.

Are you:

Not very good   or   Sort of good at jumping

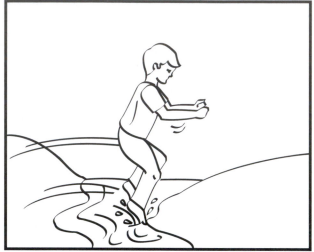

This girl can run pretty fast.

Are you:

Pretty fast   or   Really fast

This girl can't run very fast.

Are you:

Not very fast   or   Sort of fast

Figure 10.5   Select items from Ulrich's Pictorial Scale of Perceived Physical Competence.

Based on D.A. Ulrich and D.H. Collier, 1990, "Perceived physical competence in children with mental retardation: Modification of a pictorial scale," *Adapted Physical Activity Quarterly 7*: 338-354.

many sports skills were added). Ulrich and Collier's final scale consists of the following fundamental gross motor skills:

Swinging	Climbing on a jungle gym	Skipping
Running	Bouncing a ball	Jumping rope
Jumping	Kicking	Throwing
Catching		

The final scale also includes the following sport-specific skills:

Baseball	Batting a baseball	Throwing a baseball	Catching a baseball
Basketball	Dribbling a basketball	Shooting a basketball	Passing a basketball
Soccer	Dribbling a soccer ball	Kicking a soccer ball	Soccer throw-in

The PSPPC was analyzed and validated in a study by Ulrich and Collier (1990) using children with mild intellectual disabilities. Results found the PSPPC to have good internal consistency (82 percent total-scale Cronbach alpha reliability) and good test–retest reliability (77 percent for the overall mean score but somewhat lower on select individual items [26 percent on the skip and 63 percent on the dribble]). There are no norms, and validity was not cited in the Ulrich and Collier study. Care should be taken to ensure subjects completely understand the pictures as well as the skill being demonstrated in each picture. To better understand why a student responds the way she does, it is recommended that the examiner ask the following additional questions: Have you ever done this skill? When? A lot or a little? Who taught you? Do you like doing the skill? Is it fun?

PLAY BEHAVIORS

Play is a critical part of early childhood development. It allows children to have fun, use their imaginations, and appropriately occupy their free time. In addition, social play (playing with or around others) allows students to learn from peers; to take turns and cooperate with peers; and to learn different, appropriate ways to play with toys and peers (Barton, 2015). Learning to play appropriately also prevents students with disabilities from being socially rejected and avoided by their peers without disabilities (Lifter, Mason, & Barton, 2011). Unfortunately, many students with autism as well as some students with intellectual disabilities do not have developmentally appropriate play skills. These students may not spontaneously play with toys or objects that are attractive to their peers, they may not seek to play with other students, or they may not play appropriately when they do engage in play with toys or peers. Additionally, these students may react to play settings in ways that are different from what is expected of children their age (Barton, 2015; Kretchmar, 2012; Powers, 2000; Reid, O'Conner, & Lloyd, 2003). For example, when other students are excited about sharing balls in a tossing and dodging game, a student with autism may just pick up one ball, hold it tight to his chest, and then run to the corner of the gym. Similarly, when other students are laughing and having fun with a parachute, a student with autism might be holding his ears and crying.

One important goal of programming for students with autism and similar developmental disabilities is to teach them how to play more appropriately. Their present level of play behavior should be assessed, as well as their progress toward demonstrating more appropriate play behavior throughout the program. Sherrill (2004) notes that assessment should include observations of a student's spontaneous play and interactions with objects and people in her environment. Sherrill suggests the following questions to ask when observing students in play: "Do they initiate contact with people and objects, and is their contact appropriate? How long do they sustain contact? Do they demonstrate preferences for some objects and people?" (p. 499). With such baseline information, the IEP team can design a developmentally appropriate intervention plan and appropriate objectives. Additionally, the team should conduct ongoing observations to determine a student's progress toward more appropriate play behaviors. There are no formal play behavior assessments that are appropriate for physical education. The following is an example of a teacher-developed assessment specifically designed for physical education settings.

Sherrill–UVA-APE Social Play Behavior Inventory

Sherrill (2004) created a simple-to-use social play behavior inventory to measure a child's current play behaviors as well as ongoing improvement in play. This social play behavior inventory was slightly modified by the University of Virginia Adapted Physical Education Program (UVA-APE) to include four behavior levels: always, most of the time, sometimes, and rarely or never (figure 10.6). These levels allow the examiner to determine "how much" a

Case Study 4
Terry: Reluctant to Play with Peers

Terry is a seven-year-old second grader who enjoys cartoons, McDonald's Chicken McNuggets, playing with toy soldiers, and tossing and chasing a small yarn ball. Terry also has autism, and he rarely shares his favorite things with his family or peers. This is particularly noticeable in physical education, where Terry often wanders the perimeter of the gymnasium, tossing and picking up his yarn ball. He does have a teacher assistant who tries to coax him to participate with his peers, but she has not been very successful. One of Terry's global goals (a goal that all IEP team members are working toward) is to move from isolated play to more interactive play. The team has some ideas on how to help Terry become more sociable in his play, but how can they measure progress toward more appropriate play?

SHERRILL–UNIVERSITY OF VIRGINIA ADAPTED PHYSICAL EDUCATION SOCIAL PLAY BEHAVIOR INVENTORY

Child's name: _____   Evaluator: _____

School: _____   Date: _____

Use this form when first observing a child with a disability who has been referred for adapted physical education. Rate each item based on how the child compares with other children in his or her physical education class.

	Always 4	Most of the time 3	Sometimes 2	Rarely or never 1
Autistic/Unoccupied				
Shows no spontaneous play	☐	☐	☐	☐
Makes no response	☐	☐	☐	☐
Shows no object or person preference	☐	☐	☐	☐
Makes stereotyped or repetitive movements	☐	☐	☐	☐
Pounds, shakes, or mouths objects without purpose	☐	☐	☐	☐
Self-stimulates	☐	☐	☐	☐
Wanders about aimlessly	☐	☐	☐	☐
Self-mutilates	☐	☐	☐	☐
Solitary/Exploratory				
Reacts to stimuli (approaches or avoids)	☐	☐	☐	☐
Reacts to persons or objects	☐	☐	☐	☐
Understands object permanence (peek-a-boo, hide and seek)	☐	☐	☐	☐
Explores body parts	☐	☐	☐	☐
Explores objects or toys	☐	☐	☐	☐
Shows object preference	☐	☐	☐	☐
Shows person preference	☐	☐	☐	☐
Parallel				
Establishes play space near others	☐	☐	☐	☐
Shows awareness of others but doesn't interact	☐	☐	☐	☐
Plays independently with own things	☐	☐	☐	☐
Plays on same playground apparatus as others	☐	☐	☐	☐
Follows leader in imitation games and obstacle course	☐	☐	☐	☐
Associative/Interactive				
Initiates contact or play with others	☐	☐	☐	☐
Talks, signs, or gestures to others	☐	☐	☐	☐
Imitates others	☐	☐	☐	☐
Rolls or hands toy or ball to another without being asked	☐	☐	☐	☐
Retrieves objects for another without being asked	☐	☐	☐	☐
Offers to share objects or toys	☐	☐	☐	☐
Engages in make-believe play with others	☐	☐	☐	☐
Takes turns talking and listening	☐	☐	☐	☐

Figure 10.6 Sherrill–University of Virginia Adapted Physical Education Program Social Play Behavior Inventory.

(continued)

SHERRILL–UNIVERSITY OF VIRGINIA ADAPTED PHYSICAL EDUCATION SOCIAL PLAY BEHAVIOR INVENTORY *(CONTINUED)*

	Always 4	Most of the time 3	Sometimes 2	Rarely or never 1
Cooperative				
Participates in small-group games	☐	☐	☐	☐
Sustains play in group of 3 or more for 5 minutes	☐	☐	☐	☐
Follows simple game rules	☐	☐	☐	☐
Understands stop and go	☐	☐	☐	☐
Understands safety zone, boundary line, base	☐	☐	☐	☐
Understands "It" and "not It"	☐	☐	☐	☐
Understands game formations (circle, line, file, scattered)	☐	☐	☐	☐
Plays games demanding one role (fleeing)	☐	☐	☐	☐
Switches roles to achieve game goals: hide or seek, chase or flee, tag or dodge	☐	☐	☐	☐

Figure 10.6   *(continued)*

From Horvat, M., Kelly, L.E., Block, M.E., and Croce, R., *Developmental and adapted physical activity assessment,* 2nd ed. (Champaign, IL: Human Kinetics, 2019). From C. Sherrill, 2004, *Adapted physical activity, recreation, and sport,* 6th ed. (New York, NY: McGraw-Hill), 500. Used with permission of The McGraw-Hill Companies.

student shows a particular play behavior and allows for a more sensitive measurement of progress. The inventory is divided into five developmental levels of play starting with autistic or unoccupied play (shows no spontaneous play, makes no response to stimuli, play is stereotypical or repetitive) and ending with cooperative play (participates in small-group games; sustains play in a group; follows simple game rules; understands safety zones, boundaries, and rules).

To use the inventory, the examiner watches a student in settings that provide opportunities to play with (1) age-appropriate toys, (2) one or two students in both unstructured play and structured partner activities, and (3) a large group of students in a structured game. The examiner then marks the box with the description that best describes the student's behavior. To gain reliability, it makes sense to observe the student multiple times in each of the three scenarios. For example, the examiner might organize a session in which balls are provided to all students in the class. Minimal instructions are provided, and the teacher simply observes the student to see how he plays with the ball. Then other toys and equipment can be given to the students such as beanbags, hula hoops, yarn balls, jump ropes, or cones to see how the student plays with these toys. Similarly, several different opportunities to observe the student playing with a peer and playing in a group game should be arranged to get a true measure of the student's current social play behaviors.

ATTITUDES

Students without disabilities do not automatically include students with disabilities in their social play activities, including the social play of physical education, recreation, and sport activities. Nondisabled students who have positive feelings toward peers with disabilities are more likely to accept and include them in their social play activities. On the other hand, students who hold negative feelings toward peers with disabilities will be less likely to want to include these students in their social play activities. Clearly, how students without disabilities feel toward students with disabilities plays an important part in the successful inclusion of students with disabilities in general physical education and recreation.

This feeling is captured in the concept of attitudes. **Attitudes** specify one's preference to either avoid or approach someone or something (Tripp & Sherrill, 2004). Furthermore, attitudes are believed to be directly connected to intentions, and in turn intentions are believed to be directly related to behaviors (Ajzen & Fishbein, 1980).

For example, Jan doesn't like roller coasters (attitude), so she plans to avoid roller coasters (intention). When faced with a chance to ride a roller coaster, she will not ride it (behavior). With regard to students with disabilities, how a student without disabilities feels toward a peer with a disability (attitude)

Case Study 5

Measuring Attitudes Before and After Intervention

William is a 16-year-old sophomore at Washington High School. He and his friends are the "in crowd" at school. They are all athletes and very popular, and pretty much every day you can find William and his friends hanging out during breaks between classes with cheerleaders and other popular girls. Unfortunately, pretty much every day you can also find William and his friends teasing and picking on classmates who are not in the "in crowd." The most intense teasing is saved for Johnny and Tim, two boys with intellectual disabilities. William and his friends can be seen tripping and pushing these two boys in the hallway. And during physical education, they make fun of Johnny and Tim, make sure no one picks them to be on their team, and push and trip and intimidate the two boys whenever possible.

Early in the semester, the teasing and physical antics were pretty minimal, so Ms. Delgado, the general physical educator, let it go. But recently William and his friends have been more overt in their negative behaviors, and Ms. Delgado is ready to put a stop to it. However, she does not want to simply punish William and his friends. First, she wants to find out why they behave the way they do. Then she would like to try a disability awareness intervention to see whether this improves their attitudes and behaviors toward the two boys. What is a good way for Ms. Delgado to measure the present attitudes of William and his friends and then measure whether or not the intervention she implements has been effective?

reflects her intentions to play with a student with a disability, which in turn reflects whether or not she will actually play with the student with a disability when given the opportunity.

With regard to assessment, physical educators need to measure how nondisabled students feel about including students with disabilities in their physical education class. By measuring attitudes, the general physical educator will have a good idea of the behaviors to expect of the students without disabilities toward peers with disabilities (behaviors such as picking a student with disabilities to be their partner or to play on their team, helping a peer with disabilities learn a skill, or accepting modifications to games and equipment to make the activity more fair for the student with disabilities). Attitude assessments conducted early in the school year leave time for the general physical educator to do some disability awareness and acceptance activities. Such activities may change some students' negative attitudes toward peers with disabilities and prevent new negative behaviors and resentment from emerging (e.g., "Why does he have to be on my team?" and "Why does she get to shoot at a lower basket?") (Block, 2000). Assessment of attitudes can also be conducted after the disability awareness training session and occasionally throughout the year to make sure nondisabled students still have positive attitudes toward peers with disabilities. Three of the more widely used attitude inventories are presented in this section.

Children's Attitudes toward Integrated Physical Education–Revised Inventory

The Children's Attitudes toward Integrated Physical Education–Revised (CAIPE-R) is a simple-to-administer attitude inventory specifically designed for physical education (Block, 1995). It is a popular tool used in research on the effects of various interventions on changing attitudes in students without disabilities toward peers with disabilities (e.g., Campos, Ferreira, & Block, 2014; McKay, Block, & Park, 2015; Papaioannou, Evaggelinou, & Block, 2014). The purpose of the CAIPE-R is to determine attitudes of students without disabilities toward including peers with disabilities in physical education as well as toward modifications to sports typically played in general physical education.

The inventory begins with a description of a child with a disability, usually a child similar to the student to be included in the specific physical education class. In other words, if a student who has cerebral palsy and uses a wheelchair is going to join a fifth-period general physical education class, then the description of the student on the CAIPE-R should be someone who uses a wheelchair and who has similar movement abilities to a student with cerebral palsy (teachers can choose which disability description to use depending on the students with disabilities who are included). After the students read (or have read to them) the description of the targeted student, they respond to 12 to 14 statements using a four-point Likert scale (a yes answer equals 4 points, a no equals 1 point) (figure 10.7). The first seven statements on the CAIPE-R focus on generally including a student with disabilities in physical education. The last five to seven questions focus on whether or not the students would accept specific modifications to a sport played in physical education (such as

CHILDREN'S ATTITUDES TOWARD
INTEGRATED PHYSICAL EDUCATION–REVISED

Part I: General inclusion	Yes	Probably yes	Probably no	No
1. It would be okay having Mike in my physical education class.	☐	☐	☐	☐
2. Because Mike cannot play sports very well, he would slow the game down for everyone.	☐	☐	☐	☐
3. If we were playing a team sport such as basketball, it would be okay having Mike on my team.	☐	☐	☐	☐
4. Physical education would be fun if Mike were in my class.	☐	☐	☐	☐
5. If Mike were in my physical education class, I would talk to him and be his friend.	☐	☐	☐	☐
6. If Mike were in my physical education class, I would like to help him practice and play the games.	☐	☐	☐	☐
7. During practice, it would be okay to allow Mike to use special equipment such as a lower basket in basketball or a batting tee in softball.	☐	☐	☐	☐

Part II: Sport-specific modifications	Yes	Probably yes	Probably no	No
What rule changes during physical education do you think would be okay if a child like Mike were playing softball?				
1. Mike could hit a ball placed on a batting tee.	☐	☐	☐	☐
2. Someone could tell Mike where to run when he hits the ball.	☐	☐	☐	☐
3. The distance between home and first base could be shorter for Mike.	☐	☐	☐	☐
4. Someone could help Mike when he plays in the field.	☐	☐	☐	☐
5. If the ball were hit to Mike, the batter could run only as far as second base.	☐	☐	☐	☐

Figure 10.7   Children's Attitudes toward Integrated Physical Education–Revised (CAIPE-R) inventory.

From Horvat, M., Kelly, L.E., Block, M.E., and Croce, R., *Developmental and adapted physical activity assessment*, 2nd ed. (Champaign, IL: Human Kinetics, 2019). Adapted, by permission, from M.E. Block, 1995, "Development and validation of the children's attitudes towards integrated physical education-revised (CAIPE-R)," *Adapted Physical Activity Quarterly* 12: 60-77.

basketball, volleyball, or soccer). For example, modifications for basketball might include shooting at a shorter basket, not allowing anyone to steal the ball, allowing a free pass, and not calling traveling or double dribbling.

The CAIPE-R is analyzed by totaling each subscale (general physical education and sport-specific modifications) and dividing by the number of statements to get a score of 1 to 4. Scores of 1 or 2 indicate negative attitudes, while scores of 3 or 4 indicate positive attitudes. Each item on the CAIPE-R can also be analyzed to determine whether the majority of students in the class disagree with a specific part about inclusion or a specific modification. If the students feel negative about a particular statement, then the teacher can lead a discussion to determine why so many students feel that way. For example, let's say a majority of students disagree with the following statement: "If the ball were hit to Mike, the batter could run only as far as second base." The teacher can explain her rationale for the modification, find out why the class does not like this modification, and then suggest a new modification that is satisfactory to everyone.

Siperstein's Adjective Checklist

Siperstein's Adjective Checklist, a quick, simple tool that measures children's attitudes toward peers with disabilities, continues to be used in research (e.g., McKay, Block, and Park, 2015). The premise of the adjective checklist is that students will choose adjectives (e.g., *clever, crazy, healthy, weak*) that describe how they feel about a peer with a disability (this could be a real peer in the class or an imaginary student with a disability). According to the theory, students who have negative feelings toward a peer with a disability will choose adjectives that have negative connotations (e.g., *weak, sloppy, dumb*), while students with positive feelings will choose adjectives that have positive connotations (e.g., *happy, clever, cheerful*). To administer the checklist, the examiner places the name of a particular student (e.g., Sarah) or a description of a disability (e.g., student with mental retardation) on the blank line at the top of the checklist. Students circle all the words they would use to describe that person or that disability (students are directed to circle as many or as few adjectives as they wish). Figure 10.8 shows the adjectives on Siperstein's Adjective Checklist.

Factor analysis conducted on data from 2,200 children revealed three factors for the Adjective Checklist. Factor 1 (labeled *P* for positive factor) represents a bright, socially able classmate (e.g., *smart, friendly, nice*); factor 2 (labeled *N* for negative factor) represents a dull, socially inept classmate (e.g., *dumb, careless, greedy*); and factor 3 (labeled *E* for empathetic factor) rep-

SIPERSTEIN'S ADJECTIVE CHECKLIST

If you had to describe _____ to your classmates, what kind of words would you use? Below is a list of words to help you. CIRCLE the words you would use. You can use as many or as few words as you want. Here is the list:

Healthy	Clever	Crazy	Honest	Lonely	Proud
Bored	Friendly	Glad	Dishonest	Mean	Kind
Slow	Alert	Greedy	Ashamed	Pretty	Weak
Helpful	Sad	Stupid	Smart	Ugly	Bright
Sloppy	Okay	Cheerful	Neat	Cruel	
Dumb	Careful	Careless	Unhappy	Happy	

Figure 10.8 Siperstein's Adjective Checklist.

From Horvat, M., Kelly, L.E., Block, M.E., and Croce, R., *Developmental and adapted physical activity assessment*, 2nd ed. (Champaign, IL: Human Kinetics, 2019). Reprinted, by permission, from G.N. Siperstein, 2007, Adjective checklist. In *Encyclopedia of measurement and statistics,* edited by N.J. Salkind (Thousand Oaks, CA: Sage Publications, Inc.).

resents empathetic responses toward the targeted student or feelings inferred to be held by the targeted student (e.g., *lonely, unhappy, ashamed*). Scores on the Adjective Checklist show whether or not a student believes the targeted student manifests traits underlying each of the three factors. Each student's score is calculated as a proportion of adjectives selected by the total number of adjectives in each factor (17 for the P factor, 10 for the N factor, and 7 for the E factor). Results become three separate scores, each representing a ratio ranging from 0 to 1.0. Scores approaching 1.0 (e.g., 0.6 or higher) indicate a high score on that factor (Siperstein, 1980). For example, a student who chooses 7 out of 10 items on the N factor would have an N factor score of 0.7, suggesting she holds negative feelings toward the targeted student.

As was the case with the CAIPE-R, results of the Adjective Checklist should be examined and then discussed with the class. If several students describe a peer who has intellectual disabilities with adjectives such as *weak, dumb, stupid,* and *ugly*, the teacher should talk about why so many students feel that way about this student. Then perhaps an intervention should be considered, such as showing videos of Special Olympics athletes or bringing in someone with intellectual disabilities who does not meet the stereotype held by many of the students (McKay, Block, & Park, 2015).

Siperstein's Friendship Activity Scale

Siperstein believed that measuring a child's intentions to play and interact with a peer with a disability would be a strong indicator of the child's actual behaviors. Because observing a child's actual play and interaction behaviors is difficult, Siperstein created the Friendship Activity Scale to measure friendship intentions (Siperstein, Bak, & O'Keefe, 1988). The original Activity Preference Scale was made up of 30 activity statements that subjects responded to with yes, no, or not sure. A yes response received a score of 3, not sure received 2, and no received 1, yielding a possible range of scores from 30 to 90. The original scale was administered twice, first when the object of the scale was a friend and once when the object was the targeted child.

The revised scale is a shortened version of the original, with 15 activity statements judged on a four-point Likert scale (yes, probably yes, probably no, no). Scores are weighted from 4 (yes) to 1 (no), representing a range of scores from 15 to 60 (figure 10.9). The revised scale need only be administered once, with the focus on only the targeted child with disabilities. Internal consistency (Cronbach alpha coefficient) of the revised scale is 90 percent ($N = 696$ children). Again, results should be examined and then discussed with the class. For example, if several students note that they would not like to play games outside together with the targeted child after school or during recess, the teacher can ask why so many students feel this way. Information from these discussions can then be used to change behaviors of the student with the disability (e.g., students said they do not like to play with this student because he is too aggressive) or change the attitude and behavior of students without disabilities (e.g., ask these students how they would feel if no one played with them during recess or after school).

SIPERSTEIN'S REVISED ACTIVITY PREFERENCE SCALE

Monitor Instructions

[Read aloud to class] Make believe that Amy or Ben is moving into your neighborhood and will be coming into your class. What types of activities would you like to do with her or him? Below is a list of activities to help you decide. If you would like to do an activity with Amy or Ben, circle *Yes*. If you would probably do an activity with Amy or Ben, circle *Probably yes*. If you would probably not do an activity with Amy or Ben, circle *Probably no*. If you would not do an activity with Amy or Ben, circle *No*.

Remember, the answer to each question depends on you, and your answers will probably be different from other kids' answers. When you are all done, you'll probably have some yeses, some probably yeses, some probably nos, and some nos, or your answers could all be one thing. Does anyone have any questions [look around and wait for questions]?

Answer Sheet

Student's code: _____

If you would like to do an activity with Amy or Ben, circle *Yes*. If you would probably do an activity with Amy or Ben, circle *Probably yes*. If you would probably not do an activity with Amy or Ben, circle *Probably no*. If you would not do an activity with Amy or Ben, circle *No*.

1. Invite her or him to your house?	Yes	Probably yes	Probably no	No
2. Sit next to each other in class?	Yes	Probably yes	Probably no	No
3. Go sledding or ice skating together?	Yes	Probably yes	Probably no	No
4. Work on a class project together?	Yes	Probably yes	Probably no	No
5. Play games outside together after school?	Yes	Probably yes	Probably no	No
6. Eat lunch together in school?	Yes	Probably yes	Probably no	No
7. Listen to music at home together?	Yes	Probably yes	Probably no	No
8. Play together during recess or snack time?	Yes	Probably yes	Probably no	No
9. Play games inside your house together?	Yes	Probably yes	Probably no	No
10. Do errands for the teacher together?	Yes	Probably yes	Probably no	No
11. Go bicycle riding together?	Yes	Probably yes	Probably no	No
12. Play games in class together?	Yes	Probably yes	Probably no	No
13. Go on a picnic or swimming together?	Yes	Probably yes	Probably no	No
14. Play on the same team in gym?	Yes	Probably yes	Probably no	No
15. Go to the movies together?	Yes	Probably yes	Probably no	No

Thank you! You are finished!

Figure 10.9 Siperstein's Revised Activity Preference Scale.

From Horvat, M., Kelly, L.E., Block, M.E., and Croce, R., *Developmental and adapted physical activity assessment*, 2nd ed. (Champaign, IL: Human Kinetics, 2019). Reprinted, by permission, from G.N. Siperstein, 2007, Adjective checklist. In *Encyclopedia of measurement and statistics*, edited by N.J. Salkind (Thousand Oaks, CA: Sage Publications, Inc.).

What You Need to Know

Key Terms

adaptive behavior	perceived competence
antecedents	positive behavioral support
attitudes	self-concept
consequences	self-esteem
functional behavior analysis	self-perception
maladaptive behavior	social competence

Key Concepts

1. You should know the difference between adaptive and maladaptive behavior, why it is important to measure adaptive behavior, and different ways to measure adaptive behavior in students with disabilities.
2. You should be able to contrast the traditional versus the functional way to assess behavior problems. You should be able to administer a functionally based behavioral assessment for students with disabilities.
3. You should understand the concept of social competence and why it is important to assess social competence. You should be familiar with key testing protocols used to assess social competence in students with disabilities.
4. You should understand the concepts of self-concept, self-esteem, and perceived competence and why they are important. You should be familiar with key testing protocols used to assess self-concept and perceived competence in students with disabilities.
5. You should understand the concept of play and why it is important to assess play behaviors. You should be familiar with key testing protocols used to assess play in students with disabilities.
6. You should understand the terminology related to attitudes and why it is important to assess attitudes. You should be familiar with key testing protocols used to measure attitudes of students without disabilities toward peers with disabilities.

Review Questions

1. Rachel in case study 1 displays several maladaptive behaviors. How would you determine the extent of her behaviors (frequency, duration) and why these behaviors occur? Once you have more information about Rachel's behaviors, how would you create a positive behavior plan for her that would prevent her from displaying these behaviors and teach her to respond more appropriately?
2. Malcolm in case study 2 clearly displays unique behavior problems that can best be categorized as social problems. How could you determine the specific social problems Malcolm displays? What type of remedial program would you implement for Malcolm to teach him how to behave more appropriately in social situations?

3. Sarah in case study 3 appears to be having problems with how she feels about herself, or her self-esteem. How would you measure her self-esteem? What modifications to your program would you create to improve Sarah's self-esteem? How would you change how you interact with Sarah to improve her self-esteem?

4. Terry in case study 4 clearly has trouble with play behaviors. How would you measure Terry's specific developmental play level? Once assessed, how would you create a program that would improve his play behaviors?

5. William and his friends in case study 5 seem to have some problems with how they feel about their peers with disabilities. How could you measure their attitudes toward their peers with disabilities? How could you apply this information to create a disability awareness program to change their attitudes?

Sample Write-Up for Tests of Infant and Early Childhood Motor Development

Adapted Physical Education Observation and Evaluation

Name: Xena Golemis

Date: 02/15/17

DOB: 09/09/11

School: Beach Cove Elementary School

Evaluator: Martin E. Block, PhD

BACKGROUND INFORMATION

Xena is a five-year-old female who has met the Individuals with Disabilities Education Act (IDEA) and Surf County Public Schools eligibility criteria for "a child with multiple disabilities." As reported by Xena's mother as well as staff and specialists in Surf County Public Schools, Xena has mixed spastic/athetoid cerebral palsy with involvement in all four limbs (she cannot walk or use a wheelchair independently, but she is learning how to walk with a Pacer gait trainer); some level of unspecified cognitive impairment; significant speech and language deficits (she is starting to say single words such as *no* on occasion and can make requests through verbal utterances and body language); medical problems, including respiratory and eating problems as well as osteoporosis; and low vision (she has some vision loss, but it is unclear as to the exact degree).

Xena has received special education services through Surf County Public Schools since preschool. She attends kindergarten at Beach Cove Elementary School in Surf County with support from a special education teacher, full-time one-on-one nurse, speech therapist, occupational therapist, and physical therapist. She receives physical education with her kindergarten classmates in general physical education once a week with the support of her nurse.

Xena's parents, special education staff, and general physical educator were concerned about Xena's physical education program, and they sought an independent evaluation of Xena's motor skills and an analysis of her physical education needs. This evaluation was conducted by Martin E. Block, PhD, director of the master's program in adapted physical education (see attached copy of Dr. Block's vitae for validation of his qualifications). His assessment focused on a developmental evaluation of Xena's motor skills, an analysis of her functional motor abilities using various mobility apparatuses, a discussion with Xena's physical education teacher and therapists, and a discussion with Xena's mother.

Xena was tested in the therapy room at Beach Cove Elementary School. Testing lasted approximately one hour. Testing was conducted by Dr. Block with assistance from Ms. Cast, Xena's occupational therapist; Ms. Alvarez, Xena's physical therapist; Ms. Smith, Xena's general physical education specialist; and Mr. Reneeson, Xena's nurse. Xena's mother was present during the assessment to provide feedback to the evaluation team and to assist and motivate Xena as needed. Testing included the Peabody Developmental Motor Scales 2; observation of Xena in her crawler, gait trainer, and scooter; and discussion with Xena's mother. Xena's therapists, who have been working with her for several months, thought that Xena had a "good day" demonstrating her abilities, staying focused, and trying her best. Therefore, I believe the results from this assessment are a fair representation of Xena's motor skills.

PEABODY DEVELOPMENTAL MOTOR SCALES

The Peabody Developmental Motor Scales 2 (PDMS-2) is a norm-referenced motor test that was standardized on a sample of normally developing children from birth to 84 months of age. The PDMS-2 was chosen for two reasons: to obtain a baseline developmental motor score for Xena and to guide a qualitative analysis of Xena's motor patterns and motor abilities. The test is divided into six parts: reflexes, stationary, locomotion, object manipulation, grasping, and visual-motor integration. The original PDMS (from 1983) and the new PDMS-2 (from 2000) are widely accepted developmental tests used by diagnosticians, occupational therapists, physical therapists, psychologists, early intervention specialists, and adapted physical education teachers (Folio & Fewell, 2000).

The PDMS-2 norms are based on scoring each item as 2, 1, or 0. The examiner must decide how to score an item based on his or her clinical judgment of the child's performance and the specific criteria provided for each item. The general criteria for scoring items are as follows:

2   The child performs the item according to the criteria specified for mastery.

1   The child's performance shows a clear resemblance to the item-mastery criteria but does not fully meet the criteria.

0   The child cannot or will not attempt the item, or the attempt does not show that the skill is emerging.

Xena was administered the PDMS-2 in the therapy room of Beach Cove Elementary School. The test was administered by Dr. Block and other members of the evaluation team. The results of the test are listed in table A.1.

The following summarizes the results of testing.

• *Reflexes*. Reflex items focus on the presence or disappearance of early infant reflexes and the appearance of righting and protective responses. Xena still has a strong asymmetrical tonic neck reflex (ATNR), and she appears to have remnants of the symmetrical tonic neck reflex (STNR). She does not have any protective reactions or righting reactions, and she does not have the

Table A.1   PDMS-2 Test Results for Xena

Subpart	Raw score	Age equivalent (months)	Percentile rank for age
Reflexes	1	1	<1%
Stationary	2	1	<1%
Locomotion	9	2	<1%
Object manipulation	0	1	<1%
Grasping	12	3	<1%
Visual-motor integration	13	3	<1%

Landau response (when held in prone, raises head above horizontal plane, extends trunk, and attempts to extend legs). The presence of the ATNR along with the lack of righting or protective reactions is limiting Xena's ability to sit and stand independently.

• *Stationary*. Stationary items focus on trunk and head control when lying on the back and stomach and when sitting, as well as more advanced stationary skills such as balancing in standing. Xena was able to align her trunk when supported in sitting with a rounded back. However, she had very little head control in prone, supine, or sitting positions. She had almost a full head lag when pulled to sit, had a very difficult time moving her head from side to side when on her stomach, and had great difficulty keeping her head upright in supported sitting. She appears to have weak muscles in her neck that contribute to her lack of head control. Lack of head control makes it difficult for Xena to regard objects in her environment. Also, lack of head control and of righting and protective responses makes it difficult for her to sit and stand independently.

• *Locomotion*. Locomotion items focus on early leg and arm movements; early locomotor movements such as crawling and creeping; and more advanced locomotor skills of walking, jumping, and galloping. Xena was able to thrust her legs when lying on her back, turn from side to back, thrust arms when lying on her back, and momentarily bear weight in standing. She also was close to rolling over, using her opposite arm to facilitate the roll. She was unable to prop herself up on forearms, bring arms to midline when in supine, perform a complete roll, scoot on her bottom, crawl forward on her stomach, or creep forward on her hands and knees. She also was unable to stand independently, but she was able to take some reciprocal steps in her gait trainer.

• *Object manipulation*. Object manipulation items focus on catching, throwing, and kicking, with the lowest item as follows: "catches a tennis ball that is rolled to child while the child is sitting independently." Xena was unable to do any items in the object manipulation category.

• *Grasping*. Grasping items focus on grasping and releasing and the pattern the child uses to grasp objects. Xena displayed remnants of the grasp reflex, but she also was able to purposely hold and release objects with a palmar grip (using palm mostly, with fingers wrapped around object). She did not display higher levels of fingertip or pincer grasping.

- *Visual-motor integration.* Visual-motor integration items focus initially on tracking and grasping objects. Later, items focus on putting objects in and taking objects out of containers, building with blocks, cutting with scissors, stringing beads, and prewriting and drawing skills. Xena was able to track objects placed in her visual field by turning her head and by moving her eyes. She was able to regard her hands, and she attempted to reach for objects placed in her visual field. She did not display the ability to bring her hands to midline to grasp an object or to play with two objects at the same time. Her limitations in visual regard are no doubt due in large part to her ATNR.

LOCOMOTION: CRAWLER AND GAIT TRAINER

Crawling

Xena was placed for several minutes in an adapted crawling device. She attempted to move her legs when secured in this device, but she was unable to generate any of her own forward momentum. With the assistance of her therapist (support provided by her feet to assist in pushing off), Xena was able to move forward a few inches. Xena was unable to display the head-up position in the device for any length of time. Both Xena's mother and therapist noted the head-down position that Xena preferred in the crawler, and this position seemed to promote drooling. Xena began to protest being in the crawler after about three minutes.

Walking

Xena was placed in an adapted gait trainer known as the Pacer for several minutes. This gait training device provided a lot of support for Xena in the upright position with her feet hanging down to the floor. Once secured in the Pacer, Xena was able to generate enough momentum to move backward approximately three to five inches. Her therapist and mother noted that she could move much farther backward (two feet or more farther) in her Pacer than she demonstrated during testing. In addition, her mother and therapist noted that Xena could move several inches forward in the Pacer, but Xena was unable to demonstrate forward movement during testing. The Pacer seemed to be a good piece of equipment for Xena, promoting weight-bearing upright posture that would aid in postural muscle development. In addition, it appears that Xena might learn how to move the Pacer more functionally with direction and purpose in the future.

CONVERSATION WITH XENA'S MOTHER

I had a chance to have a brief conversation with Xena's mother, Jane, to find out what she would like from a physical education program. I asked her to focus on general motor goals for Xena as well as specific physical education goals and activities. In terms of general motor goals, Jane noted that functional motor skills were the most important thing for her and her family now and in the future. She specifically noted that activities and goals from the Mobility Opportunities Via Education (MOVE) program were important, including sitting independently, weight bearing in standing, assisting in pivoting, using hands and arms to assist in dressing and feeding, and mobility. In terms of specific goals for physical education, she would like Xena to use and improve her ability to move in her gait trainer while other children are doing locomotor patterns. Jane would also like to see Xena out of her wheelchair for part of physical education to work on her stretching and strengthening activities. Finally, she would like Xena to continue receiving general physical education with the support of her nurse. She would like to see peers work with and play with Xena more during these general physical education settings.

SUMMARY AND RECOMMENDATIONS

Xena is a five-year-old female whose motor skills are significantly delayed compared to her peers. Functional motor abilities are limited because of persistence of primitive reflexes, lack of balance and protective reactions, minimal strength and postural control, and mixed spastic/athetoid cerebral palsy. Xena is an outgoing, engaging child who truly loves movement. In addition, her mother and her therapists have noted small but consistent motor gains in the last few years, and they all believe she will continue to make progress toward more functional and independent movement.

Xena receives physical education once a week in the general setting with support from her nurse. General physical education can be appropriate for Xena as long as the nurse and general physical educator make sure Xena works on IEP objectives rather than simply trying to do what her peers are doing. For example, in a dodging and fleeing game, Xena can practice moving in her Pacer, and during throwing and catching activities, Xena could practice her grasping and releasing skills with small beanbags. Because of the significance of Xena's delays, I would recommend that Xena receive at least one additional day of adapted physical education in a one-on-one setting with her physical education teacher to focus on specific motor goals that might be more difficult to work on in a general physical education setting. In addition, the one-on-one session would give Ms. Smith, the general physical educator, more direct time with Xena. (In general physical education, Ms. Smith has to work with all the children, not just Xena.) This one-on-one session could include a few peer tutors to encourage social interactions and to motivate Xena.

It is also recommended that global motor goals be established that can be implemented by all members of the team, whether Xena is in general or adapted physical education, in physical or occupational therapy, in her classroom, or at home. As suggested by her mother, goals should focus on functional motor abilities (e.g., sitting and standing with a gradual reduction in support, walking in her Pacer with a gradual reduction in support, and functional use of hands and arms) and opportunities to interact with peers during motor sessions. Finally, the team should develop a home exercise program to give Xena more opportunities to improve her motor function.

Sample Write-Up for Tests of Fundamental Motor Development

Adapted Physical Education Observation and Evaluation

Name: John Dore

DOB: 09/23/2011

Evaluator: Christina Surf, APE

Date: 10/10/17

School: Rutherford Elementary School

BACKGROUND INFORMATION

John is a six-year-old male student who is repeating kindergarten at Rutherford Elementary School. John has participated in general physical education (GPE). He was referred for evaluation by Ms. Jones, who completed an initial request form with John's parents. The request form addressed concerns about John's motor skills, with the biggest concern being not alternating feet while going downstairs.

The following were used to evaluate John's skills in physical education to determine whether he requires APE: percentile ranking compared with age peers on the Test of Gross Motor Development 3, observation of John in regular physical education, and feedback from John's GPE teacher. Ms. Curry, CAPE, the APE specialist for Rutherford Elementary School, conducted the testing. All testing was conducted at Rutherford Elementary School during John's GPE class, in the hallway by the gymnasium, and in the gymnasium itself. John was observed on 10/07/17 while he participated with his kindergarten class in the gym. He was very cooperative during all testing, and he seemed to try his best in all testing situations. Dr. Martin E. Block, PhD, an associate professor at the Curry School of Education in the area of APE, was present during the TGMD-3 test to ensure the highest quality and accuracy of the test results. Therefore, these test results are a fair representation of John's skills in physical education.

TEST OF GROSS MOTOR DEVELOPMENT

The Test of Gross Motor Development 3 (TGMD-3) is an individually administered norm- and criterion-referenced test that measures the gross motor functioning of children 3 to 10 years of age. The test measures 13 gross motor skills frequently taught to children in preschool and elementary school. The skills are grouped into two subtests: locomotor and ball skills. The locomotor subtest measures the run, gallop, hop, leap, horizontal jump, skip, and slide. The ball skills subtest measures the two-hand strike, stationary dribble, catch, kick, overhand throw, and underhand roll. Each of these motor skills has been broken down into three to five components. Skills are analyzed to determine whether each component was present (1) or not present (0). Results are tallied across two trials and then totaled for the locomotor and ball skills subtests. Each subtest score is compared with a normative sample for analysis.

John scored at the 63rd percentile for locomotor skills (age equivalent of 6.9 years) and at the 50th percentile in ball skills (age equivalent of 7.0 years) compared with six-year-olds in the norm sample. John passed all the components of the run, gallop, leap, and horizontal jump, and he passed all but one component of the slide. He missed two out of five items on the hop (see table B.1 for detailed results). John passed all the components of the strike, kick, and underhand roll. He missed one out of three on the catch, one out of four on the overhand throw, and one out of two on the stationary dribble (see table B.2 for detailed results). It should be noted that, with the exception of the underhand roll, the ball skills tested on the TGMD-3 are not expected to be mastered, according to the Albemarle County physical education curriculum, until later in elementary education (second grade for the stationary dribble, third grade for the two-hand strike, fourth grade for the overhand throw and catch, and fifth grade for the kick), so it is not surprising that John did not pass all components of the ball skills. I have provided a table in this report that shows when children John's age are expected to master object control skills. Most children John's age have not mastered these object control skills. John's movements seemed fluid and precise, and he demonstrated reasonably good rhythm in locomotor skills and reasonably good eye–hand coordination in ball skills. John had the most difficulty with the stationary dribble. His stance made it easy for the ball to contact his foot and roll away from him in the middle of the dribble. During the catch, he would scoop the ball rather than catch it with two hands, so he scored only two out of three.

OBSERVATION IN GENERAL PHYSICAL EDUCATION

Following Directions and Staying on Task

I observed John in general physical education one time this fall. I also talked with Kathy Guilford, his GPE teacher. We both agreed that John is able to follow directions given by the lead teacher in a large-group setting (as many as 25 children) without any redirections. However, when John is doing warm-ups, he will not participate in any of the activities unless Ms. Guilford individually addresses him to do so. For example, the students went from stand-up stretches to floor exercises, and John realized he was the only one still standing, so he quickly sat down on the floor, continuing to do nothing until Ms. Guilford told him to do his sit-ups. He then completed two sit-ups and went back to playing with the tape on the floor. Ms. Guilford had them play a floor maze game ("Pac-Man"), and John completed every task the first time without needing any additional cues. I believe John engages in activities that grab his attention, which has nothing to do with his motor ability.

Table B.1 Locomotor Skills: TGMD-3 Results

		Trial		
		1	2	Score
Run	1. Arms in opposition to legs, elbows bent	1	1	2
	2. Brief period where both feet are off the ground	1	1	2
	3. Narrow foot placement, landing on heel or toe	1	1	2
	4. Nonsupport leg bent approximately 90°	1	1	2
Gallop	1. Arms bent and lifted to waist level	1	1	2
	2. A step forward with the lead foot followed by a step with the trailing foot to a position adjacent to or behind the lead foot	1	1	2
	3. Brief period where both feet are off the ground	1	1	2
	4. Maintains a rhythmic pattern for four consecutive gallops	1	1	2
	Locomotor skills subtest score			42
	Percentile rank			63
	Age equivalent			6.9 years

Note: Only two locomotor subitems are shown. Test results for the remaining five subitems would be shown in an actual write-up. Totals are shown.

Table B.2 Ball Skills: TGMD-3 Results

		Trial		
		1	2	Score
Two-hand strike	1. Dominant hand grips bat above nondominant hand	1	1	2
	2. Nondominant side of body faces the tosser, feet parallel	1	1	2
	3. Rotates hips and shoulders during swing	1	1	2
	4. Transfers body weight to front foot	1	1	2
	5. Bat contacts ball	1	1	2
Stationary dribble	1. Contacts ball with one hand at about belt level	0	0	0
	2. Pushes ball with fingers (not slap)	1	1	2
	3. Ball contacts floor in front of or to the side of foot on the side of the hand being used	0	0	0
	4. Maintains control of ball for four consecutive bounces without having to move feet to retrieve it	1	1	2
	Ball skills subtest score			41
	Percentile rank			50
	Age equivalent			7.0 years

Note: Only two ball skill subitems are shown. Test results for the remaining four subitems would be shown in an actual write-up. Totals are shown.

Behaviors and Social Skills

John has never displayed any inappropriate behaviors that would cause him to be considered a behavior problem by his peers or GPE teachers. I have seen him off task during warm-ups, but he is easily refocused to the task at hand, usually by the GPE teacher. I never observed him (or heard from the others who work with him more regularly) having any behavioral outbursts such as crying or getting very angry. John interacts appropriately with his peers; his personality truly comes out during every game played. Most of the physical education activities I observed were individual in nature, and the pace of the program did not lend itself to lots of social interactions by any of the children. On the other hand, John is not opposed to holding a peer's hand, being a partner with a peer, being in a group, or playing a group game.

Conversation With Ms. Guilford

I also talked with John's physical education teacher. She did not consider John's motor or fitness skills to be delayed compared to his age peers. In addition, she did not consider John to be a behavior problem. She did note that he veers off task very easily during individual activities, such as warm-ups or closing songs, but he promptly gets back on task upon her request. She further noted that John was able to keep up with his peers in various conditioning, skill-building, and game activities. Ms. Guilford believes there is something different about John, but it is definitely not motor or skill related, nor does it interfere with the education of his peers in his class.

SUMMARY AND RECOMMENDATIONS

Results from the Test of Gross Motor Development 3 (TGMD-3), observation in general physical education, and conversation with John's GPE teacher lead me to conclude that John does not qualify for adapted physical education services at this time. Even though he is repeating kindergarten, he is functioning at age level on gross motor development and on skills required by Rutherford Elementary for schoolchildren his age. He seems to follow directions very well in general physical education, he does not need anything to make his participation any more successful, and he does not exhibit any behaviors that would cause him to interfere with other children's learning. Although it was indicated in the initial request form that his balance is poor, his running is awkward, and he does not alternate feet going down stairs, I did not observe any of these things in his general physical education setting. The concerns addressed in the initial request form can be corrected within the activities that Ms. Guilford leads in her classes. Ms. Guilford includes numerous cross-lateral activities, which integrate both sides of the brain, ultimately improving John's balance and running ability. I would recommend placement in general physical education without any special accommodations or adapted physical education services for the 2017-2018 school year.

In the event that the general physical education staff believe that John is not making adequate progress or is causing a behavior problem, then the APE specialist can reevaluate the need for accommodations to general physical education.

Sample Write-Up for Tests of Motor Proficiency

Adapted Physical Education Observation and Evaluation

Name: Renee Gross

DOB: 08/23/07

Evaluator: Christina Surf, APE

Date: 10/10/17

School: Crooked Stick Elementary School

BACKGROUND INFORMATION

Renee is a 10-year-old fourth grader at Crooked Stick Elementary School. Renee has participated in general physical education. She was referred for evaluation by her parents. The request form addressed concerns about Renee's specific motor ability, balance, and coordination problems that they believe are related to her learning disability.

Given Renee's parents' specific concerns, the Bruininks-Oseretsky Test of Motor Proficiency 2 (BOT-2) was administered to Renee. In addition, she was observed in general physical education over two class sessions. All testing was conducted by Martin Jones, adapted physical education specialist for the school district, at Crooked Stick Elementary School during Renee's physical education class, in the hallway by the gymnasium, and in the gymnasium itself. Renee was very cooperative during all testing, and she seemed to try her best in all testing situations. Results are a fair representation of Renee's skills in physical education.

BRUININKS-OSERETSKY TEST OF MOTOR PROFICIENCY

The BOT-2 is an individually administered norm-referenced test that assesses the motor functioning of children from 4 to 21 years of age. The complete battery—eight subtests made up of 53 separate items—provides composite scores in four motor areas (fine manual control, manual coordination, body coordination, and strength and agility) and one comprehensive measure of overall total motor proficiency, represented as the total motor composite. Administration of the complete battery for Renee took approximately 60 minutes. Results from each of the eight subtests and battery composites are presented in this report (see table C.1).

Table C.1   Results From the Bruininks-Oseretsky Test of Motor Proficiency 2

	Total point score	Scale score	Standard score	Percentile rank	Age equivalent	Category
Subtest 1: fine motor precision	39	16			10.0-10.2 years	Average
Subtest 2: fine motor integration	37	13			8.9-8.11 years	Average
Fine manual control		**29**	**47**	**38**		**Average**
Subtest 3: manual dexterity	26	10			8.0-8.2 years	Below average
Subtest 7: upper-limb coordination	30	10			8.6-8.8 years	Below average
Manual coordination		**20**	**36**	**8**		**Below average**
Subtest 4: bilateral coordination	19	8			6.9-6.11 years	Below average
Subtest 5: balance	27	7			5.2-5.3 years	Below average
Body coordination		**15**	**33**	**5**		**Below average**
Subtest 6: running speed and agility	24	8			5.10-5.11 years	Below average
Subtest 8: strength	8	4			4.6-4.7 years	Well below average
Strength and agility		**12**	**30**	**2**		**Below average**
Total motor composite		**76**	**146**	**5**		**Below average**

Results indicate that Renee did well on fine motor control items (fine motor precision and integration). In fact, Renee scored on age level or close to age level on both subtests in this category. With a percentile rank of 38, she scored better than 38 percent of children in fine motor control. Renee did display a slight delay in manual coordination items. In manual dexterity, her score was age equivalent to 8.0-8.2 years, and in upper-limb coordination, she scored age equivalent to 8.6-8.8 years. With a percentile rank of 8, 92 percent of children would score better than Renee on manual coordination items. Renee's greatest delays were on body coordination items (bilateral coordination and balance), where her percentile rank was 5, and strength and agility items (running speed/agility and strength), in which she had a percentile rank of 2. Strength (age equivalent of 4.6-4.7 years), balance (age equivalent of 5.2-5.3 years), and running speed and agility (age equivalent of 5.10-5.11 years) were clearly her weakest areas. Results from this test suggest that Renee is significantly delayed in the area of gross motor abilities.

OBSERVATION IN GENERAL PHYSICAL EDUCATION

Renee was observed in two different general physical education sessions. At first glance, she was indistinguishable from her peers. In other words, she was not so delayed or impaired to cause her to appear significantly different from her peers. In fact, her GPE teacher was surprised that Renee was being observed and tested. He thought that she did well in most general physical education activities, was well behaved and happy, and seemed to try her best. I observed her in tagging and dodging games that were used for the warm-up. She was able to keep pace with her peers in that game, and I did not notice any limitations in functional speed, balance, or agility. I also observed her in activities that required catching and throwing with a partner. Again, although Renee's skills were not the strongest in class, her skills were not the weakest either. She demonstrated the general throwing and catching pattern, and she was accurate with her throws and successful with catching (in at least 75 percent of the trials I observed).

The second observation included a warm-up that focused more on strength (sit-ups, push-ups, mountain climbers). Again, while one of the weaker individuals in these strength activities, she was clearly not the weakest child. She seemed to try her best, and I did not see any signs of frustration in her struggle to complete 10 modified push-ups and 10 sit-ups. In a throwing and catching game that followed, Renee was as active and engaged in the activity as the other children in the class. Her throwing and catching patterns were poorer in the game setting than the skill setting observed the previous day (but this was true for many of the children in the class).

SUMMARY AND RECOMMENDATIONS

Renee is a 10-year-old at Crooked Stick Elementary School. She was recommended for testing by her parents. Results from the Bruininks-Oseretsky Test of Motor Proficiency 2 indicate that Renee is significantly behind her age peers in motor proficiency. Her strengths are in fine motor precision and fine motor integration, as well as upper-limb coordination. Her weakest areas are in strength, running speed and agility, and body coordination (balance and bilateral coordination). She was slightly delayed in manual coordination (manual dexterity and upper-limb coordination), and she did not show any significant delays in fine motor control (fine motor precision or integration). With regard to general physical education, Renee seems able to keep up with her peers in all activities. She seems well adjusted and enjoys general physical education activities. The weaknesses seen in the BOT-2 did not seem to present problems for her in general physical education.

Given that Renee did score at a level that would indicate a significant motor impairment, it is recommended that Renee receive adapted physical education services for 30 minutes per week. Since Renee does well in general physical education, this adapted session should take place at another time of the day, away from general physical education. This one-on-one or small-group session should focus on remediating some of the specific areas Renee had the most trouble with—strength and agility as well as body coordination.

Sample Write-Up for Tests of Sports Skills

Adapted Physical Education Observation and Evaluation

Name: Li Xiang   Date: 02/13/18

DOB: 01/23/06   School: East Middle School

Evaluator: Martin E. Block, PhD

BACKGROUND INFORMATION

Li Xiang is a 12-year-old male who attends sixth grade at East Middle School in Albemarle County. He attended Lewis Elementary School in West County until third grade, and he was homeschooled for the past two years. Li has qualified for special education through Albemarle County as a child with a disability. He currently participates in general physical education (GPE). Li was referred for evaluation by his special education teacher, Ms. Sey, and his GPE teacher, Ms. Luck. Specifically, Ms. Luck had concerns about Li's refusal to participate in most GPE activities. In addition, Li's mother had concerns regarding his motor skills.

The following were used to evaluate Li's skills in physical education to determine whether he qualifies for adapted physical education: evaluation of Li's skills compared to the Albemarle County middle school physical education curriculum, feedback from Li's GPE teacher, and feedback from Li. Martin Block, PhD, CAPE, an associate professor at the University of Virginia, along with Kristy McClain, a graduate student at the University of Virginia in the area of adapted physical education, conducted the testing. All testing was conducted at East Middle School in Li's GPE class on February 13, 2018, during Li's normal health and physical education time. Li was very cooperative during all testing, and he seemed to try his best in all testing situations. Therefore, these test results are a fair representation of Li's skills in physical education.

ALBEMARLE COUNTY MIDDLE SCHOOL CURRICULUM

The Albemarle County middle school physical education curriculum is a criterion-referenced curriculum that focuses on sports skills. Each skill has been broken down into three to five components. Skills are analyzed to determine whether the component is present (1) or not present (0). Results are then tallied across two trials. The curriculum also includes cognitive tests for each sport that were not given to Li at this time. Li was given a demonstration of each skill before he was asked to perform it. According to conversations with Ms. Luck, Li refused to participate in physical education during a soccer unit in the fall, and he has not yet had the chance to participate in any of the other sports skill units that are represented in this testing. Nevertheless, Li was able to demonstrate most of the components of most of the skills tested after a demonstration by the evaluator. This is rather remarkable given that Li has not had formal instruction in physical education for the past two years and has chosen not to participate in physical education so far in sixth grade.

Li's strengths were in volleyball and soccer skills. He also did well in softball and basketball skills, but there were components in these skills that Li had yet to master (e.g., shooting was a little stiff, and he used two hands rather than performing a one-hand shot; dribbling forward was a little stiff, although he controlled the ball going forward with his right hand first and then his left hand). Results suggest that Li is not delayed in sports skill development as compared with what is expected of middle school children in sixth grade (see table D.1). In fact, many of the skills that Li already mastered will not be presented and taught to Li until the seventh and eighth grades.

PHYSICAL FITNESS

Physical fitness is another important part of the Albemarle County middle school physical education curriculum. Fitness includes upper-body and abdominal strength, cardiorespiratory endurance, and flexibility. Results were collected by Ms. Luck during physical fitness testing of Li's class. However, we reevaluated Li's flexibility during our testing.

Results show that Li is significantly behind his peers in physical fitness, especially in cardiorespiratory fitness (mile run). However, Ms. Luck noted that Li walked during testing and did not try. In addition, Li has asthma, which may have affected his cardiorespiratory endurance. In fact, during our testing Li asked to go to the nurse's office for his inhaler. He seems to be a little overweight, but not so much that he stands out compared to his peers. Based on discussions with Ms. Luck, it is difficult to determine whether Li has significant fitness delays as reflected in this testing or whether these results reflect Li's lack of effort during testing.

Results of Physical Fitness Testing

Mile run	24.02 minutes (below average for sixth-grade boys)
Sit-and-reach	14 (below average for sixth-grade boys)
Pull-ups	0 (below average for sixth-grade boys)
Curl-ups	9 (below average for sixth-grade boys)

Table D.1 Results from Albemarle County Middle School Physical Education Curriculum

| | | Trial | | |
		1	2	Score
Volleyball skills				
Underhand serve	1. Preparatory position: faces net, feet shoulder-width apart; 45° forward trunk lean; holds ball in nondominant hand, with arm extended across body at waist height in front of serving arm	1	1	2
	2. Holds serving arm straight, pendular swing back at least 45° to initiate serve; then brings serving arm forward with pendular arm motion	1	1	2
	3. Strides forward with opposite foot in concert with forward motion of striking arm	1	1	2
	4. Heel of striking hand strikes center of ball held at or below waist height in line with back foot and in front of serving foot	1	1	2
Overhead pass	1. Preparatory position: faces oncoming ball, feet (set) staggered shoulder-width apart; knees slightly bent, arms and hands hanging by knees; eyes are on ball	1	0	1
	2. Moves to get under ball, with head tilted back, legs flexed; hands move up just above forehead	1	1	2
	3. Hand position: palms out, fingers apart and slightly bent	0	1	1
	4. Upon contact, head remains in tilted position, eyes focused on ball, wrists hyperextended and fingers flexed to form a diamond or triangle to absorb force of the ball	1	0	1
	5. Extends knees and arms upward on follow-through	1	1	2
	6. Passes ball to above net height	1	1	2
Forearm pass	1. Ready position: faces ball, feet shoulder-width apart; knees slightly bent, arms hanging below waist and extended in front of body, palms facing up	1	1	2
	2. Preparatory hand position: one hand placed in the other hand, with thumb of lower hand placed across fingers of upper hand, forearms together	1	1	2
	3. Eyes are on ball	1	1	2
	4. Moves to meet ball by transferring weight forward, arms together, knees bent	1	1	2
	5. Contacts ball with flat side of forearms	1	1	2
	6. Upon contact, extends knees to raise the arms upward	1	0	1
	7. Completes pass standing straight up, arms parallel to floor; hands stay together throughout entire motion	1	1	2
	8. Passes ball to a height of at least 8 ft (2.5 m) to stationary teammate	1	1	2
Softball skills				
Striking a stationary ball	1. Dominant hand grips bat above nondominant hand. Nonpreferred side of body faces the imaginary tosser with feet parallel	1	1	2
	2. Rotates hips and shoulders during swing	0	0	0
	3. Transfers weight by stepping with front foot	1	0	1
Catch	1. Preparation phase: hands are in front of the body and elbows are flexed	1	1	2
	2. Arms extended while reaching for the ball as it arrives	1	1	2
	3. Catches ball with hands only	1	1	2

(continued)

Table D.1 *(continued)*

		Trial		
		1	**2**	**Score**
Overhand throw	1. Initiates windup with downward movement of hand	1	0	1
	2. Rotates hips and shoulders to a point where the nonthrowing side faces the target	1	1	2
	3. Transfers weight by stepping with the foot opposite the throwing hand	1	1	2
	4. Follow-through beyond ball release, diagonally across body toward nonpreferred side	1	1	2
Basketball skills				
Dribble	1. Contacts ball with one hand at about belt level	1	1	2
	2. Pushes ball with fingertips (not slap)	1	1	2
	3. Ball contacts floor in front of or to the outside of foot on preferred side	0	0	0
	4. Maintains control of ball for four consecutive bounces without having to move feet to retrieve ball	1	0	1
	5. Dribbles while walking forward 15 ft (4.5 m) with dominant hand	1	1	2
	6. Dribbles while walking forward 15 ft (4.5 m) with nondominant hand	1	1	2
Shooting	1. Eyes are on basket, feet shoulder-width apart, knees flexed	1	1	2
	2. Marked flexion of knees before shooting	1	1	2
	3. Shooting hand under ball with fingers apart; holds ball slightly off center of forehead, shooting-hand side; elbow is directly under ball, pointed down; nondominant hand is on side of ball	0	0	0
	4. Coordinated extension of knees, hips, and ankles, while flexing wrist and fingers to guide the ball on release	1	0	1
	5. Follow-through with the shooting hand remaining briefly in the release position toward basket	1	0	1
Soccer skills				
Kick	1. Rapid, continuous approach to the ball	1	1	2
	2. Elongated stride or leap immediately before ball contact	1	0	1
	3. Places nonkicking foot even or slightly in back of ball	1	1	2
	4. Kicks ball with instep of preferred foot (shoelaces) or toe	0	0	0
Trap	1. Eyes are focused on moving ball	1	1	2
	2. Moves in line with the ball, weight on nontrapping foot	1	1	2
	3. Trapping foot is perpendicular to nontrapping foot	1	0	1
	4. Contacts ball at center with inside surface of foot	1	0	1
	5. Retracts foot to absorb force	1	1	2
Dribble	1. Contacts ball with any part of foot	1	1	2
	2. Ball travels no more than 2 ft (0.6 m) away from foot	0	1	1
	3. Occasionally looks up to see where he or she is going	0	0	0
	4. Maintains jogging pace	1	1	2

CONVERSATION WITH LI

After testing I had a brief conversation with Li regarding his feelings toward physical education. When asked to rate his enjoyment of physical education on a scale of 1 (hates physical education) to 10 (loves physical education), Li rated his enjoyment as a 3. He said that his least favorite activity was running, and he thought doing Tae Bo to the videotapes was stupid. However, he did say that he tried to follow the tapes. He said he liked to play pickleball but did not think the rules made sense.

CONVERSATION WITH MS. LUCK

Ms. Luck has been Li's primary physical education specialist since the start of the school year. She noted that she has been unable to determine Li's motor or fitness skills because he usually refuses to participate in physical education activities. Ms. Luck has tried to make some accommodations for Li such as allowing him to walk part of a lap if he runs part of a lap. However, she noted that Li just walks the entire way. She also noted that Li does not dress with the other boys in the locker room. Rather, he gets dressed in his special education classroom, and this usually makes him late for class. When he arrives to class, he tells Ms. Luck that he does not have to participate in the warm-up since the class has already started. During activities, Li often refuses to participate, choosing to sit in the corner of the gym. Regarding his interaction with peers, Ms. Luck noted that Li often gets into arguments with his peers and that his peers often tease Li.

SUMMARY AND RECOMMENDATIONS

Li is a sixth grader who qualifies as a child with a disability according to the Albemarle County School District. He was referred for adapted physical education by his special education and physical education teachers as well as his mother. Testing showed that Li is not delayed in gross motor development as measured by the Albemarle County middle school physical education curriculum. He is delayed in physical fitness compared to what is expected of sixth-grade boys. However, these results are somewhat suspect because it is unclear whether Li's low fitness is due to lack of practice (he chooses not to participate in physical education), lack of effort (he did not try his best), his asthma, or actual fitness delays. Li's social skills and behaviors are clearly causing problems for him (as well as his physical education teacher) in general physical education. Li's problems seem to be more behavioral than motor, and thus he does not qualify for adapted physical education services.

Glossary

1RM—The greatest amount of weight lifted for a specific exercise in one complete repetition; a measure of absolute strength.

abduction—Sideward movement or withdrawal from the midline or sagittal plane.

ACE behaviors—Attention, comprehension, and effort, the three prerequisite student behaviors for consistent, reliable assessment.

adaptive behavior—The ability to effectively meet social and community expectations for personal independence, physical needs, and interpersonal relationships expected for one's age and cultural group.

adduction—A pulling toward the midline of the body or the return movement from abduction.

administration procedures—How an assessment should be administered and scored, ideally with all conditions kept the same during repeated assessments so that any change is the result of student performance.

agency files—Records of a client's participation kept by hospitals, sports organizations, social services, and other agencies that provide services to students.

agnosia—The inability to recognize, locate, or interpret sensory information, such as touch or pressure.

alternate form—A way to test reliability by administering two equivalent forms of one test to the same group of students.

Americans with Disabilities Act (ADA)—Americans with Disabilities Act is a law that states that individuals with disability must be provided equal opportunity in all aspects of life.

antecedents—Things that happen just before a behavior occurs that may cause the behavior.

apraxia—A motor disorder caused by damage to the brain (specifically the posterior parietal cortex), in which the individual has difficulty with the motor planning to perform tasks or movements when asked, provided that the request or command is understood and he is willing to perform the task.

assessment—The process used by teachers to make informed decisions; may be used interchangeably with other terms such as *testing*, *measurement*, and *evaluation*.

asymmetrical tonic neck reflex—A postural infantile reflex stimulated by turning an infant's head to one side. The face-side extremities will extend, while extremities on the other side will flex.

attention—The ability to focus on internal or external stimuli; the length of an individual's focus, or attention span.

attitudes—One's preference to either avoid or approach someone or something, believed to be directly connected to intentions and consequently to behaviors.

auditory processing—The ability to make sense of information taken in through the auditory system.

authentic assessment—Measuring performance in real-world settings on functional skills that a child needs in order to be successful in physical education, recreation, and community sports.

balance reactions—Involuntary reactions, appearing in late infancy and early childhood, that keep an infant or child from falling over when balance is lost.

body composition—The percentage of total body weight that is fat.

body mass index—A measure of body composition, it is determined by dividing weight in kilograms by height in meters squared.

body types—The classification of the body as mesomorphic (muscular), endomorphic (round), ectomorphic (slender), or any combination of the three.

brain stem reflexes—Reflexes regulated at the level of the brain stem, such as pupillary, pharyngeal, and cough reflexes and the control of respiration; their absence is one criterion of brain death.

cardiorespiratory endurance—Fitness component that measures the ability of the heart, lungs and muscles to work for an extended period of time.

central file—Contains records kept by the director of special education, such as parent questionnaires, screening results, referrals, IEPs, test protocol files, consent forms, and doctor forms.

circumduction—Sequence of movements of a segment occurring in the sagittal, frontal, and oblique planes so that the movement as a whole describes a cone, as in arm or trunk circling.

cognition—High-level brain processes, such as attention, planning, motivation, and memory recall, that are essential for movement selection and execution.

concentration—The ability to focus one's attention on the task at hand and not be affected by internal or external distractions.

concurrent validity—Statistically measures the relationship between an existing instrument with established validity and a new instrument that assesses the same attribute.

concussion—A complex pathophysiological process affecting the brain, induced by traumatic mechanical forces and often causing structural damage.

consequences—Things that happen immediately after a behavior occurs that may reinforce the behavior.

construct validity—Evidence that what an assessment item measures is representative of a construct (i.e., traits such as sportsmanship, anxiety, general motor ability, and coordination).

content validity—Evidence supporting that what is measured by the instrument reflects what the instrument is designed to measure.

criterion (predictive) validity—Examines the degree to which one or more test scores can be used to predict performance on a future related event.

criterion-referenced instruments—Less standardized assessments that involve evaluating performance against an established set of criteria.

curriculum decisions—Determine what modifications will address a student's unique needs in the various curricula areas.

developmental landmarks—Motor skills that are achieved by most children by a certain age.

Disabled Sports USA—A program that provides opportunities for individuals with disabilities to participate in community sports, recreation, and educational programs.

dynamic balance—Equilibrium maintained either on a moving surface or while moving the body through space.

dynamic strength—The ability to apply force in a maximal or near-maximal contraction.

evaluation—The comparison and interpretation of multiple assessments to explain the changes observed; formative or summative in nature.

executive functions—Include a person's ability to self-regulate, ignore or act upon inhibitions, or perform multiple tasks simultaneously.

external rotation—Movement of a body part occurring when the posterior surface of the part is rotated away from the midline of the body.

face (logical) validity—The simplest and most subjective source of validity evidence, present when there is a direct connection between what is measured by the instrument and what is being assessed.

fine motor skills—Skills controlled by smaller muscles or muscle groups, such as movements with the hands (e.g., grasping and releasing).

flexibility—The ability to move the body and its parts through a wide range of motion without stress.

flexion—Movement at a joint that causes a decrease in the relative angle between the two segments.

fluid cognition—The ability to solve new problems, to use logic in new situations, and to identify patterns.

focal points—The components that define the established criteria for correct performance of a skill.

foot drop—Weak dorsiflexion of foot that does not allow toes to clear the surface.

formative evaluation—Ongoing assessment that focuses on shaping the performance over time to reach a desired goal.

functional behavior analysis—A process in which the IEP team attempts to determine why a student displays a particular behavior in hopes of planning a program that can prevent it.

functional fitness—Being able to accomplish daily living tasks such as lifting, stretching, or moving to promote overall function and independence.

fundamental motor patterns—Movement patterns that are necessary, or fundamental, for participation in sports.

gait cycle—The time interval or sequence of motions between two contacts of the same foot.

gross motor skills—Skills controlled by large muscles or muscle groups, such as the muscles in the legs (locomotor patterns) and in the trunk and arms (object control skills).

health-related fitness—Attributes that facilitate day-to-day function and health maintenance (e.g., muscular strength and endurance, flexibility, cardiorespiratory endurance, and body composition) as well as health components as they relate to function.

health-related records—Confidential health and medical files that outline illness history, impairments, special considerations, medications, and emergency contact information.

Individuals with Disabilities Education Act 2004 (IDEA)— IDEA 2004 is the current special education legislation mandating equity, accountability, and excellence in education for children with disabilities.

information processing speed—How rapidly an individual can input, integrate, store, and output information.

instructional decisions—The most common decisions teachers make, determining what objectives are targeted for instruction, what learning and behavioral characteristics should be considered when delivering instruction, and how students should be grouped.

internal rotation—Movement of a body part occurring when the anterior surface of the part is rotated toward the midline of the body.

interrater reliability—The consistency of the results obtained in two administrations of a test to the same group of students by different teachers.

intraclass correlation coefficient—Calculates the reliability (i.e., r value) using analysis of variance by comparing multiple rating by different raters (e.g., teachers) of the performance of a group students on a skill or one rater's repeated ratings on multiple performance trials of one group of students.

intrarater reliability—The consistency of the results obtained by the same assessor across multiple administrations.

isometric strength—Isometric strength involves a maximal voluntary contraction performed at a specific joint angle against an unyielding resistance

kyphosis—Abnormally rounded upper back.

long-term memory (LTM)—The ability to take in, store, and retrieve information over a long period (months to years).

lordosis—Forward curvature of the lumbar spine.

maladaptive behavior—Behavior that interferes with everyday activities; also known as problem behavior.

measurement—The data collected by the assessment instrument. In physical education, measurement tends to focus on either the process involved in the performance or the products produced by the performance.

motor abilities—General capacities or characteristics that are related to the ability to perform motor skills such as running, jumping, throwing, or catching.

motor development—The emergence of behaviors through maturational processes and the further development of these behaviors through learning and practice.

motor performance team—A group of APE specialists and other professionals (e.g., physical and occupational therapists) who evaluate students in the motor domain as a team to maximize efficiency and reduce the time and stress on the student being evaluated.

motor performance—Measures, such as reaction time and speed, that define the outcome of performing a motor skill.

muscular endurance—Submaximal exertion that extends over a relatively long period of time.

muscular strength—Maximal muscular exertion of relatively brief duration; it is generally measured by the amount of force a person can exert in a single maximal effort.

normative sample—Test takers from the wider population who are representative of the population a test is intended for.

norm-referenced instruments—Standardized tests designed to collect performance data that are then compared with reference standards based on normative data provided with the instrument.

norms—A description of how a sample of students performs on a test in relation to the students in the normative sample.

objectivity—A special type of reliability related to the ability of two test administrators to get the same results when giving the same test to the same group of people.

orientation—Awareness of person (awareness of self and knowing who you are), place (knowledge of where you are and how you can move about in the environment), and time (awareness of time of day, seasons, months, and passage of time).

Paralympics—Held after every Olympic Games, the Paralympics offer elite-level sport opportunities for individuals with physical disabilities, intellectual disabilities, and visual impairments.

parental insights—Information supplied by parents or guardians about their child's history (e.g., family, health, developmental, social) and out-of-school environment.

Pearson product-moment correlation—A statistical technique for calculating an r value that represents the linear relationship between two variables.

perceived competence—How competent one feels in particular activities or pursuits.

perception—The organization, identification, and interpretation of sensory information in order to represent and understand the environment.

perceptual-motor tests—Used to evaluate normal development of visual and kinesthetic perceptual systems and to determine if a student has a significant deficit in one or more subareas within these systems.

physical fitness—A state of health and well-being that allows a person to be active; divided into health-related functioning and motor functioning, or performance.

placement decisions—Determining the most appropriate instructional setting and least restrictive environment for addressing the identified curriculum needs of students who have qualified for SE.

positive behavioral support—Creating positive ways to help a student develop more appropriate adaptive behavior and become more independent.

postural control—Achieving, maintaining, or restoring a state of balance during any static posture or dynamic activity.

posture—The manner in which the body aligns itself against gravity. Correct posture is achieved when all segments of the body are properly aligned over a base of support, with minimum stress applied to each joint.

power—The muscles' ability to exert maximal force in the shortest possible time; a combination of muscular strength and speed.

process measures—Typically related to CRIs, they measure motor skill performance and judge how the skill was performed; a subjective measure.

product measures—Focus on the outcomes or products of the performance, such as the number of repetitions, distance covered, time needed to complete a task, or number of times a target was hit out of a number of trials; an objective measure.

protective reactions—Involuntary reactions, appearing in late infancy and early childhood, that cause an infant or child to extend the arms or legs to prevent injury during a fall.

psychological workups—Formal and informal assessments by school or agency psychologists that provide insights into students' psychological characteristics.

qualification decisions—Determine whether a student's performance warrants special consideration, whether it's to qualify for an award or for special education services; also known as eligibility or classification decisions.

reference standards—How the data collected during an assessment are interpreted.

reflex movements—Involuntary subcortical movement reactions exhibited after sensory stimulation such as head movement, light, touch, and sound.

reliability—The consistency of the results obtained from an assessment instrument over multiple administrations.

righting reactions—Involuntary reactions, appearing in late infancy and early childhood, that keep an infant or child's head in line with the body.

school files—Cumulative records that document students' names, addresses, IEPs, psychological assessments, and classroom modifications, among other information.

scoliosis—Lateral curve of the spine (one side: C curve; both sides: S curve).

scoring precision—A function of what is measured and the amount of skill needed to make the measurement.

screening—Informal assessments of large groups to identify students with potential problems who require more formal assessment.

self-concept—Beliefs about oneself, including personal attributes and competencies.

self-esteem—A general positive self-regard, self-worth, or overall good feeling about oneself.

self-perception—Perception of oneself; especially, self-concept.

short-term memory (STM)—The ability to take in, store, and retrieve information that was learned minutes to months previously.

social competence—The ability to get along with others; for students, characterized by basic classroom skills, basic interaction skills, getting-along skills, making-friends skills, and coping skills.

spasticity—Involuntary increased muscle tone that causes resistance to movement.

Special Olympics—An organization that offers movement training and multiple levels of sport participation for individuals with intellectual disabilities on regional, state, national, and international scales.

split half—A way to test reliability by administering a single test to one group of students and then dividing it into two forms, typically by the odd and even items.

sports skills—The skills required in specific sports, such as object control skills (e.g., throwing and catching) and locomotor skills (e.g., running and sliding).

stability—Pertains to skills executed in a static, balanced position, as opposed to locomotion.

stance phase—The part of the gait cycle when the foot is on the ground bearing weight, allowing the lower leg to support and advance the body over the supporting limb.

static balance—State of the body undergoing zero acceleration and the ability to maintain equilibrium in a stationary position.

structural deviations—Abnormalities or deformities of the skeletal system resulting from disease or injury.

student insights—Information provided by students themselves about their specific interests, needs, and challenges.

student performance variability—The variability of a student's performance from one trial or test to the next, affected by attention, comprehension, and effort.

summative evaluation—Assessments performed at established intervals, with the purpose of interpreting the performance against established standards.

swing phase—The part of the gait cycle when the foot is moving forward and not bearing weight, allowing the toes to clear the floor and making adjustments to advance the swing leg forward.

task sequencing—Performing tasks with multiple movement components in a specific order or sequence, which requires complex information and cognitive processing by the brain.

test–retest reliability—The correlation, or degree of agreement, between results when an instrument is administered twice to the same group of students.

tilting reactions—A balance reaction that keeps a child from falling when the body is tilted.

validity—The ability of a test to accurately measure what it is supposed to measure.

verbal fluency—In the context of this chapter, verbal fluency refers to a cognitive function that facilitates information retrieval from memory, requiring executive control over several cognitive processes such as selective attention, selective inhibition, and response generation.

visual processing—The ability to make sense of information taken in through the visual system.

visual search and scanning—Types of perceptual tasks requiring attention that typically involve an active scan of the visual environment for a particular object or feature (the target) among other objects or features (the distracters).

zero exclusion—Providing physical education services to everyone with disabilities regardless of the severity of the disability.

zero failure—Creating and implementing a special education program in such a way as to ensure the student's success.

References

Chapter 1

Horvat, M., Kalakian, L., Croce, R., and Dahlstrom, V. (2011). *Developmental/Adapted Physical Education*. San Francisco: Benjamin Cummings.

Horvat, M., Ray, C., Ramsey, V., Miszko, T., Keeney, R., and Blasch, B. (2003). Compensatory Analysis and Strategies for Balance in Individuals with Visual Impairments. *Journal of Visual Impairment and Blindness, 97(1)*, 695-703.

Chapter 2

AAHPERD. (1976). *AAHPERD Youth Fitness Test manual*. Reston, VA: American Alliance for Health, Physical Education, Recreation and Dance.

Folio, M, & Fewell, R.F. (2000). *Peabody developmental motor scales* (2nd ed.). Austin, TX: Pro-Ed.

Individuals with Disabilities Education Act. LRE Requirements. 20 U.S.C. 1412(a)(5).

Individuals with Disabilities Education Act. Evaluation Procedures. 20 U.S.C. 1414(b) (1)-(3), 1412(a)(6)(B).

Individuals with Disabilities Education Act. Determination of Disability. 20 U.S.C. 1414(b) (4) and (5).

Individuals with Disabilities Education Act. Child with a Disability. 20 U.S.C. 1401(3);1401(30).

Kelly, L.E. (2011). *Designing and implementing effective adapted physical education programs*. Urbana, IL: Sagamore Publishing.

Kelly, L.E., & Melograno, V.J. (2004). *Developing the physical education curriculum: An achievement-based approach*. Long Grove, IL: Waveland Press.

Kelly, L.E., Wessel, J.A., Dummer, G., & Sampson, T. (2010). *Everyone Can!: Elementary physical education curriculum and teaching resources*. Champaign, IL: Human Kinetics.

Ulrich, D.A. (2018). *Test of Gross Motor Development 2*. www.kines.umich.edu/tgmd3.

Chapter 3

Horvat, M., & Kalakian, L. (1996). *Assessment in adapted physical education and therapeutic recreation,* (2nd ed). Dubuque, IA: Brown.

Horvat, M., Kalakian, L., Croce, R., and Dahlstrom, V. (2011). *Developmental/Adapted Physical Education*. San Francisco: Benjamin Cummings.

Chapter 4

Kelly, L.E., & Melograno, V.J. (2004). *Developing the physical education curriculum: An achievement-based approach*. Long Grove, IL: Waveland Press.

Kelly, L.E., Wessel, J.A., Dummer, G., & Sampson, T. (2010). *Everyone Can!: Elementary physical education curriculum and teaching resources*. Champaign, IL: Human Kinetics.

Chapter 5

Block, M.E. (2000). *A teacher's guide to including students with disabilities in general physical education*. Baltimore: Brookes.

Kelly, L.E. (2011). *Designing and implementing effective adapted physical education programs.* Urbana, IL: Sagamore Publishing.

Kelly, L.E., & Melograno, V.J. (2004). *Developing the physical education curriculum: An achievement-based approach.* Long Grove, IL: Waveland Press.

Kelly, L.E., Wessel, J.A., Dummer, G., & Sampson, T. (2010). *Everyone Can!: Elementary physical education curriculum and teaching resources.* Champaign, IL: Human Kinetics.

Chapter 6

Alotaibi, M., Long, T., Kennedy, E., & Bavishi, S. (2014). The efficacy of GMFM-88 and GMFM-66 to detect changes in gross motor function in children with cerebral palsy (CP): A literature review. *Disability & Rehabilitation, 36,* 617-627.

Barnes, M.R., Crutchfield, C.A., Heriza, C.R., & Herdman, S.J. (1990). *Reflex and vestibular aspects of motor control, motor development and motor learning.* Atlanta: Stokesville.

Block, M. E., Lieberman, L. J., and Connor-Kuntz, F. 1998. Authentic assessment in adapted physical education. *Journal of Physical Education, Recreation & Dance, 69*(3): 48–55.

Bricker, D., Capt, B., Johnson, J.J., Pretti-Frontczak, K., Waddell, M., & Straka, E. (2002). *The Assessment, Evaluation, and Programming System (AEPS)* (2nd ed.). Baltimore: Brookes.

Brigance, A.H., & French, B.R. (2013). *Brigance inventory for early development, III.* North Billendca, MA: Curriculum Associates

Bruininks, R. H., & Bruininks, B.D. (2005). *Bruininks-Oseretsky test of motor proficiency* (2nd ed.). (BOT™-2). Bloomington, MN: Pearson Education.

Burger, M., & Louw, Q.A. (2009). The predictive validity of general movements: A systematic review. *European Journal of Paediatric Neurology, 13,* 408–420.

Burton, A.W., & Miller, D.E. (1998). *Movement skill assessment.* Champaign, IL: Human Kinetics.

Capute, A.J., Palmer, F.B., Shapiro, B.K., Wachtel, R.C., Ross, A., & Accardo, P.J. (1984). Primitive reflex profile: A quantitation of primitive reflexes in infancy. *Developmental Medicine and Children Neurology, 26*(3), 375-83.

Clark, J.E., Getchell, N., Smiley-Oyen, A.L. & Whitall, J. (2005). Developmental coordination disorder: Issues, identification and intervention. *Journal of Physical Education, Recreation and Dance, 76,* 49-53.

Cools, W., De Martelaer, K., Samaey, C., & Andries, C. (2009). Movement skill assessment of typically developing preschool children: A review of seven movement skill assessment tools. *Journal of Sports Science & Medicine, 8*(2), 154-168.

Cowden, J.E., & Torrey, C.C. (2007). *Motor development and movement activities for preschoolers and infants with delays.* Springfield, IL: Charles C. Thomas.

Darsaklis, V., Snider, L.M., Majnemer, A., & Mazer, B. (2013). Assessments used to diagnose developmental coordination disorder: Do their underlying constructs match the diagnostic criteria? *Physical & Occupational Therapy in Pediatrics, 33*(2), 186-195.

Folio, M, & Fewell, R.F. (2000). *Peabody developmental motor scales* (2nd ed.). Austin, TX: Pro-Ed.

Futagi, Y., Yanagihara, K., Mogami, Y., Ikeda, T., & Suzuki, Y. (2013). The Babkin reflex in infants: Clinical significance and neural mechanisms. *Pediatric Neurology, 49,* 149-155.

Gallahue, D.L., Ozmun, J.C. and Goodway, J. (2012). *Understanding motor development: Infants, children, adolescents, adults.* New York: McGraw-Hill.

Haywood, K.M., & Getchell, N. (2014). *Life span motor development* (6th ed.). Champaign, IL: Human Kinetics.

Haywood, K.M., & Getchell, N. (2009). *Life span motor development online student resource* (5th ed.). Champaign, IL: Human Kinetics.

Henderson, S.E., Sugden, D.A., & Barnett, A. (2007). *Movement assessment battery for children* (2nd ed.). (Movement ABC-2). Bloomington, MN: Pearson.

Jooyeon, K. (2014). Sensitivity to functional improvements of GMFM-88, GMFM-66, and pediatric mobility scores in young children with cerebral palsy. *Perceptual & Motor Skills, 119*, 305-319.

Josenby, A.L., Jarnio, G., Gummesson, C., & Nordmark, E. (2009). Longitudinal construct validity of the GMFM-88 total score and coal total score and the GMFM-66 score in a 5-year follow-up study. *Physical Therapy, 89*, 342-350.

Kelly, L.E., Wessel, J.A., Dummer, G.M., & Sampson, T. (2010). *Everyone Can!: Skill development and assessment in elementary physical education.* Champaign, IL: Human Kinetics.

Logan, S.W., & Getchell, N. (2010). The relationship between motor skill proficiency and body mass index in children with and without dyslexia: A pilot study. *Research Quarterly for Exercise and Sport, 81*, 518-523.

Moodie, S., Daneri, P., Goldhagen, S., Halle, T., Green, K., & LaMonte, L. (2014). *Early childhood developmental screening: A compendium of measures for children ages birth to five* (OPRE Report 201411). Washington, DC: Office of Planning, Research and Evaluation, Administration for Children and Families, U.S. Department of Health and Human Services.

Payne, V.G., & Isaacs, L.D. (2016). *Human motor development: A lifespan approach* (9th ed.). Scottsdale, AZ: Holcomb Hathaway.

Russell, D.J., Rosenbaum, P.L., Avery, L., & Lane, M. (2000). Improved scaling of the Gross Motor Function Measure for children with cerebral palsy: Evidence of reliability and validity. *Physical Therapy, 80*, 873-885.*

Russell, D.J., Rosenbaum, P.L., Avery, L., & Lane, M. (2002). *Gross motor function measure (GMFM-66 and GMFM-88) user's manual: Clinics in developmental medicine.* London: Mac Keith Press.

Special Olympics Basketball Coaching Guide. (2016). Retrieved from http://digitalguides.specialolympics.org/basketball/?#/36.

Squires, J., Twombly, E., Bricker, D., & Potter, L. (2009). *Ages and Stages Questionnaires, Third Edition.* Baltimore: Brookes.

Stins, J.F., Emck, C., de Vries, E.M., Doop, S., & Beek, P.J. (2015). Attentional and sensory contributions to postural sway in children with autism spectrum disorder. *Gait & Posture, 42*(2), 199-203.

Ting, L. (2013). Sensory processing and motor skill performance in elementary school children with autism spectrum disorder. *Perceptual & Motor Skills, 116*(1), 197-209.

Voress, J.K., & Maddox, T. (2013). *Developmental Assessment of Young Children, Second Edition.* Austin, TX: Pro-Ed.

Werder, J.K., & Bruininks, R.H. (1988). *Body skills: A motor development curriculum for children.* Circle Pines, MN: American Guidance Services.

Zafeiriou, D.I., Tsikoulas, I.G., Kremenopoulos, G.M., & Kontopoulos, E.E. (1998). Using postural reactions as a screening test to identify high-risk infants with cerebral palsy: A prospective study. *Brain Development, 20*(5), 307-311.

Zafeiriou, D.I. (2004). Primitive reflexes and postural reactions in the neurodevelopmental examination. *Pediatric Neurology, 31*(1), 1-8.

Chapter 7

American College of Sports Medicine. (2014). *ACSM's health-related physical fitness assessment manual* (4th ed.). Philadelphia: Lippincott, Williams & Wilkins.

Aufsesser, P., Horvat, M., & Austin, R. (2003). The reliability of hand-held dynamometers in individuals with spinal cord injury. *Clinical Kinesiology, 57*(4), 71-75.

Aufsesser, P., Horvat, M., & Croce, R. (1996). A critical examination of selected hand-held dynamometers to assess isometric muscle strength. *Adapted Physical Activity Quarterly, 13*, 153-165.

Bar-Or, O. (1983). *Pediatric Sports Medicine for the Practitioner.* New York: Springer-Verlag.

Cooper Institute, The. (2017). *FitnessGram administration manual: The journey to MyHealthyZone* (5th ed.). Champaign, IL: Human Kinetics.

Corbin, C.B., Welk, G., & Corbin, W.R. (2012). *Concepts of physical fitness* (6th ed.). Des Moines, IA: McGraw-Hill.

Croce, R., & Horvat, M. (1992). Effects of reinforcement-based exercise on fitness and work productivity in adults with mental retardation. *Adapted Physical Activity Quarterly, 9*, 148-178.

Fleck, S., & Kraemer, W. (2014). *Designing resistance training programs* (4th ed.). Champaign, IL: Human Kinetics.

Golding, L.A. (2000). *YMCA fitness testing and assessment manual* (4th ed.). Champaign, IL: Human Kinetics.

Harris, C., Wattles, A.P., DeBeliso, M., Sevene-Adams, P.G., Berning, J.M., & Adams, K.J. (2011). The seated medicine ball throw as a test of upper body power in older adults. *Journal of Strength and Conditioning Research, 25*(8), 2344-2348.

Heymsfield, S.B., Lohman, T.G., Wang, Z., & Going, S. (2005). *Human body composition* (2nd ed.). Champaign, IL: Human Kinetics.

Heyward, V.H., & Gibson, A. (2014). *Advanced fitness assessment and exercise prescription* (7th ed.). Champaign, IL: Human Kinetics.

Heyward, V. and Wagner, D. (2004) *Applied body composition assessment* (2nd ed.). Champaign, IL: Human Kinetics.

Hoeger, W.K., Hopkins, D.R., Button, S., & Palmer, T.A. (1990). Comparing the sit and reach with the modified sit and reach in measuring flexibility in adolescents. *Pediatric Exercise Science, 2*, 156-162.

Horvat, M., & Croce, R. (1995). Physical rehabilitation of individuals with mental retardation: Physical fitness and information processing. *Critical Reviews in Physical and Rehabilitation Medicine, 7*(3), 233-252.

Horvat, M., Croce, R., & Roswal, G. (1993). Magnitude and reliability of measurement of muscle strength across trials in individuals with mental retardation. *Perceptual and Motor Skills, 77*, 643-649.

Horvat, M., & Franklin, C. (2001). The effects of environment on physical activity patterns of children with mental retardation. *Research Quarterly for Exercise and Sport, 72*, 189-195.

Horvat, M., McManis, B.G., & Seagraves, E.E. (1992). Reliability and objectivity of the Nicholas Manual Muscle Tester with children. *Isokinetics and Exercise Science, 2*, 1-8.

Horvat, M., Ray, C., Nocera, J., & Croce, R. (2006). Comparison of isokinetic peak force and work parameters in adults with partial vision and blindness. *Perceptual and Motor Skills, 103*, 231-237.

Hui, S.C., & Yuen, P.W. (2000). Validity of the modified back saver sit and reach test: A comparison with other protocols. *Medicine and Science in Sports and Exercise, 32*, 1655-1659.

Johnson, R.E., Bulbulian, R., Gruber, J., & Sundheim, R. (1986). Estimating percent body fat of paraplegic athletes. *Palaestra, 3*, 29-33.

Kelly, L., & Rimmer, J. (1987). A practical method for estimating percent body fat of adult mentally retarded males. *Adapted Physical Activity Quarterly, 4*, 117-125.

Kendall, I.P., McCreary, E.K., Provance, P.G., Rogers, M., & Romani, W. (2005). *Muscles: Testing and function* (5th ed.). Baltimore: Williams & Wilkins.

Leger, L., & Lambert, J.A. (1982). A maximal multistage 20 m shuttle run test to predict $\dot{V}O_2$max. *European Journal of Applied Physiology, 49*, 1-12.

Leger, L.A., Mercier, D., Gadoury, C., & Lambert, J. (1988). The multistage 20 metre shuttle test for aerobic fitness. *Journal of Sports Sciences, 6*, 93-101.

Lohman, T.G. (1982). Measurement of body composition in children. *JOPERD, 53*, 67-70.

Lohman, T.G. (1986). Application of body composition techniques and constants for children and youth. In Pantolf, K.B. (Ed.), *Exercise and sport sciences reviews* (pp. 325-357). New York: Macmillan.

Lohman, T.G. (1987). The use of skinfolds to estimate body fatness on children and youth. *JOPERD, 58*, 98-102.

Lohman, T.G. (1989). Assessment of body composition in children. *Pediatric Exercise Science, 1*, 19-30.

Lohman, T.G. (1992). *Advances in body composition measurement.* Champaign, IL: Human Kinetics.

Lorenzi, D., Horvat, M., & Pellegrini, A.D. (2000). Physical activity of children with and without mental retardation in inclusive recess settings. *Education and Training in Mental Retardation and Developmental Disabilities, 35*(2), 160-167.

Mason, R.C., Horvat, M., & Nocera, J. (2016). The effects of exercise on the physical fitness of high and moderate-low functioning older adult women. *Journal of Aging Research.*

Norkin, C.C., & White, D.J. (2009). *Measurement of joint motion: A guide to goniometry* (4th ed.). Philadelphia: Davis.

Palmer, M.L., & Epler, M. (1998). *Fundamentals of musculoskeletal assessment techniques* (2nd ed.). Philadelphia: Lippincott.

Pitetti, K.H., & Fernhall, B. (2005). Mental retardation. In Skinner, J.S. (Ed.), *Exercise testing and exercise prescription for special cases* (3rd ed.) (pp. 392-403). Baltimore: Lippincott, Williams & Wilkins.

Plowman, S.A., & Meredith, M.D. (Eds.) 2013. *FitnessGram/ActivityGram reference guide* (4th ed.). Dallas: The Cooper Institute.

Reese, N.B. (2012). *Muscle and sensory testing* (3rd ed.). St. Louis: Saunders.

Rikli, R.E., & Jones, C.J. (2013). *Senior Fitness Test manual* (2nd ed.). Champaign, IL: Human Kinetics.

Seagraves, F., Horvat, M., Franklin, C., & Jones, K. (2004). The effects of a school-based physical activity program on work productivity and physical functioning in individuals with mental retardation. *Clinical Kinesiology, 58*(2), 18-29.

Smail, K.M., & Horvat, M. (2006). Relationship of muscular strength on work performance in high school students with mental retardation. *Education and Training in Developmental Disabilities, 41*(4), 410-419.

Smail, K.M., & Horvat, M. (2009). Resistance training for individuals with intellectual disabilities. *Clinical Kinesiology, 63*(2), 20-24.

Winnick, J.P., & Short, F.X. (2014). *Brockport physical fitness test (BPFT)* (2nd ed.). Champaign, IL: Human Kinetics.

Zetts, R., Horvat, M., & Langone, J. (1995). The effects of a community-based progressive resistance training program on the work productivity of adolescents with moderate to severe intellectual disabilities. *Education and Training in Mental Retardation and Developmental Disabilities, 30*, 166-178.

Chapter 8

Biggan, J.R., Melton, F., Horvat, M., Richard, H., Keller, D., and Ray, C. (2014). Increased load computerized dynamic posturography in prefrail and nonfrail community-dwelling older adults. *Journal of Aging and Physical Activity, 22*, 96-102.

Caciula, M.C., Horvat, M., Tomporowski, P., & Nocera, J. (2016). The effects of exercise frequency on executive function in individuals with Parkinson's disease. *Mental Health and Physical Activity, 10*, 18-24.

Cech, D.J., & Martin, S. (2012). *Fundamental movement development across the life span* (3rd ed.). St. Louis: Saunders.

Herman, T., Giladi, N., & Hausdorff, J. (2011). Properties of the 'timed up and go' test: More than meets the eye. *Gerontology, 57*, 203-210.

Horvat, M., Kalakian, L., Croce, R., & Dahlstrom, V. (2011). *Developmental/adapted physical education: Making ability count* (5th ed.). San Francisco: Cummings.

Johnson, J. (2012). *Postural assessment*. Champaign, IL: Human Kinetics.

Khanna, N.K., Baumgartner, K., and LaBella, C.R. (2015). *Balance error scoring system performance in children and adolescents with no history of concussion.* Sports Health, (4), 341-345.

Los Amigos Research and Education Institute. (2001). *Observational gait analysis handbook*. Downey, CA: LAREI.

Magee, D.J. (2015). *Orthopedic physical assessment* (6th ed.). Philadelphia: Saunders.

Payne, G.V., & Isaacs, L.D. (2016). *Human motor development: A lifespan approach* (9th ed.). Scottsdale, AZ: Holcomb Hathaway.

Perry, J., & Burnfield, J. (2010). *Gait analysis: Normal and pathological function* (2nd ed.). Thorofare, NJ: Slack Incorporated.

Shumway-Cook, A., & Woollacott, M.H. (2001). *Motor control: Theory and practical applications* (2nd ed.). Baltimore: Lippincott, Williams & Wilkins.

Sugden, D.A., & Keogh, J. (1990). *Problems in movement skill development*. Columbia: University of South Carolina Press.

Chapter 9

Army Individual Test Battery. (1944). *Manual of directions and scoring*. Washington, DC: War Department, Adjunct General's Office.

Bowie, C., & Harvey, P. (2006). Administration and interpretation of the Trail Making Test. *Nature Protocols, 1*(5), 2277-2281. doi:10.1038/nprot.2006.390. Retrieved 2017-01-10.

Chin, E., Nelson, L., Barr, W., McCrory, P., & McCrea, M. (2016). Reliability and validity of the Sport Concussion Assessment Tool (SCAT3) in high school and collegiate athletes. *American Journal of Sports Medicine, 44*(9), 2276-2285.

DTVP-3: Developmental Test of Visual Perception, Third Edition. (2014). Austin, TX: PRO-ED.

Gabbard, C.P. (2018). *Lifelong motor development* (7th ed.). New York: Wolters Kluwer.

Horvat, M., Croce, R., Tomporowski, P., & Barna, M. (2013). The influence of dual-task conditions on movement in young adults with Down Syndrome. *Research in Developmental Disabilities, 34*, 3517-3525.

Horvat, M., Kalakian, L., Croce, R., & Dahlstrom, V. (2011). *Developmental/adapted physical education: Making ability count* (5th ed.). Boston: Benjamin Cummings.

Horvat, M., Fallaize, A., Croce, R., & Roswal, G. (in press). *The use of the Trail Making Test to assess motor and cognitive functioning in intellectual disabilities.*

McCrory, P., Meeuwisse, W., Aubry, M., et al. (2013). Consensus statement on concussion in sport: The 4th International Conference on Concussion in Sport held in Zurich, November, 2012. *Journal of Science and Medicine in Sport, 16*, 178-189.

Salthouse, T. (2011). What cognitive abilities are involved in trail-making performance? *Intelligence, 39*, 222-232.

Strauss, E., Sherman, E., & Spreen, O. (2006). *A compendium of neuropsychological tests: Administration, norms, and commentary* (3rd ed.). New York: Oxford University press.

Van Biesen, D., Mactavish, J., McCulloch, K., Lenaerts, L., & Vanlandewijck, Y. (2016). Cognitive profile of young well-trained athletes with intellectual disabilities. *Research in developmental disabilities, 53-54*, 377-390.

Zakzanis, K., Mraz, R., & Graham, S. (2005). An fMRI study of the Trail Making Test. *Neuropsychologia, 43*, 1878-1886.

Chapter 10

Ajzen, I., & Fishbein, M. (1980). *Understanding attitudes and predicting social behavior.* Englewood Cliffs, NJ: Prentice Hall.

Akshoomoff, N., Corsello, C., & Schmidt, H. (2006). The role of the autism diagnostic observation schedule in the assessment of autism spectrum disorders in school and community settings. *The California School Psychologist : CASP / California Association of School Psychologists, 11,* 7–19.

Ashwood, K., Tye, C., Azadi, B., Cartwright, S., Asherson, P., & Bolton, P. (2015). Brief report: Adaptive functioning in children with ASD, ADHD and ASD + ADHD. *Journal of Autism & Developmental Disorders, 45*(7), 2235-2242.

Bambara, L.M., Janney, R., & Snell, M.E. (2015). *Behavioral support: Teachers' guide to inclusive practices* (3rd ed.). Baltimore: Paul H. Brookes.

Barton, E. (2015). Teaching generalized pretend play and related behaviors to young children with disabilities. *Exceptional Children* [serial online], *81,* 489-506.

Block, M.E. (1995). Development and validation of the Children's Attitudes toward Integrated Physical Education–Revised (CAIPE-R). *Adapted Physical Activity Quarterly, 12,* 60-77.

Block, M.E. (2000). *A teacher's guide to including students with disabilities in general physical education* (2nd ed.). Baltimore: Brookes.

Brown, F.E., McDonnell, J.J., & Snell, M.E. (2016). *Instruction of students with severe disabilities* (8th edition). Bloomington, MN: Pearson.

Bruininks, R.H., Woodcock, R.W., Weatherman, R.E., & Hill, B.K. (1996). *Scales of independent behavior - Revised comprehensive manual.* Itasca, IL: Riverside Publishing.

Campos, M.J., Ferreira, J.P., Block, M.E. (2014). Influence of an awareness program on Portuguese middle and high school students' perceptions toward peers with disabilities. *Psychological Reports, 115*(3), 1-16.

Constantino, J. N. (2012). *Social responsiveness scale* (2nd ed.). Los Angeles: Western Psychological Services.

Doobay, A.A., Foley-Nicpon, M., Ali, S., & Assouline, S. (2014). Cognitive, adaptive, and psychosocial differences between high ability youth with and without autism spectrum disorder. *Journal of Autism & Developmental Disorders, 44*(8), 2026-2040.

Harrison, P.L., & Oakland, T. (2015). *Adaptive Behavior Assessment System,* Third Edition (ABAS – III). Torrance, CA: WPS.

Harter, S. (1988). *Manual for the self-perception profile for children.* Denver: Author.

Harter, S. (2012). *Manual for the self-perception profile for adolescents.* Denver: Author.

Jansiewicz, E. M., Goldberg, M. C., Newschaffer, C. J., Denckla, M. B., Landa, R., & Mostofsky, S. H. (2006). Motor signs distinguish children with high functioning autism and asperger's syndrome from controls. *Journal of Autism and Developmental Disorders, 36,* 613–621.

Kazdin, A.E. (2000). *Psychotherapy for children and adolescents: Directions for research and practice.* New York: Oxford University Press.

Kretchmar, R.R. (2012). Play disabilities: A reason for physical educators to rethink the boundaries of special education. *Quest, 64*(2), 79-86.

Lambert, N., Nihira, K., & Leland, H. (1993). *AAMR Adaptive Behavior Scale–School* (2nd ed.). Austin, TX: Pro-Ed.

Lifter, K., Mason, E. J., & Barton, E. E. (2011). Children's play: Where we have been and where we could go. *Journal of Early Intervention, 33,* 281–297.

Lloyd, M., MacDonald, M., & Lord, C. (2013). Motor skills of toddlers with autism spectrum disorders. *Autism, 17*(2), 133–146.

Lord, C., Rutter, M., DiLavore, P. C., & Risi, S. (2001). Autism diagnostic observation schedule. Los Angeles: Western Psychological Services.

Lord, C., Rutter, M., Dilavore, P. C., Risi, S., Gotham, K., & Bishop, S. L. (2012). Autism diagnostic observation schedule, (2nd ed). (ADOS-2) (Part 1): Modules 1-4 [Manual]. Torrance, CA: Western Psychological Services.

Lord, C., Luyster, R.J., Gotham, K., & Guthrie, W. (2012). Autism diagnostic observation schedule, (2nd ed). (ADOS-2) (Part 2): Toddler module [Manual]. Torrance, CA: Western Psychological Services.

MacDonald, M., Lord, C., & Ulrich, D. A. (2014). Motor skills and calibrated autism severity in young children with autism spectrum disorder. *Adapted Physical Activity Quarterly*, *31*(2), 95–105.

McKay, C., Block, M.E., & Park, J.Y. (2015). The impact of Paralympic School Day on student attitudes toward inclusion in physical education. *Adapted Physical Activity Quarterly*. 32, 331-348.

Ming, X., Brimacombe, M., & Wagner, G. C. (2007). Prevalence of motor impairment in autism spectrum disorders. *Brain and Development*, *29*(9), 565–570. http://doi.org/10.1016/j.braindev.2007.03.002

Ogg, J. J., Montesino, M., Kozdras, D., Ornduff, R., Lam, G., & Takagishi, J. (2015). Perceived mental health, behavioral, and adaptive needs for children in medical foster care. *Journal of Child & Family Studies*, *24*(12), 3610-3622.

Paynter, J. M., Riley, E. P., Beamish, W., Scott, J. G., & Heussler, H. S. (2015). Brief report: An evaluation of an Australian autism-specific, early intervention programme. *International Journal of Special Education*, *30*(2), 13-19.

Papaioannou, C., Evaggelinou, C., & Block, M.E. (2014). The effect of a disability camp program on attitudes towards the inclusion of children with disabilities in a summer sport and leisure activity camp. *International Journal of Special Education*, *29*(1), 1-9.

Powers, M.D. (2000). What is autism? In M.D. Powers (Ed.), *Children with autism* (2nd ed.) (pp. 1-44). Bethesda, MD: Woodbine House.

Reid, G., O'Conner, J., & Lloyd, M. (2003). The autism spectrum disorder: Physical activity instruction, part III. *Palaestra*, *19*(2), 20-26, 47-48.

Sherrill, C. (2004). *Adapted physical activity, recreation, and sport* (6th ed.). Madison, WI: McGraw-Hill.

Siperstein, G., Bak, J., & O'Keefe, P. (1988). Relationship between children's attitudes toward and their social acceptance of mentally retarded peers. *American Journal of Mental Retardation*, 93, 24-27.

Siperstein, G.N. (1980). *Instruments for measuring children's attitudes toward the handicapped*. Unpublished manuscript. Center for Human Services, University of Massachusetts, Boston.

Snell, M.E., & Janney, R. (2006). *Social relationships and peer support* (2nd ed.). Baltimore: Paul H. Brookes.

Sparrow, S. S., Cicchetti, D. V., & Saulnier, C.A. (2016). *Vineland Adaptive Behavior Scales*—3rd Edition. San Antonio. TX: Pearson.

Tripp, A., & Sherrill, C. (2004). Inclusion, social competence, and attitude change. In C. Sherrill (Ed.), *Adapted physical activity, recreation, and sport* (6th ed.) (pp. 240-260). Madison, WI: McGraw-Hill.

Ulrich, D.A., & Collier, D.H. (1990). Perceived physical competence in children with mental retardation: Modification of a pictorial scale," *Adapted Physical Activity Quarterly 7:* 338-354.

Ventola, P. P., Friedman, H., Anderson, L., Wolf, J., Oosting, D., Foss-Feig, J., & Pelphrey, K. (2014). Improvements in social and adaptive functioning following short-duration

PRT program: A clinical replication. *Journal of Autism & Developmental Disorders,* *44*(11), 2862-2870.

Walker, H.M., & McConnell, S.R. (1995). *Walker-McConnell Scale of Social Competence and School Adjustment, Elementary Version: User's manual.* San Diego, CA: Singular Publishing Group.

Appendix A

Folio, M.R., & Fewell, R.R. (2000). *Peabody Developmental Motor Scales* (2nd ed.). Austin, TX: Pro-Ed.

Index

Note: The italicized *f* and *t* following page numbers refer to figures and tables, respectively.

About the Authors

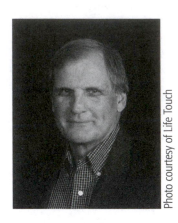

Photo courtesy of Life Touch

Michael Horvat, EdD, is a professor of adapted physical education and motor behavior at the University of Georgia, where he is also the director of the Movement Studies Laboratory and the Pediatric Exercise and Motor Development Clinic. Dr. Horvat is extensively published, having authored numerous books, monographs, chapters in books, and articles in dozens of refereed journal publications. He is also a highly sought-after speaker, having presented at more than 100 international and domestic conferences.

Dr. Horvat has been elected to many boards and councils and has professional affiliations with a number of organizations, including the International Society of Adapted Physical Activity, the North American Federation of Adapted Physical Activity, and SHAPE America. In 2005 he was named to the Honor Society of Phi Kappa Phi, and he has also been named to Who's Who in American Education.

Dr. Horvat was the Southern District AAHPERD Scholar for 1994-1995 and was named a fellow of the North American Society (NAS) of Health, Physical Education, Recreation, Sport, and Dance Professionals in 2008. He also received the 2006 Hollis Fait Scholarly Contribution Award and the 2016 G. Lawrence Rarick Research Award from the National Consortium for Physical Education for Individuals with Disabilities (NCPEID).

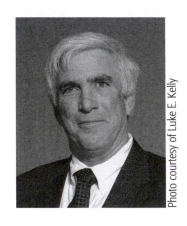

Photo courtesy of Luke E. Kelly

Luke E. Kelly, PhD, is a certified adapted physical educator, professor of kinesiology, holder of the Virgil S. Ward endowed professorship, and director of the graduate program in adapted physical education at the University of Virginia. He has 40 years of experience working with public schools in evaluating and revising their physical education curricula to meet the needs of students with disabilities. Dr. Kelly has written extensively about the achievement-based curriculum model, assessment, and the use of technology in physical education. Dr. Kelly has served as the president of the National Consortium for Physical Education for Individuals with Disabilities (NCPEID) and directed the NCPEID adapted physical education national standards project from 1992 to 1999. Dr. Kelly is a fellow of the National Academy of Kinesiology (formerly the American Academy of Kinesiology and Physical Education). He has also received the G. Lawrence Rarick Research Award and the William A. Hillman Distinguished Service Award from NCPEID.

Martin E. Block, PhD, is a professor in the department of kinesiology at the University of Virginia. He has been the director of the master's program in adapted physical education (APE) at the University of Virginia since 1993. During that time he has supervised and graduated more than 120 master's students. Dr. Block has served as an APE specialist in Virginia, working with children with severe disabilities and learning and behavioral problems.

Photo courtesy of Martin E. Block

Dr. Block has been a consultant to Special Olympics, Inc., helping to create the Motor Activities Training Program (MATP), a sports program for athletes with severe disabilities. He has authored or coauthored four books, more than 20 chapters in books, and more than 80 refereed articles, and he has conducted more than 100 international and national presentations on various topics in APE. He is the editor of the journal *Palaestra*, and he is on the editorial board of *Adapted Physical Activity Quarterly*.

Dr. Block is the president of the International Federation of Adapted Physical Activity (IFAPA) and previously served as president of the National Consortium for Physical Education for Individuals with Disabilities (NCPEID) and as chair for the Adapted Physical Activity Council and the Motor Development Academy of SHAPE America. He was named the Virginia College Professor of the Year in 2004.

Ronald V. Croce, PhD, received his doctorate in neuroscience/exercise physiology and special populations from the University of New Mexico, and he is currently a professor in the kinesiology department. His main teaching focus is applied anatomy/kinesiology and medical neuroscience, and he has been the recipient of several university teaching and research awards. Dr. Croce's research focuses on physical and motor functioning of individuals with cognitive and motor impairments as well as human neuromuscular functioning and cognition. He has over 100 published articles and is a coauthor of *Developmental/Adapted Physical Education*.

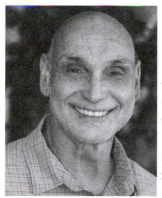

David J. Murray, ClearEyePhoto.com

About SHAPE America

SHAPE America – Society of Health and Physical Educators is committed to ensuring that all children have the opportunity to lead healthy, physically active lives. As the nation's largest membership organization of health and physical education professionals, SHAPE America works with its 50 state affiliates and is a founding partner of national initiatives including the Presidential Youth Fitness Program, Active Schools, and the Jump Rope For Heart and Hoops For Heart programs.

Since its founding in 1885, the organization has defined excellence in physical education, most recently creating *National Standards & Grade-Level Outcomes for K-12 Physical Education* (2014), National Standards for Initial Physical Education Teacher Education (2016), National Standards for Health Education Teacher Education (2017) and *National Standards for Sport Coaches* (2006). Also, SHAPE America participated as a member of the Joint Committee on National Health Education Standards, which published *National Health Education Standards, Second Edition: Achieving Excellence* (2007). Our programs, products and services provide the leadership, professional development and advocacy that support health and physical educators at every level, from preschool through university graduate programs.

The SHAPE America website, www.shapeamerica.org, holds a treasure trove of free resources for health and physical educators, adapted physical education teachers, teacher trainers and coaches, including activity calendars, curriculum resources, tools and templates, assessments and more. Visit www.shapeamerica.org and search for Teacher's Toolbox.

Every spring, SHAPE America hosts its National Convention & Expo, the premier national professional-development event for health and physical educators.

Advocacy is an essential element in the fulfillment of our mission. By speaking out for the school health and physical education professions, SHAPE America strives to make an impact on the national policy landscape.

Our Vision: A nation where all children are prepared to lead healthy, physically active lives.

Our Mission: To advance professional practice and promote research related to health and physical education, physical activity, dance and sport.

Our Commitment: 50 Million Strong by 2029

50 Million Strong by 2029 is SHAPE America's commitment to put all children on the path to health and physical literacy through effective health and physical education programs. We believe that through effective teaching, health and physical educators can help students develop the ability and confidence to be physically active and make healthy choices. As educators, our guidance can also help foster their desire to maintain an active and healthy lifestyle in the years to come. To learn more visit www.shapeamerica.org/50Million.

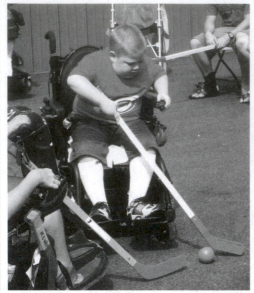

You'll find other outstanding
adapted physical education resources at

www.HumanKinetics.com

In the U.S. call 1.800.747.4457
Canada. 1.800.465.7301
Europe . . . . +44 (0) 113 255 5665
International 1.217.351.5076

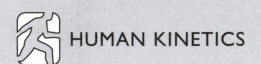

HUMAN KINETICS